W9-BRJ-458

Black Religion

By the Same Author

Edward Said and the Religious Effects of Culture

Black Religion

Malcolm X, Julius Lester, and Jan Willis

William David Hart

palgrave
macmillan

I gratefully acknowledge the following grants for permission to reprint:
From *Lovesong: Becoming a Jew* by Julius Lester, copyright 1988, reprinted
by courtesy of the author. From *Happiness Here & Now: The Eightfold Path
of Jesus Revisited with Buddhist Insights* by Elizabeth West, courtesy of
Continuum International.

First published in 2008 by
PALGRAVE MACMILLAN™
175 Fifth Avenue, New York, N.Y. 10010 and
Houndmills, Basingstoke, Hampshire, England RG21 6XS
Companies and representatives throughout the world.

PALGRAVE MACMILLAN is the global academic imprint of the Palgrave
Macmillan division of St. Martin's Press, LLC and of Palgrave Macmillan Ltd.
Macmillan® is a registered trademark in the United States, United Kingdom
and other countries. Palgrave is a registered trademark in the European
Union and other countries.

ISBN-13: 978–0–230–60537–4
ISBN-10: 0–230–60537–0

Library of Congress Cataloging-in-Publication Data

Hart, William D., 1957–
    Black religion : Malcolm X, Julius Lester, and Jan Willis / by
William David Hart.
        p. cm.
    Includes bibliographical references (p.) and index.
    ISBN 0–230–60537–0 (alk. paper)
        1. Conversion. 2. African Americans—Religion. 3. Spiritual biography.
    4. Christianity and other religions. 5. X, Malcolm, 1925–1965.
    6. Lester, Julius. 7. Willis, Janice Dean. I. Title.

BL639.H37 2008   [B]
200.92'396073—dc22   2007044336

A catalogue record for this book is available from the British Library.

Design by Newgen Imaging Systems (P) Ltd., Chennai, India.

First edition: June 2008

10 9 8 7 6 5 4 3 2 1

Printed in the United States of America.

This book is dedicated to my beloved wife,
Carrol and to our equally beloved children,
Adrienne and Kwame. They make life worth living.

CONTENTS

PREFACE

For several years, I have taught a course on "African American Religious Autobiography," the principal readings of which I make the subjects of this book—*The Autobiography of Malcolm X* (1965), written with Alex Haley; *Lovesong: Becoming a Jew* (1988), by Julius Lester, and *Dreaming Me: From Baptist to Buddhist, One Woman's Spiritual Journey* (2001), by Jan Willis. In my course, *The Autobiography of Malcolm X* is the central text, setting the agenda for the others as it does in this book. I chose to write about the autobiographies of Malcolm, Julius, and Jan not because I regard them as representative expressions, respectively, of Islam, Judaism, and Buddhism among black Americans. Whether they are representative, and they may very well be, is an empirical question, the answer to which though interesting is tangential to my inquiry. My inquiry does not depend on representation. It is an *expressive* rather than a *representational* undertaking. I write about these autobiographers because they are interesting and reveal the varieties of black religious expression. I write about them, further, because I teach them, and because of the reactions this material elicits from my students. Invariably, my black students like Malcolm X whom they regard as a cultural hero but regard his religion as deviant. They dislike Julius Lester's identity politics and regard Judaism as strange and not "black." They regard Jan Willis as bizarre, asking—"What does Buddhism have to do with black people?" My curiosity about these reactions lies behind this inquiry; especially, the narrow imagination they express, and the peculiarly normative and even "totalitarian" notion of black identity they encode.

Each autobiographer is a singular individual. Malcolm X was a prison-bred autodidact, Julius Lester is a graduate of a historically black college (Fisk University) and a professional writer, and Jan Willis is an Ivy League-educated (Cornell undergraduate, Columbia PhD) professor of Indic and Buddhist Studies at Wesleyan University. Thus, we have an autobiography written by an accomplished professional writer, on the one extreme and on the other, an autobiography written by a third party, with an autobiography reflecting, perhaps, the reserve of a highly trained academic in between. Other differences seem to track these differences: Julius is the most confessional, Jan the least confessional, and Malcolm the most strategic in what he confesses. Despite these and other differences, each autobiographer is Afro-*Eccentric* and their Afro-*Eccentricity* plays out against the counterpoint of the Black Church. Afro-*Eccentricity* is neither a comprehensive philosophy as Afro- and Africentricity claim to be, nor a principle, that is, a form of cultural essentialism applied to *black people of African descent*. Essentialism is the claim that there is some significant characteristic common to all members of a class that make them who they are. Blood, genetics, spirit, soul, language, and expressive culture have all been proposed as essence-bearers. Afro-*Eccentricity* is a critical pun and trope that mimics, underscores, and reminds us of the difference within the same, the manifold within the apparent uniformity of American black people. As Stuart Hall has argued, there is no essential black subject.[1] Improvisation, the spiritual-blues-Jazz impulse—understood in formal terms as a trope within a trope—is the engine of difference. However, this should not be taken as a backdoor argument for some deep racial/cultural essence that makes black people who they are. The improvisation of which I speak is a pragmatic reaction to contingent historical circumstances. Thus, Afro-*Eccentricity* provides a critique of the essence-bearer view that characterizes Afrocentricity; that view is descriptively wrong, a conceptual prison that is totalitarian in its consequences. The Afro-*Eccentric* interpreter rejects ahistorical notions of essence, notions that deny the trace of the different, nonidentical, and Afro-*Eccentric* other. Against the backdrop of the standard account of black religion, I accent those figures who do not conform to standard expectations of what it means to be a black person *and* a religious person, figures who are eccentric, Afro-*Eccentric*. "Afro-*Eccentric*" is synonymous with "different." *It refers to ways of "being black" that are off-center, "off-color," and outside the statistical if not "the" axiological norm.* The standard account of Black Religion often construes *black religious others* (Muslims, Jews, and Buddhists) as strange, deformed, and deviant versions of the black Christian norm. While acknowledging the differences, I contest deviant constructions of *black religious others* by familiarizing religious "deviance" and defamiliarizing the purported "normativity" of the standard account.

My approach to religion is thoroughly naturalistic—that is, religion is a "distal artifact" of evolution by natural selection. Like every other aspect of culture, it emerged because of its survival value for the human species but it persists for reasons that transcend mere survival and may become, like our "sweet tooth," detrimental to our survival. We dance with the ghosts of our evolutionary history.[2] In this view, gods are *species* of the human imagination and have no reality apart from it. My naturalism, notwithstanding, I inhabit the first-order language of my subjects without questioning every extranatural claim or placing them in quotation marks. I debunk their claims regarding religious institutions, rites, and beliefs only when I need to advance mine. This serves the purpose of avoiding tiresome repetition while reminding the reader of my naturalistic assumptions: that religion is a "distal artifact" of evolution by natural selection, that gods are *species* of the human imagination. I elaborate on my perspective at the end of the book in "Coda: My Point of View as Author." My naturalism is both methodological and metaphilosophical; thus I reject the convention regarding capitalization and use "god" in lowercase, even when god is a proper name. The only exceptions I make is when quoting, when god begins a sentence, or for emphasis.

I would like thank two people: Jeffrey Stout for reading the manuscript and offering suggestions for restructuring it, and Melvin Peters who tirelessly read many revisions of the manuscript, offered wise council, and behaved admirably as a friend. Whatever virtues this manuscript might have are due largely to him.

Notes

1. See S. Hall, "New Ethnicities," in "Black Film, British Cinema," ed. Kobena Mercer, *ICA Documents* 7 (1988): 27–31.
2. See David Sloan Wilson, *Darwin for Everyone* (New York: Bantam Dell, 2007).

ABBREVIATIONS

The Autobiography of Malcolm X (AMX)
Lovesong: Becoming a Jew (L)
*Dreaming Me: From Baptist to Buddhist, One Woman's
    Spiritual Journey* (DM)

CHAPTER ONE

Afro-Eccentricity *and Autobiography*

This book traces the spiritual journey of Malcolm X. After tracing that journey as described in his autobiography, I explore the spiritual journeys of Julius Lester and Jan Willis[1] whom I construe as Malcolm's spiritual legatees. I *trace* what is known about Malcolm, Julius, and Jan by analyzing their autobiographies. In contrast, I also *explore* what is relatively unknown and establish connections between the three auto-biographers that may not be obvious and that some readers may view as counterintuitive. In this regard, my analysis is "constructive." The "spiritual" in spiritual journey refers to those events (artistic, drug-induced, sporting, sexual, violent, political, and religious) that grab, lift, and transport us to another dimension of imagination, if not of space and time, beyond the placid surfaces, gray zones, and temperate climates of our everyday lives.

Malcolm's autobiography iterates a set of themes that the autobio-graphies of Julius and Jan reiterate. While there are direct relations between Malcolm's narrative and those of Julius and Jan, most of the thematic connections I pursue are matters of affinity and interpreta-tion. They are what students of comparative literature call a "reading." These thematic connections include the intersection of religious eccen-tricity, the politics of racial identification, and the allure of the black freedom struggle. I contend that this intersection provides the spiritual ground for their radical transformations. In this light, I explore the complexities of Malcolm's multileveled passage from Christianity to Islam. I then extend that exploration to the passages of Julius and Jan: that of Julius from Christianity to Judaism, of Jan from Christianity to Buddhism. Again, I take their narratives, which reveal their own complexities, as reiterating the thematic ensemble (religious, racial, and political) that I call radical transformations. In my account, Julius and Jan are "spiritual children" of Malcolm X. The stories of each autobiographer exemplify the difference within the sameness of black identity, the diversity of the black "cosmographic imagination," that is, the many ways in which black people have written their own meanings onto the cosmos, thus constructing a life they could live.

A Special Note on *The Autobiography Malcolm X*

As the center of gravity and focus of this book, *The Autobiography of Malcolm X* merits special attention. Unlike the autobiographies of his spiritual legatees, Malcolm's autobiography was not written by the "author." He "authorized" it but did not write it. Because it is an "as-told-to" autobiography, there will always be some uncertainty about its authorship. As we know from the writings of Michel Foucault, even when the writer and author are the same, authorship is still a complex and vexing issue. After all, "What is an author?" Fortunately, I do not need to answer this question. But I am aware of the irremediable gap between the self-written and as-told-to forms of autobiography. Malcolm died before his autobiography was published. He did not have final editorial control. However, we should not exaggerate the difference. Any writer who has worked with an editor knows that there is no such thing as "final" editorial control. Without denying the differences between self-written and as-told to texts, every autobiography has an as-told-to quality. Every autobiography is ghostwritten by the prevailing discourse. If there is a gap between author and writer in an as-told-to autobiography, and if that gap interferes with the transparency of the narrative, then there is also a gap (editors and discourse) between the author of a self-written autobiography and what she writes. In either case, there is no transparency. We "see through a glass darkly." Language does not provide an unmediated and unproblematic portrait of the author. It does not "mirror" the self it describes nor does the self escape *différance,* the deferring and differential play of language.[2] Neither the author of a self-written autobiography nor the author of an as-told-to autobiography has a privileged access to his or her own mind. The authors' autobiographical representation of themselves is one performance of their "real self" out of many possible performances.

A second major difference between Malcolm's autobiography and those of Julius and Jan is the volume of the secondary literature. A vast secondary literature enhances my interpretation of Malcolm, while the secondary literature on Julius and Jan is virtually nonexistent. This difference speaks volumes about the cultural status of *The Autobiography of Malcolm X* in relation to Julius' and Jan's autobiographies. Along with Malcolm's greater cultural importance, the volume of the secondary literature accounts for the length and detail of my analysis of his narrative.

Autobiographical Narrative and Religion Study

There is something about religion scholarship that leaves one dissatisfied and even suspicious. Consider the following questions: Since there is always a gap between what we know and what we believe, what does the scholar *really* believe, however unscholarly, naïve, and embarrassing? How should he describe the relations between what he believes and what she knows, between his viscera and intuitions, on the one side and on the other side, the reflective, considered claims that she makes as a scholar? Is there a gap between the two? If there is, what is that gap? How does he distinguish the visceral side of that gap from the reflective? Can she? How can we trust the scholar unless he enacts this distinction in his work, before our very eyes, where we can track the moves that he makes, discounting his claims where appropriate? Even as I address these questions, there are other questions: Why does the autobiographical voice seem unavoidable? What does the genre of autobiography, narrative, and confession allow one to say that other forms do not? Why is it especially important for religion scholars, on occasion, to speak in this voice? According to James Olney, an influential student of autobiography, "What one seeks in reading an autobiography is not a date, a name, or a place, but a characteristic way of perceiving, of organizing, and of understanding, an individual way of feeling and expressing that one can somehow relate to oneself."[3] Richard White offers a cautionary note about the knowledge that autobiographies provide. "For while an autobiography relates the facts of an individual's personal history, there is nothing definitive about the way in which these facts are organized or held to be important or irrelevant—this is all determined by the autobiographical performance, and by definition no performance can ever be definitive."[4]

Paul Ricoeur argues that historical and fictional narratives comprise narrative identity. Human lives become more readable when presented in story form. The epistemological status of autobiography seems to confirm this intuition. He thinks it plausible, therefore, to assert the following: As an interpretative act, self-knowledge privileges narrative mediation, borrowing equally from history and fiction. The story of a life, whether described as fictive history or historical fiction, differs little from the marriage of history and fiction in the "biographies of great men."[5] Against those who say that autobiography places too much emphasis on the "I," Ricoeur offers the following: "The phrase 'I am nothing' must maintain its paradoxical form; 'nothing' would not mean anything if it were not assigned to an 'I.' For what indeed is an 'I' when I say that it is 'nothing,' if not a self deprived of the aid of sameness?" We sometimes experience dramatic, even terrifying events that call our personal identity into question, with conversion being one such event. "In these moments of extreme self-divestiture, the empty response, far from rendering the question empty, reinforces this question and maintains it as a question. What cannot be abolished is the question, 'who am I?' "[6]

In *The Voice within: Reading and Writing Autobiography*, Roger Porter and H. R. Wolf offer the following observation:

> Autobiography is one attempt to solve problems of identity: in the writing of autobiography the author either postulates a new identity or reinforces an already existing one, and in it he asserts that the patterns he has found in his experience reveal truths about himself. The writing style he chooses will reveal his personality and show different sides of himself, sides that may sometimes be in conflict. The "real me" is often an artistic construct, a series of labels or metaphors serving some specific purpose for the autobiographer, who may idealize or disparage the character he calls the "self," leave things out, or overwhelm or overcomplicate. Truth is a highly subjective matter, and no autobiographer can represent *exactly* "what happened back then," any more than a historian can definitively describe the real truth of the past. But *how* he describes his past—distant or immediate—reveals who he thinks he is.[7]

Autobiography defies the conventions of a literary genre. Equally uncanny, religion study defies the conventions of an academic discipline. Is this merely a structural similarity or does it cut deeper? Is autobiography especially suited to religion study? For me these are open questions. But I cannot help remarking on what autobiography and narrative allow me to do. They allow me to traverse the multiplicity of theories and approaches to the study of religion that appeal in different ways to my own multiplicity as devotee, skeptic, scholar, and "Curious George." An autobiographical approach allows me to establish a narrative unity while simultaneously acknowledging my subjective multiplicity and the irreconcilability of the theories and approaches to the study of religion that I employ as a scholar. This approach, moreover, seems ideal when negotiating and dissolving the insider/outsider, knower/known, subject/object dualities. The question of whose perspective (participant or observer) should prevail when assessing religious phenomena is boldly answered by the very form of autobiography, which insists on being both inside and outside, of being torn between participation and observation, of being both the subject and the object of knowledge and the interpreter of both.

As a final point about autobiography, consider the remarks of the literary theorist and critic, Henry Louis Gates. According to Gates, the black autobiographical tradition, rooted in the slave narrative, endeavors to narrate the collective history of a people whose history was denied. Black Americans expressed their desire for power through a mode of writing that allowed them to create "a black self in words." As the predominance of first-person narrative shows, even black fiction reveals "the impulse to testify, to chart the peculiar contours of the individual protagonist on the road to becoming." As Gates remarks: "Constructed upon an ironic foundation of autobiographical narratives written by ex-slaves, the African-American tradition, more clearly and directly than most, traces its lineage—in the act of declaring the existence of a surviving, enduring ethnic self—to this impulse of autobiography."[8]

Character and Characterization in Religious Autobiography

The relationship between character and characterization, the ethical character of the autobiographer and how she reveals her character through characterization of self and others, is a central issue in assessing religious autobiographies. In this section, I provide a summary of John D. Barbour's essay, "Character and Characterization in Religious Autobiography."[9] Barbour begins with the issue of truth and truthfulness. If truth is a matter of fact, then truthfulness is not the same as factual accuracy. In the work of self-evaluation, the autobiographer may omit, misremember, and consciously distort some facts but still reveal what is central to her character. Truthfulness is primarily a matter of avoiding self-deception, especially regarding one's own moral failings.[10] The work of moral acknowledgment can be illuminated by factual accuracy but can also be obscured by the facts. Selection, which entails the omission of some facts, is essential to truthfulness. A good autobiographer does not ignore the facts but also does not allow too many facts to get in the way of the truthfulness of the truth.

The issues of truth and truthfulness play out in the difference between history and text. Truthfulness connects directly with the difference between the historical self and the textual self. Contemporary theorists of autobiography distinguish between the two. According to Barbour, "Autobiography is treated as a process of fictional characterization in which there are, at the very least, crucial differences between the textual version of the self and the writer's actual experience."[11] At its most radical, this theory denies a preexisting self; rather, the self is created through the narrative. Some claim that autobiography is impossible since it presupposes what is impossible, an unmediated access to the self. The self, they claim, is a series of metaphors, shaped by the conventions and traditions of writing. As an example of this view, Barbour cites Louis Renza whose view he characterizes as follows: "Autobiography cannot fully communicate the privateness of the self or the feeling of pastness; it forces the writer to adopt a persona."[12] In his autobiography, Julius Lester uses the term "Persona" to characterize Julius Lester the writer as distinguished from the Julius Lester of actual experience whom he calls "Soul." In my presentation of Julius' autobiography, I criticize this move.

My assessment of Julius' move brings us back to the issue of character. If character and characterization are related but different, then I cannot avoid assessing the acts of characterization by Malcolm, Julius, and Jan. According to Barbour, the authors of classic autobiographies (he regards *The Autobiography of Malcolm X* as an example) recognize the "conscious artistry and techniques of fictional characterization" in their text.[13] Take, for example, Malcolm's and Haley's use of the composite character "Shorty." Characterization reveals character imprecisely due to "unintentional distortion, misplaced emphasis, rationalization, and self-deception."[14] However, the good autobiographer reveals her character at the time of writing by forcing the fictions of characterization to service the facts of character. Thus assessing the character of my autobiographical subjects means assessing their acts of characterization. Through their characterizations of self and others, autobiographers reveal their own characters in myriad ways. To use Hayden White's language, they reveal character through the way they emplot their narrative; through the kind of story—romance, tragedy, comedy, satire—they choose to tell. "Character is revealed in the unique tone of voice of the autobiographer: bitter, wry, self-deprecating, evasive, loftily dignified, or defensive."[15] Autobiographers reveal character through the beliefs and convictions they articulate and through their illusions, fantasies, and dreams; for example, Jan uses a recurrent dream about lions to structure her narrative. Autobiographers also reveal character through the models—metaphors of the self—they choose.[16] Malcolm cites the Apostle Paul and the boy-bird Icarus as models before questioning their adequacy. Julius cites the Catholic monk Thomas Merton and describes Malcolm X as a man against whom to measure oneself. In addition to her gurus, Jan cites *The Life of Milarepa*, a Buddhist narrative, as a model.[17] Further, citing her mother's comments, Jan regards Malcolm X as a person against whom to measure herself.

If literary theorists are primarily interested in the fiction of characterization and theologians in the ethics of character, then Barbour does more than merely split the difference. While affirming the relations between the facts of character and the fictions of characterization, he shows why the whole project of autobiography collapses without a distinction between the two. Interest in autobiographies and the authority they command rely on the distinction between fact and fiction (as the controversy over James Frey's *A Million Little Pieces* reconfirms), a distinction that literary theorists covertly affirm even as they overtly proclaim the autonomy of the text. Barbour illustrates this point by reference to *The Autobiography of Malcolm X*. Like other great autobiographers, Malcolm grapples with "issues of truthfulness and self-deception, authenticity and bad faith."[18] He characterized his life as a series of theatrical-like roles. "Each of the many names and nicknames he assumed corresponds to a distinct interpretation of his character at a stage in his life: Malcolm Little, 'Homeboy,' 'Detroit Red,' 'Satan,' Malcolm X, and El-Hajj Malik El-Shabazz."[19] The success or failure of his autobiography (and of Julius' and Jan's autobiographies) has everything to do with how he grapples (and they grapple) with the issues of truthfulness, self-deception, authenticity, and bad faith. Often, my critique of the autobiographers assumes an ironic voice, offering commentary on their self-representations and deceptions.

Finally, I cite the following:

> The autobiographer must be concerned with character assessment or we sense a kind of frivolousness and an evasion of the central aspect of self-knowledge. But the autobiographer who cannot see his self-portrayal as partly a matter of characterization—as involving selection, perception, imaginative projection, and imitative

patterning according to literary types and figures—seems to lack insight into his own activity as a knower and writer of the self.[20]

What Barbour says about the autobiographer is also applicable to persons such as me who write about them. I make various ethical-political judgments about Malcolm, Julius, and Jan, where my tone and the modulation of my voice express judgment. As a critic, I offer these judgments. In turn, I expect to be judged.

The Problem

The Standard Narrative of Black Religion poses a problem for the story I wish to tell. In this narrative, the black Protestant Church is virtually conterminous with Black Religion. It defines Black Religion. Every other form of black religious expression is normatively peripheral and culturally suspect. In relation to the Standard Narrative and its Black Church rhetoric, Malcolm's autobiographical expression of Black Religion is eccentric, off-color, and "deviant"—it is Afro-*Eccentric*. The Black Church is a barrier to understanding Malcolm's narrative and the Afro-*Eccentric* narratives of Julius Lester and Jan Willis. The term "Black Church" embodies the presumption that church is a synonym for religion. The Standard Narrative constructs "church" as a universal term, an ideal type describing the institutional dimensions of a religious tradition, no matter how nonchurchly or antichurch it may be.[21] Black Church stereotypes our expectations of what "Black Religion" is and what religion study ought to be. It is a term that screens some things into our field of vision and other things out. In the language of Kenneth Burke, the Black Church is a *terministic screen*. It influences our perceptions of normality and propriety as well as our ability to even recognize certain narratives as part of black religious expression. It encourages us to look for the wrong thing and to discover "lack" where is there is "difference." Either we do not see these kinds of narrative or we "normalize" them under the category of the Black Church. The Black Church functions like the mythical bed of Procrustes, stretching and cutting the eccentric narratives to fit. Such is the case with the Islam of Malcolm X. This stretching and cutting, where there is not outright suspicion or bewilderment, also characterizes typical reactions to the Afro-*Eccentric* choices of Judaism and Buddhism. The subjects of these choices are construed as weird or inauthentic. Against the backdrop of the Standard Narrative of Black Religion, Malcolm, Julius, and Jan struggled and became who they are: a black Muslim, a black Jew, and a black Buddhist.

There are basically two overlapping versions of the Standard Narrative of Black Religion. W. E. B. DuBois' *The Souls of Black Folks* (1903) is the foundational text for what I call the *Black Religion as the Soul of Black Folks Narrative.* The tenth chapter, "Of the Faith of the Fathers," provides a prototype for studies of Black Religion, and is the precursor of the Black Church Narrative. DuBois' essay establishes the following conventions: that religion is the essence, genius, or soul of black folks; that slavery, Jim Crow, and Christianity transformed this religion of African origin into the religion of Afro-Americans; that "the Preacher, the Music, and the Frenzy" reveal the distinctive characteristics of Black Religion; that the Black Church is the most important institution and social center in the black community, and that the church teeters between resistance to white supremacy and submission, between "manliness" and "effeminacy."[22]

Much of this DuBoisian wisdom is still evident in contemporary studies of Black Religion. DuBois' brief narrative provides a metaphysic, an existential phenomenology, and a historical sociology that continue to influence our understanding of Black Religion. The history of black religious studies is a series of footnotes to "Of the Faith of the Fathers." Metaphysically, within this interpretive tradition, Black Religion is the preeminent revelation of the character, "soul," or "inner ethical life," as DuBois puts it, of black people. Phenomenologically, Black Religion is distinguished by its theatricality, mesmerizing music, kinetic orality, passionate physicality, and combative spirituality.[23] As historical sociology, Black Religion bifurcates geographically between north and south, dispositionally between militant church and submissive church, and ethically-politically between fashionable, if trivial, pursuits and hard questions. DuBois describes the Negro as "a religious animal"—deeply emotional and instinctively oriented toward the supernatural:

> [W]e must realize that no such institution as the Negro church could rear itself without definite historical foundations. These foundations we can find if we remember that the social history of the Negro did not start in America. He was brought from a definite social environment—the polygamous clan life under the headship of the chief and the potent influence of the priest. His religion was nature-worship, with profound belief in invisible surrounding influences, good and bad, and his worship was through incantation and sacrifice. The first rude change in this life was

the slave ship and the West Indian sugar-fields. The plantation organization replaced the clan and the tribe, and the white master replaced the chief with far greater and more despotic powers. Forced and long-continued toil became the rule of life, the old ties of blood relationship and kinship disappeared, and instead of the family appeared a new polygamy and polyandry, which, in some cases, almost reached promiscuity. It was a terrific social revolution, and yet some traces were retained of the former group life, and the chief remaining institution was the priest or medicine man. He early appeared on the plantation and found his function as the healer of the sick, the interpreter of the Unknown, the comforter of the sorrowing, the supernatural avenger of wrong, and the one who rudely but picturesquely expressed the longing, disappointment, and resentment of a stolen and oppressed people. Thus, as bard, physician, judge, and priest, within the narrow limits allowed by the slave system, rose the Negro preacher, and under him the first Afro-American institution, the Negro church. This church was not at first by any means Christian nor definitely organized; rather it was an adaptation and mingling of heathen rites among the members of each plantation, and roughly designated as Voodooism. Associations with masters, missionary effort and motives of expediency gave these rites an early veneer of Christianity, and after the lapse of many generations the Negro church became Christian.[24]

DuBois was a product of the Victorian, racial, and religious discourses of his time. While one might quibble here and supplement there, this is still the dominant narrative of Black Religion at the beginning of the twenty-first century. In the same year he published *The Souls of Black Folks,* he also published an edited volume, commissioned by Atlanta University, entitled *The Negro Church.*[25] The first important study of its kind, it was followed by a number of studies that define Black Religion as the Negro Church and later as the Black Church. The influence of DuBois' black church studies on subsequent analyses, both theological and social-scientific, is apparent. Examples of the former include the work of Howard Thurman and James Cone. Examples of the latter include Carter Godwin Woodson's *The History of the Negro Church* (1921), Benjamin E. Mays and Joseph W. Nicholson's *The Negro Church* (1933), Arthur Fauset's *Black Gods of the Metropolis* (1944), Ruby Funchess Johnston's *The Development of Negro Religion* (1954), E. Franklin Frazier's *The Negro Church in America* (1964), C. Eric Lincoln's, *The Black Church since Frazier* (1974), Hart Nelsen and Anne Kusner Nelsen's *Black*

Church in the Sixties (1975), Ida Rousseau-Rousseau-Mukenge's, *The Black Church in Urban America* (1983), C. Eric Lincoln and Lawrence Mamiya's *The Black Church in the African American Experience* (1990), and Andrew Billingsley's *Mighty like a River* (1999).[26]

The Soul Narrative provides great insights into black American religious life. However, when not associating it with a transhistorical spirit, DuBois associates this narrative exclusively with the Black Church. The Soul Narrative, we might say, morphs into the Black Church Narrative. The Soul Narrative is not wrong. In fact, it gets many things right. But we now recognize that it is too simple and not quite messy enough. In its simplicity and narrowness, the Soul Narrative makes it more difficult to see the kinds of narratives represented by figures such as Malcolm X and his early American Muslim predecessors. *The Souls of Black Folks as Black Religion Narrative* screens from view the Islamic prehistory of black Americans, and its residual presence among slaves and throughout the postslavery generations. When it morphs into the *Black Church as Black Religion Narrative,* it carries this defect with it.

In the view that I am attributing to the proponents of this narrative, Protestant Christianity and *normative* black identity are mutually constitutive. Though rarely expressed explicitly, this claim shouts to the reader between the lines of more typical rhetorical formulations. In the Standard Narrative of Black Religion, black religious "others," including Muslims, Jews, and Buddhists, are deemed eccentric, if not weird, racially inauthentic, and culturally deviant. In short, they are perceived through the terministic screen of the Black Church. Ignorance, the inability to see the religious otherness of black religious others, the fear that their religious eccentricity could undermine black solidarity and thus the ongoing struggle against white supremacy, and a generalized distaste for difference compels the proponents of the Standard Narrative to adopt an authoritarian conception of blackness. Though I wish to contest the Standard Narrative, I do not claim that it is wrong in all respects as an account of the Black Church. Nor is it all wrong as an account of Black Religion. However, it is inadequate and it screens important matters from our collective view. In my view, *Black Religion is a consequent not an antecedent reality, an artifact not an essence.* Black Religion is *blue.* "Blue" is a musical term that refers to notes outside the "normal," diatonic scale. These blue notes—flattened thirds, fifths, and sevenths, simultaneously melancholic and joyful—challenge our expectations of how music should sound. They introduce dissonance and improvisation. Like jazz, Black Religion "blues" the cultural raw materials that it encounters and thereby challenges our expectations of normality and propriety. The product of what people identified as black have created and are now creating, Black Religion cannot be defined exclusively by the "African sacred cosmos" or the Black Church. As I shall argue, *The Autobiography of Malcolm X* "*blues*" the Standard Narrative. It is Afro-*Eccentric*.

Itinerary

In part I "The Spiritual Journey of Malcolm X," I explore his multidimensional pilgrimage to Islam. Malcolm describes his life as a series of changes. I follow these chameleon-like changes and map the passages across the domains of personal identity, religion, and politics. In the two chapters that constitute part I (chapters 2 and 3), I use Muslim words *Jahiliyyah* (darkness), *Jihad* (struggle), *Hijrah* (flight), and *Hajj* (pilgrimage) to describe various stages of Malcolm's life. I do so fully aware that these terms are controversial within Muslim circles and that some will find my use of them offensive. My purpose is not to offend. However, reverence is not a virtue in the academic study of religion, not when it undermines the truthfulness of the truth.[27] Further, I use these terms with a certain polemical intent. I assert that these categories are available to anyone who claims Muslim identity and, even more controversially, to scholars and non-Muslim interpreters attempting to make sense of their subject matter. As a scholar, I do not police the boundaries of a tradition by determining "who is in" and "who is out." I assume that the tradition is contested and I make that contestation an object of study. Part of my polemical intent in using Muslim categories is to challenge *Arabcentrism*, that is, an Arabcentric monopoly on interpretation that regards Sunni Islam as "orthodox," Shi'a Islam in its many varieties as "heterodox," and the Islam of black American Muslims, especially those who are neither Sunni nor Shiite, such as the Nation of Islam, as beyond the Muslim pale. Like reverence, "orthodoxy" and "heterodoxy" are dogmatic categories, terms of praise and abuse within a religious tradition. They have little utility for the scholar of religion and certainly cannot bind her judgments. I am not bound by the dogmatic assertions of those who claim that "Black Muslims" in their many varieties are not true Muslims.

To reiterate, my approach is to renarrate the life of Malcolm X using interpretive categories that he did not use but that I take as a compelling way of describing his life. These categories describe (1) Malcolm's pre-Nation of Islam period, a time of Jahiliyyah or pre-Islamic "paganism" and darkness; (2) his Nation of Islam period, a time of Jihad (struggle) against white supremacy, including idolatrous conceptions of religion where whiteness is god; (3) his post-Nation of Islam period of Hijrah (flight from the enemies of Islam, which imitates the Prophet Muhammad's flight from enemies in Mecca) and; (4) Hajj, which symbolizes Malcolm's pilgrimage from nationalist to Sunni Islam.

Though the debate on the use of the term Jahiliyyah is contentious, I find the term suggestive, metaphorically rich, and useful in illuminating Malcolm's perceptions of his pre-Nation life. However, I reject those who use Jahiliyyah as a term of abuse for those they disagree with or dislike. Sayyed Qubt's *Milestones* (1963) exemplifies the position I do not take. Qubt uses Jahiliyyah not only in reference to the "pre-Islamic age of pagan ignorance" but as a term of abuse for non-Muslim societies and for Muslims whose view of the world differs from his—those, in his estimation, who have succumbed to modernism and Western decadence. In Qubt's view, the entire world, non-Muslim and ostensibly Muslim alike, is a sea of Jahiliyyah with an island of submission to Allah here and there. This radically Manichaean view underwrites a violent Jihad against non-Muslims whom Qubt presents with two options: either submit to the word of Allah or be *converted* "by the sword or the death penalty."[28] I emphatically dissociate myself from this use of the term. I offer neither aid nor comfort to those who use Jahiliyyah as an anti-Semitic, antimodern, and crudely anti-Western epitaph or as a way of policing Muslim "orthodoxy." In relation to Qubt's use of Jahiliyyah, my use is a provocation rather than an affirmation. No less provocative, perhaps, is my use of the word Jihad. Jihad (inadequately and contentiously translated as "holy war") describes Malcolm's multileveled struggle against his own baser inclinations, and his struggle on behalf of the Nation of Islam, against the Nation of Islam, and against white supremacy. In chapter 2, I explore Malcolm's life under the controversial categories of Jahiliyyah and Jihad. In chapter 3, I continue the provocative appropriation of Muslim terms where I use Hijrah and Hajj to describe Malcolm's post-Nation of Islam life and death, his flight (Hijrah) from the FBI and the Nation of Islam, and pilgrimage (Hajj) to Sunni Islam.

A note on narrative structure: the reader should be alert to a documentary narrative in the form of excerpts from Malcolm's FBI file. I weave this narrative into the primary narrative to graphically illustrate the circumstances under which Malcolm's spiritual journey occurred. This provides a parallel and, at one-time, clandestine account of Malcolm life. From prison-release to assassination, this documentary narrative is the official voice of the United States Government and the precursory activities of its Counter Intelligence Program (COINTELPRO). COINTELPRO was originally designed to undermine the effectiveness of the Communist Party. In concert with the FBI's white supremacist orientation, COINTELPRO's anticommunism irradiated surveillance of the black freedom movement. Indeed, the FBI originally suspected Malcolm of being a communist.[29]

In "Part II: The Spiritual Children of Malcolm X" that consists of chapters on Julius Lester and Jan Willis, I continue this Afro-*Eccentric* account of Black Religion. "Spiritual Children" is a riff on "The Angry Children of Malcolm X,"[30] Julius' description of the "Black Power" generation. Their ambivalence notwithstanding, I regard Julius and Jan as "spiritual descendants" of Malcolm X. This ambivalence cuts in different directions and with different degrees of intensity and depth, but the more important point is a shared double-mindedness regarding Malcolm: the attraction and the aversion. I trace this ambivalence in chapter 4, where I use the Hebrew term *Teshuvah* and in chapter 5, where I use the Buddhist (Sanskrit) term *Duhkha*. This usage compliments my use of Muslim (Arabic) terms—Jahiliyyah, Jihad, Hijrah, and Hajj—in chapters 2 and 3. Teshuvah means atonement in English. Chapter 4 explores Lester's quest for atonement for his revolutionary activism, his authoritarian notion of "blackness," and his anti-Semitic past. Duhkha means "unsatisfactoriness" in English. Often translated as "suffering," duhkha describes the inherent frustrations of life, which is transitory, imperfect, and metaphysically empty. Chapter 5 explores Willis' struggle against various forms of duhkha in her life: the unsatisfactoriness of family, friendship, and religion.

The primary affinities between Malcolm's narrative and the narratives of Julius and Jan are their respective attempts to negotiate their Christian heritage, especially around the person of Jesus, their quest for a form of politics that responded adequately to the crisis of white supremacy as they understood it, and their efforts to honor their religious commitments, given the realities of racial identification and what they experienced as the demands of racial solidarity. Each autobiographer negotiated tensions between "roots" and "routes." They struggled with an ensemble of issues and tensions that I present as a set of questions: Is there a "natural" relation between race and religion? Are some religions "blacker" than others? Do some religious commitments deracialize and culturally deracinate black people, demanding an either/or choice? If Islam is the "black man's" religion, as Malcolm claims or if Christianity is the "black man's" religion as Jan's parents suggest, then does that mean that black Christians are brainwashed? Or that black Jews and black Buddhists are not black? Or that they are inferior in their blackness? Or that they are inauthentically black? These questions, which the journey of Malcolm X poses and the journeys of Julius Lester and Jan Willis reiterate, revise, and elaborate, lead in their turn to questions about the very nature of black identity and the adequacy of the Standard Narrative. Like Malcolm's narrative, the narratives of Julius and Jan reveal their Afro-*Eccentricity* with respect to the Standard Narrative. Whereas Malcolm describes a multidimensional pilgrimage from childhood Christianity into the multiple worlds of Islam, the religious itineraries of Julius and Jan take them from childhood Christianity into the religious worlds of Judaism and Buddhism, respectively. These narrative accounts of cosmographic creativity, spiritual restlessness, pilgrimage, and radical transformation cast a different light on the meaning of Black Religion. We should no longer assume that Black Religion equals the Black Church, or that it has a definitive, essential, and transhistorical shape.

In this book, I provide an interpretation of the spiritual journey of Malcolm X and the recapitulation of its themes in the autobiographies of Julius Lester and Jan Willis.

PART I

The Spiritual Journey of Malcolm X

How are you going to be nonviolent in Mississippi, as violent as you were in Korea?

I'm one of the 22 million black people who are the victims of Americanism....I don't see any American dream; I see an American nightmare.

You can't separate peace from freedom because no one can be at peace unless he has his freedom.

I'm a Muslim, which only means that my religion is Islam. I believe in God, the Supreme Being, the creator of the universe. This is a very simple form of religion, easy to understand.

Malcolm X[1]

CHAPTER TWO

Jahiliyyah *and* Jihad

Biographical Particulars

Malcolm X was born in Omaha, Nebraska in 1925 to Earl and Louise Little. He had several siblings, including three older, half sibling[1] and a younger, half brother. Malcolm spent his childhood and adolescence in Omaha, Lansing, Boston, and New York City before his incarceration in the Massachusetts State Prison for larceny in 1946. He was released from prison in 1952 and began working with the Nation of Islam. This organization gave him an opportunity to hone his leadership skills and he rose rapidly through the ranks, becoming a valued lieutenant and surrogate son of Nation of Islam leader Elijah Muhammad. Indeed, he became Muhammad's spokesperson, minister–at–large, and agent. With his wife Betty Shabazz, Malcolm fathered six daughters: Attallah, Qubilah, Ilyasah, Gamilah, Malikah, and Malaak. Malcolm's popularity and influence provoked petty jealousies and led to tensions with members of Muhammad's Family. Rumormongering by these family members and other Nation of Islam officials, facilitated by the clandestine agent provocateurs of the FBI, drove a wedge between Malcolm and Muhammad. Muhammad suspended Malcolm, using the latter's irreverent comments about the assassination of President John F. Kennedy as a pretext. Malcolm responded by denouncing the Nation of Islam; he also founded a rival organization, Muslim Mosque Inc., made the Hajj to Mecca, and converted to Sunni Islam. When he returned to America he founded the Organization of Afro-American Unity, which would serve as the political arm of his new revolutionary nationalist movement. Many people thought that Malcolm was on the cusp of his most fruitful period of leadership. But before he could sink his teeth into the work of unifying a strong critique of white supremacy with a critique of American colonialism and capitalism (and, assuming his continued personal growth, a critique of the American gender system), he was assassinated on February 21, 1965. After his death, Malcolm became an icon for a younger generation of black radicals and revolutionaries. He is often viewed in tandem with Martin Luther King, Jr. as the Janus-faced presentation of leadership possibilities ("by any means necessary" or massive, nonviolent civil disobedience) in the black freedom struggle, during the middle of the twentieth century.

In this chapter and in chapter 3, I trace Malcolm's Afro-*Eccentric* spirit using the Muslim categories of Jahiliyyah, Jihad, Hijrah, and Hajj.

Ancestor Piety

Surah 24: Al-Nur (The Light)

Or (the Unbelievers' state) is like the depths of darkness in a vast deep ocean, overwhelmed with billow topped by billow, topped by (dark) clouds: depths of darkness, one above another: if a man stretches out his hands, he can hardly see it! For any to whom Allah giveth not light, there is no light!

Qur'an 24:40

Here is an enlightened, post-*Jahiliyyah* Malcolm reflecting on the darkness of his drug use:

Cocaine produces, for those who sniff its powdery crystals, an illusion of supreme well-being, and a soaring over-confidence in both physical and mental ability. You think you could whip the heavyweight champion, and that you are smarter than anybody. There was also that feeling of timelessness. And there were intervals of ability to recall and review things that had happened years back with an astonishing clarity. (AMX 155–6)

Long before cocaine gave Malcolm K. Little a false clarity—a pseudo-Enlightenment—and sent his life spiraling down a rat hole of criminality, he experienced a great trauma. His father, the Reverend Early Little died on an Omaha, Nebraska night in 1931. Was he murdered as Malcolm claims or was his death an unfortunate accident? Did he die at the hands of white men or is this the preferred memory of a man who even then suffered and would suffer again the closed fist of a white supremacist society? Memory works in strange ways; often brilliant and vivacious, yet wrong. What we remember with clarity is sometimes inaccurate. Remembering what did not happen and failing to remember what did happen constitute two sides of the same reality. Perhaps we misremember or repress memories because of their traumatic associations. Or we misremember because some memories do not interest us or because we are cognitively limited and cannot remember everything. Memory is selective. There is a complex and ambiguous relationship among memory, accuracy, factuality, and truth. This is especially true when considering "autobiographical memory," those memories selected and ordered by our desire to represent our life in a particular manner. Such memory provides both the medium and text of this study.

Malcolm remembers his father as a Baptist preacher[2] and a black Zionist, preaching the gospel of Jesus Christ and the gospel of African redemption. To say that Malcolm venerated his father understates the case. As an adult, remembering his life as a young boy, Malcolm describes his father—big, very black, and fearless—in the heroic language of Greek tragedy (AMX 4). This imagery tempts one to think of Freud's description of his father as a "titan." Titans, of course are gods, the predecessors of the Olympians. Freud took his godlike father as an archetype of "the father" in human culture, which provides the prototype for how we image god.[3] By pursuing this Freudian line of inquiry, we might better understand an apparent paradox. Early Little behaved like an ogre; he beat Louise and she beat the children.[4] Whether the children, in the proverbial sense of "shit running down hill," kicked the family dog is unclear. One of Malcolm's biographers supplements this—the portrait of a man who brutalizes his family—with the following: Earl "was notoriously unfaithful to Louise—'a natural-born whoremonger,'" who beat his girlfriends as badly as he did his wife; a poor or indifferent provider, he enjoyed pleasing others at the expense of his family, which often went hungry. He had a criminal record and behaved like a confidence man; he behaved, in the African American vernacular, like a "jackleg" preacher.[5] Yet Malcolm venerated him. How do we explain this paradox? Freud's oedipal theory, a totem-based account of human culture, provides one explanation.[6]

Freud's theory is based on a "conjectural" rather than a "factual" history; it is a thought experiment in which he speculates on the origins of human civilization using Darwin's reference to a "primal horde." In this speculative view, Freud characterizes primitive human society as a "horde" comprised of an alpha male, subordinate males, and females. The subordinate males are the sons of the dominant couple; the female offspring are their sisters. The alpha male exercises tyrannical control of the horde, which includes monopolizing sexual access to the females. The sons seethe with desire and envy; they cower before the alpha male who maintains his sexual monopoly through deadly violence, killing any one who challenges his sexual rights. The sons are ambivalent. They both love and fear their father. They envy him too, since they want what he has, namely, sexual access to the females. Burning with incestuous desire, the brothers grow green with envy, and blush red with rage. Eventually they put an end to this intolerable arrangement by killing their father. This act of patricide causes them to feel sad and guilty: sad because they truly loved and admired their father, guilty because they envied and hated him. Now they fear that one of them might aspire to the tyrannical status of alpha male. They fear that the same love-hate relationship will develop; the same death wish as a repetition compulsion drives them to reenact the primal murder (of the father), and thus reproduce the initial trauma. Their fear and desire threaten to pile fratricide on patricide. As foresight is the better part of desire, the brothers decide to renounce their incestuous instincts by prohibiting relations with any females in the horde. Henceforth, sexual desire would be satisfied exogamously, that is, with nonclan members. This act of instinctual renunciation, especially the exclusion of mother as sexual object, causes pain. The maintenance of this act requires something stronger than law. Hence the incest taboo and the guilt associated with it, which enforces the renunciation of oedipal desires. Through this cunning of desire and guilt—the compromises that comprise the incest taboo—the immediate problem of sexual tyranny and violence is more or less addressed. But these compromises leave something unresolved: a nagging sense of guilt. To reiterate, the brothers both love and hate their father. They express their hatred by killing him, their love by eating his body. By cannibalizing their father, eating his flesh and drinking his blood, a primordial act of communion (*religio*), they identify with him. Through identification (cannibalistic communion) and transference (idealization), the brothers diminish their sense of guilt for their murderous aggression. Through the dreamwork of memory, they forget the tyranny and terror of their actually living father. Repressing their envy and fear, they make father larger than life, covering him with a halo, as they actively repress the knowledge of how amoral he had been. In short, they deify him.[7] Their father becomes god.

The inadequacy of Freud's theory notwithstanding, it does shed some light on father-son relationships. Malcolm deified his father with bits of ambivalence poking through the subterfuge. He depicts his father's death as murder at the hands of white men who feared his political effectiveness, even though some evidence suggests that his death was accidental.[8] Earl Little, the alpha male of the Little horde was struck down by the envy of evil white men. This is Malcolm's account. Deviating somewhat from the Freudian script, his mother conspired, no doubt for her own ambivalent reasons, in deifying her abusive husband. "Her insistence that her husband had been a victim of political assassination provided her children with a father-image of which they could at last be proud."[9] Malcolm's veneration of his father foreshadows his deification of Muhammad, clearly a surrogate father for a man who had become fatherless at a tender age. One can "hear a gleam" in Malcolm's voice, which one might have seen in his eyes, when he describes his father's great work—the pride and privilege he felt being involved, being about his father's business, even though he was no older than six and had not reached the age of Christian accountability (AMX 9). In his early, childhood religious world, the gospel of Jesus and the gospel of black liberation were interchangeable: one world, one faith, one baptism, and "one race, one nation, one destiny." In a sense, the Reverend Earl Little and Marcus Garvey, black Christianity and the black Zionist religion of Garveyism meld into a single reality.[10] Princes shall come out of the biblical Egypt and from the American Egypt, Ethiopia and the descendants of black slaves will stretch forth their hands to God (AMX 9).

Though he venerates his father, Malcolm is not blind. I think it significant that he does not repress the knowledge of his father abusing his mother, even if he seems remarkably bereft of moral judgment. Consider how common it is for religious people to exempt god from moral judgments they routinely make of humans. If god did it, it is right. Think of the strained arguments they make, the logical absurdities they are willing to tolerate. Anything to avoid the conclusion that god behaved as badly as any bad man. If you extend Freud's primal horde allegory in this direction, it might provide insight into Malcolm's reticence where normative ethics demands judgment.

Without minimizing the Reverend Earl Little's culpability, what begs closer attention is the interreligious conflict that fueled much of this abuse. Malcolm's father was Baptist and his mother's religious proclivities were those of a Seventh Day Adventist, whose dietary habits she found attractive.[11] This conflict between spouses was among other things a conflict between so-called mainline Christianity and sectarian Christianity. It circles the most crucial and intimate of human behaviors, the desire to eat. Based on a biological need, this desire is so powerful that it sometimes cannibalizes the desire for sex, as eating is sexualized and sex is conceived as a meal. This explains the "rabbit incident" in which Malcolm's father, in an angry huff, ripped off the head of a rabbit and tossed it at the feet of his wife with the demand that she cook it for dinner. Rabbit along with pork was on her religiously proscribed list of food. In the view of this most Jewish of all forms of Christianity, such meat was taboo. The stability of Earl and Louise's marriage, the trauma of seeing his mother beaten, the patterns of repetition such trauma often produces transgenerationally, and the destabilization of family life, circled in significant ways interreligious disagreement that involved the most basic human activity of all.

Immediately after the "rabbit incident" as Earl blew out of the house like a thunderstorm, Louise had a premonition of his death. Earl was found near the railroad tracks with his left arm crushed and left leg nearly severed, bleeding to death[12]—the victim, it appears, of a tragic accident or, if Malcolm is correct, of a racially-inspired murder. Earl Little's death devastated Malcolm. From an object-relations[13] point of view where the mother is the primary object for the infant and thus the prototype of god, one is impressed by Malcolm's primary attachment to his father. Is this attachment to father and relative detachment from mother related to the abuse? Could this abuse, at least as a working hypothesis, be implicated, perhaps by its very absence from Malcolm's account, in his mother's descent into mental illness? In Malcolm's account, his mother's mental decline follows the death of his father, the bleak prospects for a Negro widow in depression-era America, and the humiliating help and annoying surveillance of state welfare workers. Louise Little suffered under their prying eyes and inquisitorial manner. As a charity case, she suffered from wounded pride. She suffered, no doubt, from her family's sharp decline in social status—once the wife of a preacher and "race man" and the mother of his children and now the object of charity. Perhaps she recalled her salad days, when she was young and everything seemed possible, when as Louisa Langdon Norton she met Early Little in Montreal at a UNIA (Universal Negro Improvement Association) meeting in 1918. Both she and Earl were "devoted followers of Garvey." They were married in Montreal the following year and then moved to the United States. Their oldest child, Wilfred was born in Philadelphia in 1920.[14] Earl led the Omaha branch of UNIA[15] and Louise wrote for the organization's paper—*The Negro World*. Now, ten years later, things were in chaos. Her kids had become unruly: Malcolm had embarked on a career of petty crime. His incipient criminality comprised one of a dozen pressures on his mother that exploded in a sad conclusion.

Malcolm seamlessly weaves a fascinating account of his mother's insanity with an account of her religious fervor. Under pressure, her Seventh Day Adventist convictions had only grown. A depression-era Negro widow, the mother of several children who refused to accept charity in the form of a recently butchered pig, Louise could only be understood by the black farmer who offered the gift, the welfare workers who apparently heard about her refusal of the gift, and by her kids who desperately wanted her to accept the gift as sure evidence that she had gone crazy. Religious people were crazy, especially when they refused good meat. Was this not the same judgment that Earl Little was making when he ripped off the head of the rabbit with his strong, bare hands and tossed the bleeding carcass at Louise's feet? His religious dispute with her led to a dramatic act of contempt. The incredulity of the state welfare workers led to the charge that she was insane. Her views were eccentric, Afro-*Eccentric*. One wonders how this affected the young Malcolm X, then known by his birth name of Malcolm K. Little. One thing is clear. It did not constrain him from hunting rabbits with his deceased father's 22 caliber rifle, which surely broke his mother's heart. Maybe his mother's pain was part of his desire, since, according to one biographer, he had a cautious and distant relationship with her.[16] Malcolm claims that she hated his color and believed that she hated him.[17] If Malcolm was his father's favorite child, then he was her least favorite. Or so he claims. Like many troubled kids, Malcolm misbehaved and underperformed in school. After his father death and the family's decline, he was knocked for a further psychological loop when he discovered in 1938 that his mother was "knocked-up." This irrefutable evidence of "illicit" sexuality embarrassed her and the children. Consequently, her depression deepened. Malcolm does not mention this fact in the *Autobiography,* or its possible relation to his mother's insanity, or the doubts about his own paternity, given his father's dark skin, Malcolm's light skin, and rumors of his mother's "promiscuity."[18] Several events marked Louise Little's mental decline: her husband dead, possibly murdered, frequently fired from jobs when employers discovered that she was half-black;[19] her kids increasingly out of control, eventually becoming wards of the state; jilted by a lover after a year-long relationship; the scandal of an out-of-wedlock pregnancy, and the birth of Malcolm's half-brother "Butch."[20]

Christianity

Malcolm associates the disintegration of his family not with his father's death but with his mother's mental breakdown, with the pervasive, panopticon-like intrusiveness of the state and with his own growing propensity for crime. Though he insisted that he loved his mother, the subtext of his claim suggests that he did not behave as a loving son. Louise's husband beat her and thrust forbidden food in her face. Malcolm hunted this same unclean animal as food and became a juvenile delinquent (AMX 22). By his own account, Malcolm's delinquency preceded his mother's insanity. He ties his emerging criminality closely, even integrally with various forms of Christianity he encountered and with the larger Christian world in which he lived. Malcolm's conflation of Christianity and crime disturbs one of his biographers immensely.[21] The biographer, however, substituting peevishness for an argument, fails to show the implausibility of Malcolm's claim. For the sake of simplicity, I shall consider Malcolm's Christianity and his criminality separately.

Malcolm's first extended characterization of his early religious life is the following passage:

> My brother Philbert, the one just older than me, loved church, but it confused and amazed me. I would sit goggle-eyed at my father jumping and shouting as he preached, with the congregation jumping and shouting behind him, their souls and bodies devoted to singing and praying. Even at that young age, I couldn't believe in the Christian concept of Jesus as someone divine. And no religious person, until I was a man in my twenties—and then in prison—could tell me anything. I had very little respect for most people who represented religion. (AMX 7)

That Malcolm Little was reared as a Christian is beyond serious dispute. His father was a Baptist preacher; his mother a member of the greater Seventh Day Adventist tradition, and like many young people, as this passage suggests, Malcolm neither enjoyed church nor understood doctrine. But how seriously can we take his claim? I do not question his goggle-eyed reaction to the theatricality of his father's pulpit manners. Perhaps these antics embarrassed Malcolm. If he was embarrassed, he would not be the first child of a preacher to feel that way. I do not question his apparently visceral reaction to the ecstatic physicality[22] of black Protestant Christianity, especially in its Pentecostal incarnations.

He is not the first child to be frightened, amused, or otherwise baffled by these displays of spirit. *If I might be permitted a personal observation: Even as an experienced, fully-formed adult, I am startled, slightly unnerved, and depending on their duration, irritated by such displays. I am hardly unusual in this regard.* There is nothing strange or unique about Malcolm's reaction. (We might call his reaction to the shouting tradition of the Black Church, Afro-*Eccentric;* it does not conform to the normative expectations of the Standard Narrative.) What I question, however, is the following phrase: "Even at that young age, I couldn't believe in the Christian concept of Jesus as someone divine." Here is a case of "autobiographical memory"[23] of which we are rightly suspicious. The claim that a six-year-old, however precocious, could understand such a complex point of doctrine is suspect. Many mature Christians go to their graves never having understood the doctrine that Jesus simultaneously is truly human and truly divine (I doubt that this doctrine can be persuasively explicated). I am not suggesting that Malcolm believed what he claims not to have believed; rather, I regard his state as one of ignorance, conducive to neither belief nor disbelief. Malcolm's profession of unbelief reads like an act of retrospection, an interpolation of current views driven by current purposes. Here one discerns the editorial hand of Malcolm X, the ex-Christian and soon-to-be ex-member of the Nation of Islam who redacts his former views to bring them in line with current views. "We were much better off," he continues, "than the town Negroes who would shout, as my father preached, for the pie-in-the-sky and their heaven in the hereafter while the white man had his here on earth" (AMX 8). This sentence also reads like an editorial redaction of memory, especially the last clause, which comes straight out of Nation of Islam theology in which the white man's heaven is the black man's hell.[24]

The death of Malcolm's father brought greater religious freedom for his mother. Her semisuppressed Seventh Day Adventism was liberated and began to flower. She acquired new Adventist neighbors with whom she met frequently, discussing no doubt the contours of the Adventist tradition and various points of doctrine. She spent a lot of time with them, giving full range to religious dispositions that clearly predated the death of Earl Little. Malcolm describes his mother's growing attraction to the Adventist tradition in the following passage:

> Like us, they were against eating rabbits and pork; they followed the Mosaic dietary laws. They ate nothing of the flesh without a split hoof, or that didn't chew a cud. We began to go with my

mother to the Adventist meetings that were held further out in the country. For us children, I know that the major attraction was the good food they served. *But we listened too* (emphasis mine). There were a handful of Negroes, from small towns in the area, but I would say that it was ninety-nine percent white people. The Adventist felt that we were living at the end of time, that the world was soon coming to an end. But they were the friendliest white people I had ever seen. (AMX 20–1)

I can only speculate on how Louise Little acquired these disposi- tions. But what we know about black communities during the nineteen thirties includes the explosive growth of black Jewish sects some of which observed kosher dietary rules.[25] Perhaps she encountered one or more of these sects before or during her marriage to Earl. Black Islamic sects with similar dietary habits and even hybrid Christian-Jewish, Christian-Islamic, and Jewish-Islamic groups emerged around the same time, any of which may account for her religiously derived dietary habits. We cannot know for sure. But we do know that the Adventist tradition is a common affiliation among blacks and a prior encounter with this Christian sect may be sufficient to explain her disposition. Before Earl's death, Louise's dietary habits anticipated the restrictions of the Seventh Day Adventist faith she later adopted. Malcolm's Muslim aversion to pork, therefore, had a Jewish and a Christian prehistory. (Though surely part of the Black Church tradition, even if he encoun- tered it in a white context, Malcolm's Seventh Day Adventism veered in an Afro-*Eccentric* direction.) That Malcolm's encounter with Seventh Day Adventism was formative rather than fleeting is suggested by the sentence that I emphasized in the passage above where he describes his reaction and that of other children to the Adventist Church. Good food was the main attraction: *But we listened too*. A claim such as this should be given a lot of credence since it cuts against the retrospective, anti- Christian narrative Malcolm otherwise constructs.

The disintegration of Malcolm's family contributed to his childhood encounter with a diversity of Christian religious expressions. His fos- ter family, the Gohannases, was Holiness Pentecostal, what Malcolm calls "sanctified Holy Rollers."[26] Malcolm describes his new church as "even louder than the Baptists I had known," as preachers and con- gregants jumped high, shouted and sung with full-throated intensity, as they swayed, rocked and rolled, chanting, moaning, and crying, while beating tambourines until they screamed (AMX 24). Though unaware of its significance, Malcolm also describes how the tradition of *conjure* (so-called black folk religion) was present side by side with conventional, black Christianity.[27] Malcolm, elaborating on his Pentecostal encounters, has this to say: "It was spooky, with ghosts and spirituals and 'ha'nts' seeming to be in the very atmosphere when finally we all came out of church, going back home" (AMX 24).

Rebellion, Crime, and Punishment

Malcolm describes himself as a black brainwashed Christian. He credits the move from Lansing to Boston, where he fell in with the "criminal element," with saving him from the mindless and soulless hypocrisy of black Christianity (AMX 46). Malcolm associates his youthful Christianity with ignorance and degradation: ignorance of Christian duplicity and hypocrisy in the oppression of black people, in denying his worth as a black man, and for repressing the glorious truth of Islam. In Malcolm's view, criminality and degradation characterized the underside of Christianity. The criminal life allowed him to see just how criminal Christianity was. To put it paradoxically, Malcolm was saved from Christianity by crime. Illicit sex, drugs, and robbery provided the conditions that made possible his redemption from life as a black brainwashed Christian. It was in this condition of Jahiliyyah (pre-Islamic ignorance, barbarism, and darkness), while sitting in a prison cell where he called himself Satan that he would first encounter the truth of Islam. There Allah, the giver of light, would first give him—through a glass darkly, to mix an Islamic image with a Christian metaphor—the first light of a new religious day.

Malcolm's pilgrimage from Christianity to crime began in petty fashion before mental illness separated his mother from her senses: before her lover jilted her, her last chance, perhaps, after the death of her husband for a "happy life," and before the pressure of caring for several rambunctious children became too much. During this time of trial and tribulation, Malcolm began to shoot and eat rabbits and to steal. His thievery attracted the unwanted attention of the state welfare department whose caseworkers decided to remove him from his birth home and place him with a foster family. He was not long with his foster family, the Gohannases, before further unruly, though not necessarily criminal behavior landed him in reform school. In retrospect, he would describe himself during these reform school years as the mascot of white folks' amusement. Though frequently addressed as "nigger," this seems to have been a happy time in his life, when he experienced many of the wonders, joys, and growing pains of people that age. It was also during this period that he met his older half sister, Ella Collins, who would provide crucial support throughout his life. He first encountered Ella on a visit she made from Boston to Lansing. Clearly impressed by her physical stature, blackness, confidence, and dominance, he regards her with awe. She reminds him of their father.[28] We get a sense of who Ella is when she takes her younger siblings to the state hospital to see their mother, a woman who was not Ella's mother and whom she presumably had never met but whose importance to her essentially orphaned, younger half brothers and sisters she surely understood. That summer Malcolm went to Boston to visit Ella. When he turned fifteen, she arranged the transfer of his custody from the State of Michigan to herself. Malcolm went to Boston to live with her permanently (AMX 19, 21, 24, 30, 34–5, 39–41, 45–6).

From Boston Malcolm took a short train ride to the "Big Apple." Only aged seventeen, he got a job as a dishwasher aboard the "Yankee Clipper"—the New York, New Haven and Hartford train—by lying about his age. Ella was pleased because she thought this would break up his relationship with Sophia (a pseudonym for Bea), a white woman whom he pursued to the detriment of his relationship with Laura. Laura was a black girl whom Ella had met and liked. She was safe. In contrast, Sophia represented danger and, perhaps, she stoked the fires of Ella's resentment. After all, they lived in a society where white men routinely lynched black men for consorting with white women. To that injury add a further insult: the ideology of white womanhood plus an aesthetic preference for the white female body went hand in hand with the denigration of black women such as Ella. Malcolm's dishwasher job aboard the Yankee clipper put money in his pocket and his body in Harlem. There he honed a hustler image, aesthetic, and ethic that Spike Lee memorializes in his 1992 biopicture, *Malcolm X*. In Harlem, Malcolm recognized who he was: not a respectable, law-abiding, upwardly mobile "striver" as many of Harlem's residents were, but a denizen of Harlem's underworld of depravity, parasites, and hustlers. "This world," Malcolm remarked, "is where I belonged." New York was heaven. Harlem was Seventh Heaven and Small's Paradise was a favorite hangout. Harlem was Blacktown. "Blacktown crawled with white people, with pimps, prostitutes, bootleggers, with hustlers of all kinds, with colorful characters, and with police and prohibition agents." New York City—Harlem, Blacktown, Seventh Heaven—functioned as Malcolm's graduate school of vice. In what sounds like boasting, Malcolm remarks: "I was thus schooled well, by experts in such hustles as the numbers, pimping, con games of many kinds, peddling dope, and thievery of all sorts, including armed robbery" (AMX 82–3, 85, 89, 94, 96–7).

Malcolm's most influential professor in the ethics of vice was Sammy McKnight a.k.a. "Sammy the Pimp."[29] As one would expect of any successful pimp, Sammy carefully observed female behavior and had an intuitive understanding of heterosexual female psychology. He knew which women were vulnerable, what they lacked, and how to fill their emptiness. One night, Sammy's intuition was rewarded when he saw a blonde nicknamed the "Alabama Peach" at the Savory Ballroom. Without speaking to her, merely by observing as she stood on the sidelines watching Negroes dance, "he could tell." There must have been something in the way that she appeared, and the way she looked at Negro men, something about her body language that subtly told Sammy the Pimp that she was ripe. He plucked her like a peach from the tree of her emptiness and desire, as he would pluck others. As it was, the Alabama Peach had been a sexually precocious grade-school girl fascinated by the mythology of Negro-male anatomy and sexual prowess. Under the "hothouse" conditions of lynch law and the "forbidden fruit syndrome," she had extorted sex from her father's Negro male employee, threatening to scream rape if he did not comply. She now pursued her desire for black flesh in a degraded context that mirrored the degradation of her youthful sexual exploits and exploitive behavior. This was Malcolm's first lesson: women, especially white women are treacherous. Lesson two was taught by the kind of women that Sammy "employed." Malcolm claims that he learned more about women from prostitutes than from anyone else. He learned that most women could not be trusted; that "church ladies" were often whores in drag; that domineering, hectoring, and psychologically castrating wives drove their men into the beds of prostitutes; that the greatest desire of men was to be men and not be pushed around by their women; that men needed to know what pimps knew—women should alternately be babied with affection and severely disciplined. Tender loving care followed by a slap in the mouth was a time-honored management technique in this rough trade. "These tough women," he remarks, "said that it worked with *them*. All women, by their nature, are fragile and weak: they are attracted to the male in whom they see strength." Lesson three: white women are practical and not the least bit sentimental. While they would "screw" Negro men and might even fall insanely in love with them, they would never marry them (AMX 103–4, 106–8, 111). As remarkable and *alarming* as the details of Malcolm's account is the absence of any evidence in his pre-Nation of Islam, Nation, or post-Nation life that he ever questioned this hustler's ethic or the "truth" of these lessons. He would go to his grave with a suspicious regard for women— the Eves, Sirens, and Pandoras of the species. Malcolm's gender views were retrograde, even by contemporary standards.

From the dark world of the sex worker to the dark world of the hustler, it was the same world under a different description. As a hustler, Malcolm ran numbers (an illegal form of gambling) and steered those who desired illicit, socially unacceptable, and "perverted" forms of sex to the appropriate provider. He also consumed copious amounts of drugs. In the *Autobiography*, Malcolm describes himself as if he were a significant hustler, a celebrity well known by leading figures in the Harlem underworld. One biographer disputes Malcolm's status and suggests that his account of why he left Harlem may be a self-aggrandizing exaggeration.[30] I will come back to this point in a moment after describing a sequence of events that Malcolm claims forced him to flee Harlem. First, according to Malcolm, he got a little sloppy. Owing to inattentiveness or, perhaps, excessive drug use, he apparently confused a set of numbers that he had played earlier with the winning number and thus had been paid three hundred dollars by the notorious West Indian Archie. A big time hustler, who once worked as an enforcer for the Dutch Schultz crime syndicate and now worked as a big-time numbers runner, Archie confronts Malcolm at his home and demands his misappropriated money. Taking on faith Malcolm's claim that his number had "hit," Archie in effect had extended Malcolm credit by paying him immediately out of his own pocket as he did with all his good customers.[31] While an unusual practice, this was clearly good customer service as it reduced the time between winning and being paid. It involved a fiduciary relationship, a relationship of "criminal trust," an act of "criminal faith" between runner and player. Apparently, Archie believed that Malcolm had "played" him. A hustler does not like to be hustled. His very status as a hustler depends on his ability to "play" and not get "played." Oozing with anger, Archie was determined to get to get paid, if not revenge. He stood before Malcolm with a 32-20 in his hands. Frightened, Malcolm tried to persuade Archie that a man as smart as he could not have made the mistake of paying someone who had not won, whose number had not "hit." The confrontation is suddenly defused when Archie backs out of the door giving Malcolm until noon the next day to repay the money.

Malcolm describes this confrontation as "a classic hustler code impasse," though impasse does not appear to be the right word since it implies a balance of power whereas Archie, gun in hand, subjected Malcolm to his mercy. In any event, the hustler code as Malcolm describes it was all about " 'face' and 'honor' " and had little to do with money. In Malcolm's view, Archie had aged and was slipping. An old hustler, Archie was intent on sending a message to young hustlers such as Malcolm, dreaming of the day when they would knock the old man from his perch. He had to show them that he was still in the game and they had best beware. In the dog-eat-dog world of the street, hustling a hustler before he hustled you and especially if he *had* hustled you was a way of sending that message. On the other hand, Malcolm does consider the possibility that he did make a mistake and had inadvertently misappropriated Archie's money but he does not admit that he cheated. The real issue, however, was honor and face, not allowing the other dogs to think that you were vulnerable, a top dog on his way to becoming an underdog. If there is no honor among thieves, then there is little pity among dogs. Malcolm's conflict with Archie, therefore, was all about dog psychology. Subdominant dogs short-circuit deadly conflict by submitting to the top dog. But where a subdominant dog will expose his throat as a sign of subordination, Malcolm chose to flee. With his Boston friend "Shorty" to the rescue and behind the wheel of their getaway car (in the *Autobiography*, "Shorty" is usually a fictional composite of several real-life people but in this case he is one Malcolm Jarvis[32]), Malcolm beat a quick path home. Or did he? There is no question that Malcolm Little left New York and returned to Boston. But one biographer finds little evidence that Malcolm was fleeing a trap constructed by West Indian Archie, disgruntled, "tough-looking *paisanos*" who believed he had "ripped them off," and by a scared kid hustler whom he had assaulted (AMX 144, 146–8, 152–3).[33]

Dr. Fanon's Couch

There was a time we use to drool in the mouth over white people. We thought they were pretty because we were blind. We were dumb. We couldn't see them as they are.

Malcolm X[34]

Out of the blackest part of my soul, across the zebra striping of my mind, surges this desire to be suddenly *white*.

I wish to be acknowledged not as *black* but as *white*.

Now—and this is a form of recognition that Hegel had not envisaged[35]—who but a white woman can do this for me? By loving me she proves that I am worthy of white love. I am loved like a white man.

I am a white man.

Her love takes me onto the noble road that leads to total realization. . . .

I marry white culture, white beauty, white whiteness.

When my restless hands caress those white breasts, they grasp white civilization and dignity and make them mine.

                                                    Frantz Fanon[36]

One of the curious aspects of the *Autobiography* is Malcolm's obsession with white women, an obsession that he displaces quite frequently onto others. Malcolm *loved* white women or, rather, what they represented. With white women he experienced a kind of metamorphosis: the ugly, black caterpillar became a beautiful, white butterfly; a crawling worm took flight. So it was in the white supremacist world in which Malcolm lived where whiteness symbolized everything valuable, everything good and beautiful. The mythology of white supremacy invested this goodness and beauty in white women who, as the privileged bearers of cultural values, exemplified the best that white civilization had to offer. Surely this must have been true. For did they not lynch black men for having sex with white women?[37] Had not countless black men tasted their own severed and bleeding genitals for less, for merely looking at white women with lust in their eyes? Did not such intercourse violate, deflower, despoil, degrade, and blacken white women? Was this not, as the French say, a case of *viol*,[38] *viol*ence, *viol*ation, rape? Was not sex between black men and white women by definition rape? If, as Fanon suggests, one could have intercourse under these conditions and not lose one's life, would that not be transcendence?

Malcolm was dancing the Lindy Hop with his black girlfriend Laura when he first saw her, a fine-looking blonde. Just as suddenly, his interest in Laura ran as flat as an old soda on the Roseland ballroom floor. Malcolm was "sprung," enthralled, bewitched by "this fine blonde" who for the sake of anonymity he called Sophia. Malcolm, as the cliché goes, dropped Laura like a bad habit when he dropped her off at home. He and Sophia were off and running. That she was no common whore, he knew instantly. Her clothes were too expensive and, perhaps, she did not have that worn-down and worn-out look of the typical whore. By all appearances, she was not for sale. So Malcolm had "a status symbol of the first order" and he felt very lucky. He had a "Beacon Hill chick," which increased his status in black downtown Roxbury. "[W]ith the best-looking white woman who ever walked in those bars and clubs," he became the target of other hustlers who envied him and wanted to steal his "fine white woman" (AMX 78–80).

Malcolm "drooled in the mouth" for white women.[39] His remark that he had never "seen a black man that desired white women as sincerely as Shorty did" seems to cry out for psychoanalysis. Is Malcolm talking about Shorty or about himself? Was Malcolm merely talking about Shorty's fascination with "two-dollar white chicks" or was he describing his own fascination as well? When he refers almost breathlessly to the "most glamorous white women I'd ever seen" is he not referring to his own aesthetic appraisal and sexual desire? Was he not among the throng of Negro men in Roxbury that he describes as engaging in "a little freelance lusting" with equally enthusiastic white women? Was he not speaking of his own desire when he assumed that his brother "Reginald, like most of the Negroes" he knew, "would go for a white woman"? (AMX 54, 56, 58, 64, 130, 156–7). Is this not confirmed by the way Sophia swept him off his racially inferior and insecure feet? Even though he does not appear to have loved her or to have treated her with respect, and even if he exaggerated her beauty (yes, I know, beauty is in the eye of the beholder), was not her white skin a source of pride and honor in a world where his racial identification as a black man was dishonorable? As a descendant of slaves, ghetto dweller, criminal-in-the-making, and brutish, potential rapist of white women (I refer, of course, to the prevailing stigmata associated with black men), was not Malcolm miraculously transformed, racially elevated, and spiritually transfigured through a curious act of transference when he cupped Sophia's white breasts in his black hands? Is not this kind of transference precisely what we otherwise call idolatry?

Dreamwork

The itinerary of Malcolm's life included the following dark passages: youthful Christianity to thievery, reform school to illegal gambling and gun-toting drug abuse; peddling drugs to peddling sex, which (if we can believe the claims of one biographer) included, in the language of the street, brokering "the sell of other people's ass" and perhaps "the sell of his own ass."[40] Internet "whispers" about the so-called gay Malcolm X are powerful reminders of his iconic status.[41]

Malcolm was no longer a black, "brainwashed" Christian. Even Ella, he says, could not believe how much of an *atheist* he had become. Malcolm had become a cocaine addict, and this addiction would play a large role in his second tour of Boston. Drugs and religion have a long and intimate relationship. Both are modalities of transcendence, ways of becoming larger than oneself, getting beyond oneself, losing and thereby finding one's true self, a new and a higher self. Both are ways of escaping a world that on its own terms is intolerable. Both are ways of seeing things that cannot be seen with an unaltered mind, which is why drug-induced ecstasy is part of the visionary rites of many traditions, which in turn is tied up with the common view that dreams are a source of divine revelation and knowledge. But drug-induced knowledge can be deceptive as exemplified by a new turn in Malcolm's criminal career. He became the leader of a burglary ring. In addition to his friend "Shorty," the ring included Malcolm's girlfriend Sophia, her sister and now Shorty's "woman," and Rudy, the son of an Italian mother and Negro father. Malcolm's leadership was confirmed when he played Russian roulette in front of his crime partners. Apparently, Malcolm was prepared, in the street vernacular, "to pay the cost to be the boss." After this display of recklessness, the gang consented to his leadership.[42] Malcolm claims that the burglary ring was successful until his drug problem, with its false knowledge, courage, and euphoria got in the way. The following passage is a companion piece to the epigraph at the beginning of this chapter:

> Drugs [Malcolm said, referring to his fear of being caught] helped me push the thought to the back of my mind. They were the center of my life. I had gotten to the stage where every day I used enough drugs—reefers, cocaine, or both—so that I felt above any worries, any strains. If any worries did manage to push their way through to the surface of my consciousness, I could float them back where they came from until tomorrow, and then until the next day. (AMX, 162–5, 169–70)

Here I analogize from conditions in sixth century Arabia to Malcolm's criminality. Muslims refer to this period as *Jahiliyyah*, the pre-Islamic age of pagan darkness. As scholars note, robbery, female infanticide, the abuse of women, and "vendetta justice" governed social relations. Malcolm lived this kind of life: disregarding the interests of others, disdaining law and morality. Malcolm was a parasite, feeding off black and white hosts alike, bereft of self-love, knowledge, and light. As the Qur'an puts it, to those whom Allah does not give light, there is no light. As a result of his drug use and the false enlightenment it produces, Malcolm got sloppy and got caught. He was trapped like an animal, caged like a beast—in the courtroom where he, "Shorty," Sophia, and her sister stood before a judge, and later as he sat in the darkness of a prison cell, where one could easily imagine him humming "What did I do, to be so black and blue?" The law and the narrow dimensions of a prison cell were not insubstantial matters; cocaine could not transcend the tensile strength of steel bars. Trapped, caught, and convicted, Malcolm would spend his early twenties in a prison cell. His life had become the mid-twentieth-century American equivalent of life in the Arabian Peninsula before the Prophet Muhammad began to receive the revelation of Allah. As the jury said "Guilty!" and the door of Malcolm's prison cell clanked shut, the darkness of Jahiliyyah closed around him.

Atheism

Along with his crime partner "Shorty," Malcolm arrived at Charlestown State Prison in February 1946. As a new inmate, he was a "fish" and a "number"—22843. In his *Autobiography*, Malcolm implies that prison was very traumatic, affecting the mind in paradoxical ways. On the one side, prison blotted out certain memories while, on the other side, it burnt memories indelibly into his brain: the bars of his cell, its coffin-like dimensions, and the omnipresent smell of feces. Malcolm could not tolerate these conditions. In the vernacular of the drug culture, he went "on a mission," seeking escape from intolerable conditions through a "good high." He discovered that you could get high on nutmeg. Better yet, corrupt prison guards served as a reliable conduit for illegal drugs such as Marijuana, Nembutal, and Benzedrine, which they smuggled into the prison under the authority of their badge and against the meaning of their oath. Law-breakers and law-enforcers benefited mutually from this illicit arrangement. Guards supplemented their meager incomes and prisoners got high (AMX, 176–7).

Malcolm discovered his atheism while a prisoner of the state of Massachusetts. His atheism was a conclusion not a presupposition. Considering the arc of his own life, he regarded his atheism as a consequence of the life that black men were fated to live in a white Christian society. Typecast as a criminal, white supremacy scripted his life as it had the lives of black men before him and as it would the lives of black men after him. The three *Fates* of white supremacy, Christianity, and family disintegration had tracked him down like a black Oedipus. Prison was his *fate*. Physically miserable, suffering the pain of withdrawal, Malcolm was "as evil-tempered as a snake," the proverbial, mythical snake in the Garden of Eden. Malcolm describes himself as the personification of evil. His "antireligious attitude" led other inmates to call him Satan (AMX 176–7).

By his own admission, Malcolm's atheism lacked an adequate, philosophical foundation. He does not put it this way but we could imagine him asking, "What does it mean to say that one is an atheist?" His fellow inmate and "friend" John Elton Bembry referred to in the *Autobiography* as "Bimbi" had apparently given this question considerable thought. His atheism was part of a coherent framework (AMX 178). He had done the cognitive work that allowed him to describe himself as an atheist matter-of-factly, without anger, rancor, or defensiveness. His atheism was coolly reasoned. It was mellow, mature, properly aged like a fine wine. Absent from his self-presentation was any evangelical spirit or excessive zeal or the sense that he had to convince others of the truth of his belief before he could believe it himself, if he were really to believe and hold that belief with conviction. His convictions did not require applause, an Amen Corner. In contrast with this attitude of Bimbi, it was precisely audience approval and confirmation that Malcolm sought when he cursed viciously and proclaimed his atheism loudly. The loudness of his proclamation stood in inverse relation to the strength of his convictions. His atheism seems thin and poorly thought-out when compared with the nonbelief of other black people in the Americas, across several generations, and through the many dark passages of their history. From the Middle Passage to the present, these black people chose to "curse god and die." As an example of this sentiment, consider Countee Cullen's poem "The Black Christ," the inspiration for which was the lynching of a black man and god's apparent indifference. The blaspheming narrator has had enough of this god, who demands praise but never answers prayers. As the Blasphemer puts it, "God is a toy; put Him away."[43]

Given cosmic indifference to black suffering, it is hard not to conclude that God is a white racist.[44] Rather than revere and depend on that god, it would be better to create one's own god from wood or stone. Better yet, one should recognize god as an idealized, though mortal construction of the cultural self as in the following poem by Cullen:

> Better my God should be
> This moving, breathing frame of me,
> Strong hands and feet, live hearts and eyes;
> And when these close, say then God dies.[45]

We should not hold Malcolm to the standards of poetry. Cullen mastered a medium and worked with skills that Malcolm (and Haley) did not have. This important caveat notwithstanding, the difference in seriousness, thoughtfulness, and conviction between Malcolm and Cullen's Blasphemer is apparent. Cullen published this poem the year that Malcolm turned four years old. He protested the same social conditions that led Malcolm's father to become a proponent of Marcus Garvey's back-to-Africa movement. The atheism in Cullen's poem is a form of social protest, an index of black suffering. Malcolm's atheism is more narrowly existential and self-referential. When one thinks of Malcolm, one thinks of Russian characters such as Raskolnikov and Ivan Karamazov, not so much their intellect but their self-obsession, if not solipsism. Malcolm appears to be thinking of no one but himself. Malcolm is no Camusean "rebel"; his atheism does not appear to be a form of "metaphysical rebellion" driven by cosmic injustice. His atheism is individualistic. It seems to have everything to do with his personal demons.

Cullen's poem helps us think about some other aspects of Malcolm's atheism. I explore the various permutations of Malcolm's professed atheism in relation to the following statement by the historian Louis DeCaro: "Bembry's atheism was a confident abandonment of all forms of theism, including Christianity; Malcolm's was only a street-hardened contempt for the Christian church and its members."[46] I think that DeCaro is right but only if we put the qualifying word "only" in quotation marks. Relying on a dictionary understanding, DeCaro associates atheism with the abandonment of all forms of theism. Historically, atheism is more complicated than he thinks. In imperial Rome, Jews and Christians were regarded as atheists because they refused to acknowledge the gods of Rome. In contrast, Christians regarded the Romans as atheists because they worshiped many gods, which was tantamount to worshiping no god at all. Both saw the other as denying what mattered most: for Romans, the plurality of deity and the centrality of the Roman cult; for Jews and Christians, the singularity and exclusivity of deity, the notion that god is one. In failing to pay homage to the local Roman cult, Jews and Christians were impious, antisocial, and misanthropic, as they showed contempt for the well-being of Rome and the citizens of the empire.[47] By requiring such homage, Rome showed contempt for the exclusivity of the Jewish and Christian gods. Each, Roman on the one side, Jew and Christian on the other, regarded the other as atheists.[48]

When Malcolm describes himself as an atheist and as Satan, his claims are perfectly comprehensible. Antagonism and contempt are standard modalities of atheism. Apart from any denial of the existence of god, which is only one modality of atheism, antagonism and contempt suggest that god and the gods do not merit our devotion. Atheism takes the form of the refusal to worship; thus expressing contempt for the moral attributes and power of the gods. The protagonist of Cullen's poem expresses such contempt when he describes god as a toy to be put away. (But he is doing something qualitatively different when he describes god as a mortal body with a black face. He asserts his own dignity and agency. In the language of Feuerbach's German idealism, the protagonist of Cullen's poem reappropriates his own alienated self when he sees god as merely the manifestation of his highest self.) In describing himself as Satan, Malcolm appropriates the most powerful symbol he can imagine to communicate his contempt of white Christian culture. This symbol proves all the more important when we consider the fact that Christian demonology, iconography, and imagery often portray Satan as a black man. Satan operates as the powerful, mythical-other within Christianity, the figure against which Christianity defines its virtues. Satan is the prototypical antichrist. As the black Satan, Malcolm is the *accuser*[49] of white America and its "ideology" of Christianity. He accuses white Christian America of enslaving black people, justifying their enslavement as god's will, and brainwashing them; therefore, in proclaiming the fatherhood of god and the brotherhood of man, Christian America behaves hypocritically. Christian virtues lie.

DeCaro takes Malcolm's anxiety over the nature and existence of god, evidenced by his profane outbursts before Bimbi, as giving the lie to Malcolm's atheistic self-description. Presumably, a genuine atheist is resolute, emotionally undivided and has no need to fight with god. Were this true, we would not be able to account for philosophical atheists who spill considerable ink questioning the existence, power, and moral attributes of god. Their compulsion to analyze in minute detail the nonexistence of god or question his attributes betrays its own anxieties. Philosophizing about god and the gods, albeit, with a better vocabulary, may be another

way of cursing, another way of looking for an audience and their confirming applause. Malcolm may not be so different from the philosophers
after all. He certainly does not appear different from those whom I call
"practical atheists"; those who live as if god or the gods do not exist. As
a theoretical matter, such a person might acknowledge certain propositional beliefs. But, practically speaking, this person lives with indifference to the existence or nonexistence of the gods. If there are any gods,
they do not affect this person's life in any noticeable way. "God is dead."
To say that god and the gods are dead is to enter a different world of discourse. The practical atheist does not refute standard arguments for the
existence and nature of god. No attempt is made to refute them because
they are matters of indifference. New habits of action have made god and
the gods irrelevant to how this person lives.

In a sense, Malcolm was a practical atheist. He first described himself
as an atheist when he and "Shorty" were driven out of Harlem. He said
that Ella could not believe how big an atheist he had become:

> I believed that a man should do anything that he was slick enough,
> or bad and bold enough, to do and that a woman was nothing
> but another commodity. Every word I spoke was hip or profane.
> I would bet that my working vocabulary wasn't two hundred
> words. (AMX 155)

Compare this account of his atheism as a Boston freeman with his
prison atheism:

> I served a total of eleven years in prison.[50] Now, when I try to
> separate that first year-plus that I spent at Charlestown, it runs all
> together in a memory of nutmeg and other semi-drugs, of cursing
> guards, throwing things out of my cell, balking in the lines, drop-
> ping my tray in the dining hall, refusing to answer my number—
> claiming I forgot it—and things like that. (AMX 177)

Strictly practical and behavioral, Malcolm's atheism lacked a cognitive,
theoretical, or reflective quality. He did not have the stomach for the
coolly theoretical atheism of Bimbi;[51] when that kind of atheism takes
hold, the impulse to shake one's fist angrily at heaven or to curse god
and die loses it allure. You understand the impulse but you recognize
its absurdity as well. The inappropriateness of cursing a phantom makes
you giggle. Malcolm's atheism was of the fist-shaking, god-cursing
variety.

Finally there is the paradoxical atheism in which god is the projection and personification of humanity's multifarious encounter with nature. Malcolm read a lot in prison. But we have no evidence of influence by the highly theoretical atheism of Feuerbach, Marx, and Freud. Feuerbach claimed that god was merely a projection of man's ideal self. Marx claimed that god was a subterfuge for the operations of capital. Freud claimed that god was the projection of our father image onto the big screen of the cosmos. God, they claimed, is our creature. Indeed, there is a triangular relation among human imagination, the nature that surrounds us and is us, and god.[52] Malcolm's atheism never reached this level of seriousness and sophistication.

Demonology

In 1948 Malcolm heard of an obscure group called Muhammad's Mosque, also called the Nation of Islam. He was introduced to the Nation of Islam by his brother Philbert, an inveterate religious explorer. Malcolm said that Philbert was "forever joining something," first a holiness church and now the Nation. He was clearly a "seeker" and now he sought to introduce to Malcolm the "natural religion for the black man." Philbert told Malcolm that god's true name was Allah. Following Philbert's letter, Malcolm received a letter from his younger brother Reginald who told him not to eat pork or smoke cigarettes. Something strange was happening. A hustler knows a hustle when he hears one. Malcolm had developed a sixth sense about such things. So what game was Reginald trying to run? How, Malcolm thought, could he exploit this hustle? Then he discovered that Reginald, Philbert, and all his siblings in Detroit and Chicago had converted to the Nation of Islam. Now their missionary eyes were watching him (AMX, 179–181).

Reginald introduced Malcolm to the ways of the Nation. He taught that god was a man and that the Devil was a man too! God's name was Allah. His name was also Fard. Wallace D. Fard Muhammad was "god in person." As the *avatar* or *incarnation* of Allah, Fard had given his prophet the Honorable Elijah Muhammad a message of hope and salvation for the black man and the Lost-Found Nation of Islam in this wilderness called North America. As Malcolm learned, the way of Allah was strict: no drugs, alcohol, or tobacco; no pork; nothing that injured the body or corrupted the mind. The black man had to free his mind by throwing off the yoke of Christian tyranny. Christianity was the slave master's religion, the Devil's ideology holding black people captive.

Christianity had brainwashed the so-called Negro and made him forget his name. It had "rape-mixed" the Negro into an ignorance of his own god. Christianity had the so-called Negro bowing down before a blue-eyed, white-skinned god, a blond-haired slavemaster-god. The Devil is a white man; white people are devils (AMX 183–4, 187–8).

Hilda, Malcolm's sister, explained the mysteries of this devil race, including the invention of the white man by the first Uncle Tom. In this wretched tale of scientific curiosity-gone amuck and of racial betrayal, the villain is the "big-head scientist, Mr. Yacub." This big-head brother was a natural-born killer, peace-breaker, and all-round troublemaker. He made trouble for the tribe of Shabazz who descended from Original Man, the first humans who were a black people and founders of the Holy City of Mecca. It is from the tribe of Shabazz that the so-called Negroes of America descend. Original Man, the tribe of Shabazz, the American Negro—this order of descent and decline was profoundly affected by Mr. Yacub whose dissatisfaction with Allah led him into the streets of Mecca where he preached an incendiary message that led to his exile to the Island of Patmos. This is the same island where John, the biblical visionary, had strange visions and wrote a strange book called Revelations. (Presumably, John's story occurs much later. We can only guess since the author of the Yacub story does not explain the relationship between Yacub and John.) Embittered, Mr. Yacub put his genetic expertise to nefarious uses by selectively breeding the Devil, that is, the white race. (Apparently, Dr. Yacub had developed a black science of genetic engineering before white scientists stole his idea. Thus genetic engineering, along with the wonders of ancient Egypt is one more "stolen legacy.") In any case, he augmented selective breeding with eugenics. Black babies were killed by inserting a needle into their brain. Cremation erased any evidence of their birth. The rise of white supremacy was the consequence. This is "Yacub's History" or as Malcolm characterizes it, the "demonology" of the Nation of Islam (AMX 190–3). Though highly racialized, Yacub's History is Afro-*Eccentric*; it places the origin of black people (Original Man) in the biblical lands of Asia Minor not in Africa.

In the language of comparative religion, Yacub's History is a myth of "lesser origins," an etiological myth[53] that explains why black people, the so-called Negroes, do not live in paradise. It explains why evil exists. As Malcolm observed, every religion has a demonology. This claim is generally true. Religions give an account of the dis-ease, sickness, and death that haunt human existence. They often personify or "demonize" these "evils." Demonology refers to knowledge of demons.

Demons are impious, irreverent, and lacking in *religio*. They personify dispositions contrary to the ways of the gods. Usually portrayed as enemies of the gods, demons are sometimes their agents, attack dogs on a long leash that torment wayward humans and those who fail to perform the proper rites or who otherwise fail to give the gods their due. Demons are malevolent spirits associated with physical and mental illness. Literally and figuratively unclean, demons are associated with disease—leprosy, cancer, HIV-AIDS—and with ritualistic impurity. They defile sacred things. They incite "unnatural" desires such as incest and cannibalism. They make people go crazy. When visible, demons are often ugly and grotesque, which corresponds to their lack of moral goodness. Their aesthetic deficiencies and ethical deficiencies mirror one another. Demons personify the worst that humans can imagine.

To demonize is to see others in the worst possible light—enemies of god, spawn of the Devil, the invention of the first Uncle Tom. In calling white people devils, Malcolm demonized them. Under the influence of the Yacub narrative, Malcolm rewrote his own history, reimagining various encounters with white people in the worst possible light: "Hymie the Jew," welfare bureaucrats, his father's "murders," the white people who committed and confined his mother in an insane asylum. The white judge who split his family; Mr. Ostrowski, his eighth grade schoolteacher who called Malcolm a nigger and laughed when Malcolm said proudly that he wanted to be a lawyer—all suddenly morphed into devils. The Swerlins, white cops, white criminals, "the Jew jeweler" who helped to trap him for the police; white people who wanted black sex and "a taste of Negro *soul*," white prisoners, guards, and officials, all are devils. Even if she was his lover and crime partner, Sophia was a devil too (AMX 184–5). In what appears to be a clear case of "autobiographical memory," Malcolm forgets a history of humane interactions with white people however rare they may have been. He represses memories of occasional acts of kindness, thus denying the genuine goodness of some white people. All white people began to look alike. Their behavior became indistinguishable. One can almost hear Malcolm chanting, "White people are devils. All of them, without exception, not one."

The desire to demonize is sometimes irresistible. It is not difficult to imagine why Malcolm found it hard to resist. The demonology of the Nation of Islam is reactive, a counterdemonology. It inverts common representations of black people as devils. Medieval Europeans portrayed the Devil as a large black man often with horns and a tail. During the Salem witchcraze of 1692 and in early modern England, white Americans and the English described the Devil as a black man.[54] In folklore and popular imagery, the Devil is still represented as a black man.[55] The rock opera "Jesus Christ Superstar" caused quite a ruckus when the Devil was played by a black actor. This popular and powerful imagery persists. The near universal association of blackness with night and of night with danger and terror partially explains the power and persistence of this imagery. The color symbolism and chain of associations extended as night, darkness, and blackness came to symbolize evil.[56] Psychoanalysis extends this chain of associations to various fantasies about dirt, which the popular imagination associates with excrement.[57] Given the dominant color symbolism, it is not surprising that the Devil, the ultimate personification of evil would be represented in the popular Euro-American imagination as a black man:

> The Devil appears in many colors, principally, however, in black. The black color presumably is intended to suggest his place of abode. Racial hatred had, however, much to do with the dark description of the Devil. There is no warrant in biblical tradition for a black devil. Satan, however, appeared as an Ethiopian or Moor as far back as the days of the Church fathers. Descriptions of the Devil as black in color will be found in the Acts of the Martyrs, the Acts of St. Bartholomew, and in the writings of Augustine and Gregory the Great. A black face was a permanent feature of medieval representations of the Devil. "Of all human forms," Reginald Scot tells us in his *Discoverie of Witchcraft* (1584), "that of a Negro or a Moor is considered a favorite one with demons." Satan figures as king of the Africans in John Bunyan's *Holy War* (1682). In modern literature, the devil appears as a Black Bogey, among others, in Washington Irving's "The Devil and Tom Walker" (1824), in Robert Louis Stevenson's "Thrawn Janet" (1881) and in Anatole Frances' *le Livre de mon ami* (1884). It is a common belief still to-day [1931] in Scotland that the Devil is a black man.[58]

Some of this color symbolism is innocent. But there is a guilty part as well. This symbolism was given an embodied, social-historical twist with the advent of the transatlantic slave trade and the rise of white supremacy and European colonialism in the modern period. The Devil was not merely a specter, a character in sacred texts or popular tales. The Devil walked among "us." He was the black excremental-body: the black skin and black heart of black people.[59]

There is little evidence that Malcolm was aware of this color symbolism and the way that European colonialism and the globalization of European culture amplified and transformed it. But he was surely aware, even if he did not have the words to say it, of the demonization of black people, especially black males. Malcolm was born in 1925 only thirteen years after D. W. Griffin's movie *Birth of a Nation* played across the country before record audiences of white people. Based on the novel *The Clansman: a Historical Romance of the Ku Klux Klan*, this movie affected audiences so powerfully that it led to the rebirth of the Ku Klux Klan and presumably to Klan-like groups such as the Black Legion that Malcolm mentions in the *Autobiography*. *Birth of a Nation* seared into the white imagination a demonic image of the black male as a sexual predator and grave threat to white Christian civilization. The villain-demon in this movie was a black man (a white man in black face) who raped a white woman. This "fiend" violated the best that white civilization had to offer. Further, he violated the natural order of things since sexual intercourse between a black man and white woman was tantamount to bestiality. Mutuality provided no defense as sexual intercourse between a black man and white woman by definition violated the purity and sanctity of white womanhood. It was a desecration and abomination, simultaneously a civil crime and a crime against the sacred order. The only way to properly deal with the fiendish perpetrator (black buck) was through a rite of exorcism. The preferred method of exorcizing the contaminating presence of the black devil was through the rite of lynching, especially when the purifying acts of burning him at the stake and castrating the offending member were part of the ceremony.[60]

As I noted earlier, Malcolm's relationship with Sophia disturbed Ella. I suggested that as a white woman in a lynch-happy society, she represented danger, which partly explained Ella's hostility toward her. To support this view, we have Malcolm's own words—his remark that his and "Shorty's" relations with Sophia and her sister disturbed and fascinated white officials in the criminal justice system. How, they wanted to know, did Malcolm and Shorty meet these white girls and did they sleep with them? "Nice white girls...goddam niggers—" (AMX 173). This was 1946. The frequency of lynching was declining, especially in the north, but they still occurred with enough frequency to strike terror in the minds of black people. The popular white imagination represented black males as brutish and sex-crazed. They were disposed to criminality, and were the prototypes of the "usual suspects" whom the cops could always round up on the assumption that they were guilty of something until proven innocent. Black people were the walking and talking embodiment of a problem. Their problems were not emblems of their full humanity but evidence of their subhumanity. Or, as Cornel West puts it, black people were a problem people. The Negro Problem, as it was called, expressed itself in an unacceptable way when black men cavorted with white women. As the judge told Malcolm, "You had no business with white girls!" (AMX 173). By the time Reginald finished schooling him in the demonology of the Nation of Islam, Malcolm was ready to agree with him. Though their reasons were different, Malcolm concluded that Reginald and the judge were right. He had no business with white girls. Though beautiful, Sophia was a devil too.

Malcolm had once described himself as Satan (AMX 178). Now, under the influence of the Nation of Islam, he "flipped the demonizing script," so to speak, proclaiming that white people were the Devil. Inversion and subversion of the dominant categories, in this case the category of racial demonology, are always the first option (hopefully not the last) of the oppressed. Where white people constructed the Devil as a black man, white people were now constructed as a devil race. Where the state convicted Malcolm as a criminal, the Nation of Islam now convicted white people as a criminal race.[61]

Apparition of the "Asiatic Man"

> When God struck me dead with his power I was living on Fourteenth Avenue. It was the year of the Centennial. I was in my house alone, and I declare unto you, when his power struck me I died.
>
> Anonymous[62]

Like the anonymous speaker in the epigraph, Malcolm had his own numinous experience:

> It was the next night, as I lay on my bed, I suddenly, with a start, became aware of a man sitting beside me in my chair. He had on a dark suit. I remember, I could see him as plainly as I see anyone I look at. He wasn't black, and he wasn't white. He was light-brown-skinned, an Asiatic cast of countenance, and he had oily black hair.
> I looked right into his face.

I didn't get frightened. I knew I wasn't dreaming. I couldn't move, I didn't speak, and he didn't. I couldn't place him racially— other than that I knew he was a non-European. I had no idea whatsoever who he was. He just sat there. Then suddenly as he had come, he was gone. (AMX 215)

Malcolm K. Little

Malcolm describes this "pre-vision," apparition, and visitation after writing a letter to Elijah Muhammad defending his brother Reginald whom the Nation of Islam had suspended. This must have been an especially traumatic event for Malcolm, given Reginald's role in introducing him to the Nation. Malcolm says as much. The bad things that Reginald said about Elijah Muhammad confused Malcolm. The Messenger's counter-accusation that Reginald had behaved indiscreetly put Malcolm in a bad position. According to Malcolm, the Messenger suspended Reginald for illicit sexual relations with the secretary of the New York Temple. Reginald's "immorality" revealed his lack of discipline. In response to Malcolm's letter inquiring about his brother's status, Muhammad remarked that truth is truth, either you believe or you don't. Reginald's behavior placed him among the unbelievers. With the zeal of the new convert, Malcolm bowed before the authority of Allah's Messenger. Suppressing any doubts, Malcolm withdrew the hand of brotherhood from his own brother and offered a cold shoulder (AMX 214–16).

Was Allah chastising Reginald? Malcolm certainly thought so at the time. Reginald had questioned Allah's Messenger and as a result the Messenger had cast him into darkness. The darkness of exile took a sad and dramatic turn as Reginald descended into madness: a species of the same malady that had struck down his and Malcolm's mother. He saw snakes where he should have seen the wiry hairs of Malcolm's beard and proclaimed himself the "Messenger of Allah." Megalomania set in when he proclaimed "I am greater than Allah." In a curiously philosophical mood, Malcolm remarks—"I believe today, that it was written, it was meant, for Reginald to be used for one purpose only: as a bait, as a minnow to reach into the ocean of darkness where I was, to save me." In this egocentric, if face-saving interpretation, Reginald's madness was providential, Allah's way of saving Malcolm from the darkness of Jahiliyyah (AMX 216–17).

It's impossible to dream, or to see, or to have a vision of someone whom you have never seen before—and to see him exactly as he is. To see someone, and to see him exactly as he looks, is to have a pre-vision.

> I would later come to believe that my pre-vision was of Master W. D. Fard, the Messiah, the one whom Elijah Muhammad said had appointed him—Elijah Muhammad—as his Last Messenger to the black people of North America. (AMX 218)

Which Malcolm should we believe? The Malcolm in the throes of love for Elijah Muhammad and the Nation of Islam who believed, retrospectively, that this apparition was an encounter with Master Fard (Allah incarnate) or the Malcolm who denies the possibility of a prevision? Perhaps a better question is "How do we assess Malcolm's experience, his eventual conclusion that it was Master Fard he saw, and his current view that it was not?" During his period of recruitment and during his prison years as a Muslim convert, Malcolm undoubtedly heard many stories about W. D. Fard. His prevision has the psychological concept of "suggestion" written all over it. That Malcolm had an encounter with an "Asiatic"-looking man is not surprising given the Muslim lifeworld, Afro-*Eccentric* to be sure, that increasingly defined how he lived. A quick survey of William James' *The Varieties of Religious Experience* (1902) or *God Struck Me Dead* (1969), from which the epigraph introducing this section is taken, shows that "religious experiences" conform to cultural expectations. In a predominantly Protestant Christian culture, the subjects of these experiences did not describe encounters with Olorun, Wakan Tanka, Vishnu, Buddha, or Muhammad, not even with the Virgin Mary; rather, they followed a culturally mediated script.[63] When *Allah struck Malcolm dead*, when he saw Allah's power manifest in a prison cell, it followed the Nation of Islam's script of what constituted a "religious experience." Though the Nation of Islam emerged out of the Garveyite, back-to-Africa commonwealth, its Masonic traditions were Arabized and thoroughly Afro-*Eccentric*.

★   ★   ★

THE FEDERAL BUREAU OF INVESTIGATION, SUBJECT: MALCOLM LITTLE. (# 100-399321; Section 1; Serial 1-17; report date: 4/5/53). This is the first FBI file on Malcolm X as a member of the Nation of Islam. It is the first installment of a "documentary narrative" of Malcolm's life from the point of view of his enemy. Obtained under the Freedom of Information Act and now part of the public domain, this file and subsequent files can be found at http://foia.fbi.gov/foiaindex/malcolmx.htm. Unless otherwise indicated, all references to Malcolm's FBI file are to this source. It was during the high tide of

Islam), was their *deen* or what we in the Euro-American West call religion.

As with the Bodhi Tree Model, Malcolm's conversion story appears to have little in common with the Mount Hira Model of Transformation. Consider Muhammad's account: the event was unexpected as it disrupted customary behavior; it occurred in solitude, the double darkness of the night and the cave; it involved a presence that was perceived bodily, a voice that was audible, and an angelic visitation that was visible; finally, it occurred within the context of conventionally defined religious activity or, rather, after that activity was completed since Muhammad, who retreated to the cave to fast, pray, and give alms had apparently fallen to sleep after the intensity of this activity. It was during sleep a common time for "religious experiences," when the soul travels or is otherwise especially susceptible to divine encounters and influences, that Muhammad first began receiving the revelation of Allah. In contrast, Malcolm's initial submission occurred within the context of the illegal activity (Reginald's hustle) that he anticipated. Malcolm's first "pre-Islam submission" as he describes it was his refusal to eat pork. Though he calls it a "pre-Islamic submission," Malcolm acknowledges that his abstention from pork (he also abstained from smoking cigarettes) was hardly an acknowledgment of Allah. The affirmation "There is no god but Allah" was not the point, which is underscored by the pride that Malcolm felt in confounding the stereotype apparently held by white convicts that Negroes could not resist pork. Abstaining from pork enabled him simultaneously to perpetrate a fraud and to express racial pride. Malcolm can call his abstention from pork a "pre-Islamic submission" only as an act of retrospection ("If you will take one step toward Allah—Allah will take two steps toward you") that is generous, given his motives (AMX 181).

The Road to Damascus Model of Transformation

Once again Saul of Tarsus threatened the "followers of the Way," a small group of troublemakers who had a fish for a symbol and worshiped a man whom the Roman authorities had crucified several years earlier. His caravan had nearly reached Damascus when suddenly a brilliant light beamed from heaven. It was as if the sun filling the entire sky had grown a million times its normal size. Suddenly he realized that he was on the ground. He had been knocked off his high horse when a he heard a voice say: "Saul! Saul! Why are you persecuting me?" "Who are you, sir?" Saul asked. And the voice replied, "I am Jesus, the one you are persecuting! Now get up and go into the city, and you will be told what you are to do." After Ananias laid his hands on him, Saul regained his sight, was filled with the Holy Spirit, took the name Paul, and began preaching that Jesus was the son of god.

Ironically, there is some evidence within Malcolm's own account for the Road to Damascus Model. This is how Malcolm describes his early encounter with the Nation of Islam:

> Many a time, I have looked back, trying to assess, just for myself, my first reactions to all this. Every instinct of the ghetto jungle streets, every hustling fox and criminal wolf instinct in me, which would have scoffed at and rejected anything else, was struck numb. It was as though all of that life merely was back there, without any remaining effect, or influence. I remember how, some time later, reading the bible in the Norfolk Prison Colony library, I came upon, then I read, over and over, how Paul was on the road to Damascus, upon hearing the voice of Christ, was so smitten that he was knocked off his horse, in a daze. I do not now, and I did not then, liken myself to Paul. But I do understand his experience. (AMX 188–9)

According to Malcolm, the truth of the Nation of Islam "was like a blinding light" (AMX 189). Light, especially the sun, the primordial and preeminent source of light is an important object, symbol, and trope in the history of religions. And a blinding light, which is paradigmatic for conversion narratives in the Christian West, is an important element in Paul's Road to Damascus experience. In narrating his own conversion to the Nation of Islam, Malcolm drew on resources that were available to him. Gautama's experience under the bodhi tree and Muhammad's experience on Mount Hira were not part of Malcolm's cultural repertory that he could draw on effortlessly to make sense of his religious encounter. In contrast, the Road to Damascus Model of Transformation provided an interpretive gird that was part of Malcolm's "cultural common sense," even if this sense was derived from his days as a black brainwashed Christian. The truth of the Nation of Islam had knocked Malcolm from his antireligious high horse. Blinded by the light, he had to struggle to make sense of things and to reorient his life in the blinding light of a newly received truth. Like Paul, Malcolm proclaimed the truth of his new revelation: there is no god but Allah who appeared on earth in the person of Master Wallace D. Fard Muhammad, and the Honorable Elijah Muhammad is his Messenger.

★ ★ ★

THE FEDERAL BUREAU OF INVESTIGATION, SUBJECT: MALCOLM X_LITTLE. This FBI file (# 100-399321; Section 2; Serials 18-20; report date: 23/4/57) reveals annoyance if not anxiety about Malcolm's political theology, especially his demonology:

[T]he guest speaker was MALCOLM LITTLE, Minister of temple No. 7, New York City. By selecting several words and combining various roots in a manner to produce words or combinations of words, attempted to prove that the government of America was evil.

To illustrate this point, LITTLE used two words: demon "which means devil" and "krasy," which according to LITTLE is Greek and means government. LITTLE dropped the letter "n" from the word demon thereby producing "demo." He then indicated that the Greek letter "k" is represented in English by the letter "c." Therefore, the Greek word "krasy" becomes "crasy" when translated into English. By combining the two words, demo and crasy, he produced the word democracy.

LITTLE then added "his syllogistic reasoning" and stated that the word meant devil government.

[H]e then continued to pursue the Muslim line of reasoning which states that all white people are devils and their government is a devil government. LITTLE said that this is why the United States is identified with the concept of democracy more than any Caucasian civilization.

★ ★ ★

Shirk

Conversion is akin to falling in love. There is a period of infatuation and transference (idealization) in which the beloved can do no wrong. Malcolm certainly goes through this process as revealed in his account of "falling out" with his brother Reginald as he "fell in" with Elijah Muhammad and the Nation of Islam. As is true with most religious people, Malcolm did not reason himself into the Nation. As is true of conversion generally, reason is infatuation's slave. Consider these passages:

> I was totally unprepared for the Messenger Elijah Muhammad's physical impact upon my emotions.

> I had more faith in Elijah Muhammad than I could ever have in any other man upon this earth.

> I had to restrain my impulse to run and bring a chair for the Messenger of Allah.

> And I worshiped him. (AMX 226–30)

Malcolm uses terms such as "galvanized" and "awed" to describe his attitude toward Elijah Muhammad. He thought that Mr. Muhammad, as he called him, should be above physical labor since a man of such deep spiritual wisdom who knew the true history of the black man's religion was too valuable to waste on mundane activities such as sweeping the floor. Of course, his willingness to sweep the floor provided evidence of his humility—"that little humble lamb of a man." In describing Muhammad, Malcolm drew on the apocalyptic imagery of a lamb whose truth was so powerful that its tongue appeared to be a two-edged sword. He imagined Muhammad's teaching as that very sword, cutting the black man's mind free from the grip of white supremacy. Malcolm describes his adoration of Muhammad as a form of worship. Muhammad was the first man that he ever feared, feared in the way that religious people fear what they regard as holy. "Religious fear" (awe) is a kind of magnetic attraction and repulsion, the desire simultaneously to approach and to flee a holy presence. It is not the kind of fear that one has of a man with a gun but you tremble just the same. Malcolm feared Muhammad the way a prudent person fears the awesome power of the sun: one looks obliquely lest one be blinded by the light (AMX 235–6, 239, 243–4). Elijah Muhammad shined on the dark places of Malcolm's life as he experienced, metaphorically, what many humans have experienced since the beginning of time: that god is light, fire, the sun.

From the perspective of Sunni, Shi'a, and sectarian Muslims of many kinds, Malcolm's adoration of Elijah Muhammad might exemplify *shirk*. Shirk is idolatry, blasphemy, and associationism.[72] To claim that Allah has associates is shirk. To speak ill of Allah is shirk. To worship any god but Allah is shirk.

Malcolm often spoke of black brainwashed Christians who worship a white blue-eyed god. Essentially he regarded the worship of a white god as shirk, for in worshiping the white god, black Christians worshiped whiteness. The concept of shirk is related to the Prophet Muhammad's triumph in Mecca. After capturing Mecca for realm of Islam, he had the 360 "idols" in the Ka'aba destroyed. Among these idols were those representing Al-Lat, Al-Uzza, and Manat who were widely regarded in pre-Islamic Arabia as the daughters of Allah. To claim that Allah has daughters, sons, wives, or any relations is shirk. This is the traditional Muslim view. Traditions are historical artifacts. People "invent" traditions to address specific historical contingencies such as the pre-Muslim consensus that Allah had three daughters, which after the revelation becomes a source of embarrassment. In the "incarnation theology" of the Nation of Islam, Allah is said to be a man—Master Wallace D. Fard Muhammad. This tradition, no doubt, is a response to the contingencies the Nation of Islam faced, namely, the power of the "incarnation" idea in a predominately Christian culture. From a traditionalist point of view (whose tradition?), this would appear to be among the most spectacular examples of shirk, as associationism, in the history of Islam. This theological innovation by the Nation of Islam, the notion that Allah has a human avatar is, to say the least, eccentric within the broad sweep of Islamic traditions. It is Afro-*Eccentric*, reflecting the improvisational work of black American Muslims, who *blue* both Islam and American culture. Sectarianism, innovation, and eccentricity are hardly foreign to Islam. Indeed, some might argue that Islam itself is an innovation, a new expression of essentially Jewish and Christian ideas, which themselves were part of a larger set of traditions that circulated in the Arabian Peninsula at the time of the Prophet Muhammad. Given their reliance on common traditions, especially their veneration of the patriarch Abraham, many scholars regard Judaism, Christianity, and Islam as sister traditions and some refer to them as "Abrahamic Religions." Islam is the child of innovation.

Closely connected with associationism is blasphemy. If the Nation of Islam's claims about Master Fard, which Malcolm propagated with great fervor, are regarded by many Muslims as the shirk of associationism, it might also exemplify the shirk of blasphemy. In the view of most Muslims, to say that Allah is a man is to speak ill of Allah. Shirk as blasphemy is illustrated well by the "Incident of the Satanic Verses," a myth that inspired Salman Rushdie's brilliant (and quite funny!) novel *Satanic Verses*. The "Incident" refers to an Islamic tradition that holds that Satan may have misled the Prophet Muhammad during the early period of the revelation. This Satanic seduction occurred before the preservation of the Qur'an in written form. According to tradition, Satan appeared to Muhammad in the form of the archangel Gabriel and revealed to him that Al-Lat, Al-Uzza, and Manat, three "pagan," pre-Islamic goddesses were daughters of Allah and worthy intercessors between Allah and humanity. Muhammad recited these satanically inspired verses for a time before the archangel Gabriel told him that he had been deceived and must disavow the false revelation. Muhammad complied, which is why there are verses in the Qur'an that are widely viewed as *abrogating* the Satanic Verses or as referring to their prior *abrogation*. Some take these verses as negative evidence in support of the view that the Incident of the Satanic Verses actually occurred.

The major difference between the traditional account of the Satanic Verses and Rushdie's account is "why" Muhammad recited these verses. In the traditional account, Satan deceives Muhammad. In Rushdie's account, Muhammad chooses to include the Satanic Verses in his recitation. Further, he includes them for self-interested reasons. If the Muhammad of tradition is deceived then Rushdie's Muhammad is calculating. He knows exactly what he is doing. He makes a crass, anti-religious "business decision." Here we have, to play on Max Weber's concept of the "Protestant Ethic and the Spirit of Capitalism, a case of the "Mercantile Ethic and the Spirit of Islam."

Rushdie's account might offend *some* Muslims, even those with a sense of humor. It certainly offends those who reject the liberal-Enlightenment virtue of irreverence, think it fine to offend others but cannot tolerate being offended, or who claim that respecting a Muslim's right to believe is not enough and that one must respect their beliefs. Rushdie rightly disagrees. In *Satanic Verses,* therefore, he depicts Muhammad as weak, unreliable, calculating, crudely self-interested, in short, of poor character. This depiction appears to undermine Allah's power and perfection and the authority of the Qur'an. It confounds Allah and Satan, angels and demons, true and false prophets. The Prophet seems less resolute and committed to Allah than his followers, Khalid, the warrior, Salman, the Persian, and Bilal, the muezzin.[73] Even the Prophet's enemy, Hind, the wife of Abu Simbel, the "Grandee" of Jahilia (the City of darkness and fun, whose very name is a play on *Jahiliyyah!*) seems to understand the true nature of Allah better than the Prophet. The Prophet seems foolish. And there are many, to make a sharp transition, who regarded

Elijah Muhammad as foolish and his claim to be "the Messenger" as blasphemous. As the chief architect of the Nation of Islam, Malcolm played a pivotal role in propagating the notion that Elijah Muhammad was Allah's Messenger. In Malcolm's sermons, through close association and verbal slights of tongue, Elijah Muhammad, "the Messenger of Allah" obscures if not displaces Muhammad ibn Abdullah, "the Prophet of Allah." The association between Elijah and Abdullah is as close as the association between Master Fard Muhammad and Allah. To be sure, from the point of view of most Muslims, these are blasphemous and offensive representations. But members of the Nation of Islam do not agree

"Muhammadolatry" is a play on the term "Mariolatry," which is a polemical, Protestant term for the veneration of Mary in Catholicism. According to this constipated view, such veneration is idolatrous. Some might charge Malcolm with Muhammadolatry, with idolizing the man he called "savior." This appears to be Malcolm's goal in the latter part of the *Autobiography* as what began as a hagiography of Elijah Muhammad is transformed under the pressure of contemporaneous events (namely, the schism between Malcolm and Elijah Muhammad) into a critique of idolatry. Even as he constructs a glowing portrait of Elijah Muhammad, he is already redacting that account by interpolating bits of criticism and anticipating a greater critique. His account reads like a battleground between hagiography and iconoclasm, between the old Malcolm who worshiped Elijah Muhammad and the emerging Malcolm who despised him.

★　★　★

THE FEDERAL BUREAU OF INVESTIGATION, SUBJECT: MALCOLM X_LITTLE. (File No. 100-399321; Section 4; Serials 23-33; report date: 7/2/1958). The FBI heightened its surveillance of Malcolm X designating him as a "key figure," which triggered a special set of protocols for those so designated, including separate Security Index cards on him:

Inasmuch as Little has been designated a key figure, you should obtain and forward to the bureau a current photograph of him as well as suitable handwriting specimens. You should carefully review that part of section 67D of the Manuel of Instructions relating to key figures.

★　★　★

Building the Nation

When did the infatuation end and a more sober assessment of the Nation of Islam and Elijah Muhammad begin? What were the telltale signs of Malcolm's growing restlessness and even dissatisfaction? Highly placed people within the Nation were talking about him and the talk was not good. He first heard negative remarks and innuendoes in 1961. They said that Malcolm wanted to take over the Nation and build an empire. They said he was a big shot and knew it. They said that he took credit for what Elijah Muhammad taught (AMX 234). Maybe he wanted the position of Messenger for himself. Was he planning a "coup de' jihad?"

During his roughly eleven years as a member of the Nation of Islam, Malcolm X would engage in an unrivaled jihad of the tongue, pen, and the spirit against the oppression and tyranny of white supremacy and *Herrenvolk* (master class) democracy. In the service of Allah, his jihad would be of both the "Lesser" and the "Greater" variety as he risked his home, wealth, reputation, and ultimately his life.

Only two years removed from prison, Malcolm had already become the most charismatic and effective member of the Nation of Islam. He interacted frequently and intimately with Elijah Muhammad. They appeared to have developed a surrogate father and son relationship. The Messenger must have been flattered by the adoration of his young lieutenant and grateful for his hard work. As Elijah's most enthusiastic "fisher of men," Malcolm recruited more people into the Nation than anyone else. His energy and personal gifts led to the growth of Detroit Temple 1 and Chicago Temple 2. He organized Boston Temple 11 and Philadelphia Temple 12 (in the early years of the Nation, mosques were called temples). To describe him as the architect of the Nation of Islam is accurate, since Malcolm played "Paul" to Elijah Muhammad's "Jesus." Malcolm visited old ghetto haunts, employing the language of the street to fish men from its murky depths. He went looking for former criminal compatriots Sammy the Pimp and West Indian Archie to recruit them, but he discovered that Sammy was dead and Archie near death. Rarely did Malcolm speak of recruiting women. He said nothing about the many prostitutes who he claims were companions and among his greatest teachers. Nor did he recruit his former girl friend Laura, even though he held himself partly responsible for her descent into the netherworld of drugs and prostitution. His lifelong distrust of women appears to have affected the pattern of his recruitment.

The peculiarities of Malcolm's courtship and marriage to Betty X reveal his distrust of women. "I guess by now," he says, belatedly confessing his love for Betty, she being one of the few women he ever trusted.[74] Like Protestant Christianity, Islam does not treat marriage as a sacrament. Still, it is ironic that Malcolm and Betty married in a civil rather than a Muslim ceremony. The person who officiated at their wedding was not a black man of Allah or even a black brainwashed Christian. They married under the authority invested in a white devil. Malcolm does not describe the color of his eyes (AMX 264–7).

Marriage did not alter the pace of Malcolm's activities on behalf of the Nation. The previous year, he had organized a Temple in Los Angeles. The year following his 1958 marriage to Betty found him actively involved in defending the honor of the Nation after an incendiary documentary, "The Hate That Hate Produced," aired on the CBS television network. The Nation of Islam exploded into the consciousness of white America. In what undoubtedly is an exaggeration, Malcolm compares its impact with the public reaction to Orson Welles' 1930 radio adaptation of H. G. Wells' science fiction novel *War of the Worlds*. On the heels of this controversy, C. Eric Lincoln's *The Black Muslims in America* (1960) generated a new controversy. The modifier "black" in the book's title made Malcolm and the Nation unhappy. The reasons for their disaffection are not altogether clear. Their preference, however, for the descriptor "Asiatic" rather than "Negro" may tell us something significant. However we interpret its significance, in defending the Nation in the face of these controversies, Malcolm's public profile was enhanced. As a subject of media attention, he had already eclipsed the "Honorable Elijah Muhammad." In a moment of retrospection when recalling his enthusiastic support and hard work on behalf of the Nation, Malcolm remarks: "Mr. Muhammad and I are not together today only because of envy and jealousy" (AMX 227–8). Was it then—in the glare of the bright lights and flashing cameras, as journalists jockeyed for interviews, producers competed to book him on their radio and television programs, and most quoted Malcolm as if he were the leader of the Nation of Islam—that the seeds of envy and jealousy were planted?

Malcolm defended the Nation from white devils, Uncle Toms, house Negroes, black brainwashed Christians, the "Right Reverend Bishop Chickenwing," and black Ph.D. puppets. In doing so, his penchant for demonizing his foes both in and outside the black community was in full effect. Undoubtedly, this demonizing is the worst part of Malcolm's legacy; it narrows the scope of legitimate disagreement and promotes an authoritarian notion of black solidarity whose consequences continue to reverberate in harmful ways four decades after his death. Indeed, it is hard to think of a person who bears greater responsibility for the rhetoric of demonization among black people than Malcolm X. If the wickedly great, big-headed scientist Dr. Yacub is responsible for unleashing the hounds of hell (white devils, the system of white supremacy, and a horde of Uncle Toms) into the pristine world of Original Man-black man-the Asiatic tribe of Shabazz, then Malcolm pioneered a form of intraracial demonizing that has metastasized since his death.

Malcolm said that "Christianity is the white man's religion." He asserted that the Bible is a great ideological weapon that white people use to enslave nonwhite people. Under white interpretations, the Bible paves the way for conquest before the fact and justifies the conquest of "heathens' and pagans" after the fact. Malcolm summarized his critique as follows: Christianity is a miracle worker. Its greatest miracle is that it has succeeded in making the black man docile; 22 million black people have not *risen up* in violent protest against their white oppressors. Would their revolt not be justified by every standard of morality, including America's democratic tradition? That black people are so meek and mild—fervently believing that they ought to turn-the-other-cheek, and persistently affirming the "heaven-for-you-after-you-die philosophy," is a miracle. It is a miracle that black people are still peaceful, given "centuries of hell that they have caught, here in white man's heaven!" Ph. D-sporting Negroes, puppet leaders, and preachers have grown fat off the quiet suffering of their poor black brothers and sisters. Meanwhile, white marionettes continue to pull their strings. That is a miracle! (AMX 283–4).

Some miracles do come true. Considering his own life, Malcolm knew the power of the Messenger of Allah and of the message. The message of black redemption had transformed his life and the lives of many others who like him had run afoul of the law or were addicted to drugs, alcohol, or to habits that destroyed families and communities. Malcolm describes with satisfaction the Nation of Islam's "six-point" therapeutic program for drug addicts. Table 2.1 shows the similarities between that program and the "twelve-step" program of Alcoholics Anonymous.

Unlike the therapeutic program of Alcoholics Anonymous, rooted culturally in Protestant Christianity, the Nation of Islam's program roots in the religious ideology of Islamic nationalism. If Alcoholics Anonymous begins with the notion that the addict is "not god," a version of what Paul Tillich called the "Protestant Principle," then the Nation of Islam's therapeutic program begins from the opposite direction. Rather than the idolatrous inflation of the alcoholic self that

Table 2.1 Similarities between Nation of Islam's program and the "twelve-step" program of Alcoholics Anonymous

Six Points of the Nation of Islam	*Twelve Steps of Alcoholics Anonymous*
1. The addict first was brought to admit to himself that he was an addict.	1. We admitted we were powerless over alcohol—that our lives had become unmanageable.
2. Second, he was taught why he used narcotics.	2. Came to believe that a Power greater than ourselves could restore us to sanity.
3. Third, he was shown that there was a way to stop addition.	3. Made a decision to turn our will and our lives over to the care of God as we understood Him.
4. Fourth, the addict's shattered self-image, and ego, were built up until the addict realized that he had, within, the self-power to end addiction.	4. Made a searching and fearless moral inventory of ourselves.
5. Fifth, the addict voluntarily underwent a cold turkey break with drugs.	5. Admitted to God, to ourselves, and to another human being the exact nature of our wrongs.
6. Sixth, finally cured, the ex-addict completes the cycle by "fishing" up other addicts whom he knows, and supervising their salvaging (AMX, 299).	6. Were entirely ready to have God remove all these defects of character.
	7. Humbly asked Him to remove our shortcomings.
	8. Made a list of all persons we had harmed, and became willing to make amends to them all.
	9. Made direct amends to such people wherever possible, except when to do so would injure them or others.
	10. Continued to take personal inventory and when we were wrong promptly admitted it.
	11. Sought through prayer and meditation to improve our conscious contact with God, as we understood Him, praying only for knowledge of His will for us and the power to carry that out.
	12. Having had a spiritual awakening as the result of these Steps, we tried to carry this message to alcoholics, and to practice these principles in all our affairs.[a]

[a] http://www.alcoholics-anonymous.org (last accessed on December 24, 2007).

preoccupies Alcoholics Anonymous, the Nation of Islam focuses on the negative, deflationary effects that white supremacy has on the black self. The black self has been degraded and devalued, which leads black people to addiction and to other self-destructive behavior. During the painful process of withdrawal cold turkey, Muslims would encourage the addict saying, "Baby, knock that monkey off your back! Kick that habit! Kick Whitey off your back!"... "Don't hold nothing back! Let Whitey go, baby!" (AMX 299–301). Perhaps this is why Malcolm regarded Christian churches as prime fishing holes for the Nation of Islam. Their members were addicted to white supremacy, to a blond-haired, blue-eyed Jesus, to the white man's god.

Malcolm and the Muslim Jesus

Malcolm often condemned the slavishness of black Christians held captive by the image of a white Jesus, which blond-haired and blue-eyed white men had taught them to worship. Not only did they worship a Jesus who did not look like them, they also worshiped a god who *was against them*. (Here Malcolm anticipates arguments by the Christian theologian James Cone, in *A Black Theology of Liberation* (1970), who wrote that either Jesus was for blacks and against white people or he was a murderer whom black people must kill.[75]) If worshiping a white Jesus in a white supremacist society was not bad enough, the white man had assaulted truth and good taste by perverting the simple message of love that the Prophet Jesus taught through word and deed (AMX 253, 329). With a hint of astonishment, Malcolm remarks:

> Audiences seemed surprised when I spoke of Jesus. I would explain that we Muslims believe in the Prophet Jesus. He was one of the three most important Prophets of the religion of Islam, the others being Muhammad and Moses. In Jerusalem there are Muslim shrines built to the Prophet Jesus. I would explain that it was our belief that Christianity did not perform what Christ had taught. I never failed to cite that even Billy Graham, challenged in Africa, had himself made the distinction, "I believe in Christ, not Christianity." (AMX 329)

This may be the best description of the Muslim Jesus in the writings and recorded speeches of Malcolm X. The Muslim Jesus is Jesus as he appears in Muslim sacred texts such as the Qur'an and Hadith and in Muslim popular piety. According to Tarif Khalidi, *The Muslim Jesus* (2001), there is the Jesus of the "Muslim gospel" and the Qur'anic Jesus, with the former rooted in the latter. The Qur'anic Jesus is a revolutionary figure, a "Protestant" and polemical figure in relation to the biblical Jesus. From the viewpoint of the Qur'an, the biblical Jesus distorts the real Jesus who was always already a Muslim, that is, one who submits to Allah. The true evidence of Jesus's submission is his strict refusal to *associate* himself with Allah. Only Allah is Allah. He has no associates, spouses, or children. Jesus is the "word" of Allah and the "spirit" of Allah but he is not Allah. The Qur'anic Jesus is controversial. "He is the only prophet in the Qur'an," according to Khalidi, "who is deliberately made to distance himself from the doctrines that his community is said to hold of him." In other words, the Qur'anic Jesus is a polemic against the biblical Jesus, the Jesus whom Paul and the author of the Gospel according to John say was Allah in the flesh. The Qur'anic Jesus denounces the Christian concept of the Trinity as "tritheism," a peculiar form of polytheism. Even more controversial, perhaps, the Qur'anic Jesus is not crucified. His miraculous birth rather than a "phony" Passion is the center of the Qur'anic representation of Jesus. Just as Jesus submitted to Allah, the true followers of the Prophet Jesus and of all the prophets *"have always been and will always be 'Muslims.'"*[76]

In contrast with the Qur'anic Jesus, the Jesus of the Muslim Gospel is the Jesus of Muslim popular piety, contained in noncanonical works of Arab Muslim literature from the earliest days of Islam through the eighteenth century. In these texts, Jesus is commonly represented as "a patron saint of Muslim asceticism."[77] Assuming his awareness of these traditions (I have found no evidence), Malcolm might have found them especially congenial given his own penchant for asceticism.

Both Qur'anic and popular representations of Jesus probably influenced Malcolm's Muslim Jesus. If the Qur'anic Jesus functions controversially as a polemical critique of biblical representations of Jesus, then Malcolm's Muslim Jesus provides a polemical critique of white American Christian civilization. Malcolm's Muslim Jesus is "black." He is a Jesus with a difference, the difference that the Prophet Jesus acquires in his racialized American habitat. This Jesus embodies a critique of white supremacy, black degradation, and inferiority, and of the horrible ways—slavery, lynching, Jim and Jane Crow, racial cleaning, disenfranchisement, economic exploitation, psychic denigration, denial of responsibility, and the minimization of injury—that characterizes the way that many white Christians have treated black people.

A Sermon

They charged Jesus with sedition. Didn't they do that? They said he was against Caesar. They said he was discriminating because he told his disciples: Go not the way of the gentiles but rather go to the lost sheep. Go to the people who don't know who they are, who are lost from the knowledge of themselves and who are strangers in a land that is not theirs. Go to those people. Go to the slaves. Go to the second class citizens. Go to those who are suffering the brunt of Caesar's brutality. And if Jesus was here in America today he wouldn't be going to the white man. The white man is the oppressor. He would be going to the oppressed. He would be going to the humble. He would be going to the lowly. He would be going to the rejected and despised. He would be going to the so-called American Negro.[78]

This is an example of the rhetorical and theological place of Jesus in Malcolm's religious imagination. To be sure, Malcolm's Jesus is a Muslim. But he is also the Jesus familiar to generations of black Christians, the Jesus of slave ancestors and of postslavery freedom fighters, the Jesus of Malcolm's father. This Jesus is on intimate terms with black people. He is of them, with them, and for them.

★   ★   ★

THE FEDERAL BUREAU OF INVESTIGATION, SUBJECT: MALCOLM X_LITTLE. This file (100-399321; Section 9; Serials 64-79; report date 15/11/63) is an index of the FBI's success in fermenting dissention within the Nation of Islam. However, they did not create tensions from whole cloth but exploited preexisting tensions between Malcolm and the "royal family"—the family of Elijah Muhammad. As the caption "Animosity between Subject and the family of ELIJAH MUHAMMAD" suggests things were getting hot. The report claims that an April, 1963 edition of *New York Times* implied that Malcolm overshadowed an ailing Elijah Muhammad, which stoked the "hostility and resentment" of the "royal family." In May, 1963, agents reported that things had cooled after the subject (Malcolm X) "had written an apologetic letter to Elijah Muhammad" and Elijah expressed his desire that they work together.[79] The "good times" did not last. The FBI documents Malcolm's suspension from the Nation of Islam by Elijah Muhammad after his joyous reaction to the assassination of President Kennedy:

Malcolm Little, who spoke at a rally held by the NOI in New York City on December 1, 1963, stated that the late President Kennedy had been "twiddling his thumbs" at the slaying of South Vietnamese President Ngo Dinh Diem and his brother, Ngo Dinh Nhu. Little added that he "never foresaw that the chickens would come home to roost so soon." He also stated, "Being an old farm boy myself, chickens coming home to roost never did make me sad; they always made me glad." Elijah Muhammad, National Leader of the NOI [Nation of Islam], was scheduled to speak at this New York rally but canceled his appearance out of respect to the death of President Kennedy and instructed noi members to make no comments concerning the assassination of the President.

★　　★　　★

As was their practice, the FBI report ended with this description: "The NOI is an all-Negro, anti-white, semi-religious organization which advocates complete separation of the races and teaches extreme hatred of all white men."

CHAPTER THREE

Hijrah *and* Hajj

Surah 22: Al-Hajj (The Pilgrimage)

And proclaim among men the Pilgrimage: they will come to you on foot
and on every lean camel, coming from every remote path.

Qur'an 22:27

Surah 4: An-Nisâ' (The Women)

He who forsakes his home in the cause of Allah, finds in the earth
Many a refuge, wide and spacious: Should he die as a refugee from home
for Allah and His Messenger, His reward becomes due and sure with
Allah: And Allah is Oft-Forgiving, Most Merciful

Qur'an 4:100

The death talk was not my fear. Every second of my twelve years
with Mr. Muhammad, I had been ready to lay down my life for
him. The thing to me worse than death was the betrayal. I could
conceive death. I couldn't conceive betrayal—not of the loyalty
which I had given to the Nation of Islam, and to Mr. Muhammad.
During the previous twelve years, if Mr. Muhammad had committed any civil crime punishable by death, I would have said and
tried to prove that I did it—to save him—and I would have gone
to the electric chair, as Mr. Muhammad's servant.

Malcolm X, *Autobiography of Malcolm X*, 352

Mecca and Medina

In 1964 Malcolm fled. One step ahead of spies and assassins, he fled the political and religious confines of the United States. His trip to the Holy City of Mecca appears as both a pilgrimage and a search for refuge, both Hajj and Hijrah. This chapter is an extended meditation on the introductory epigraphs.

Muslims regard Mecca as the holiest city in Islam. It sites the Ka'aba, a rectangular shaped shrine one of whose walls embeds a sacred black stone. Scholars are not certain about the origins of this stone. But it may have fallen to earth as a meteor, which may account for its status as a scared object. The stone had become a site of religious pilgrimage long before the Prophet Muhammad began receiving the revelation of Allah on Mount Hira. Before the Prophet, "pagans" and "polytheists" consecrated the Ka'aba as a site of pilgrimage, performing the Hajj as an act of worship. "Idols" of three hundred and sixty gods, corresponding to the days of the year, surrounded the Ka'aba. Pilgrims brought these idols from places throughout the Greco-Roman world. They performed certain rites at the Ka'aba, the most important of which was *tawaf*, comprising seven counterclockwise circumambulations of the sacred stone. What these circuits meant before the revelation of the Qur'an gave them an Islamic meaning remains murky. After the revelation, they signified the oneness and centrality of Allah. The Ka'aba symbolized the Divine House in the Seventh Heaven; in circling it one circled the Throne of Allah, on the axis of which cosmos, angels, and every creature rotate.[1]

According to tradition, Abraham and his son Ibrahim constructed the Ka'aba as the first shrine to Al-Llah, the one true god. Another tradition holds that Adam built the first Ka'aba and Abraham rebuilt it. Others have reconstructed the Ka'aba several times. According to the standard account, Arab tribes eventually lost their knowledge of the oneness of Al-Llah and began to worship the gods of the merchants and pilgrims who passed through Mecca. In time Al-Llah became merely one god among many, even if worshipers accorded him the status of "high god." Like some Arabs, Muhammad believed that this god was the same god in whose honor Abraham had originally constructed the Ka'aba, the same god worshiped by Jews and Christians. But idolatry and polytheism had corrupted true worship. By the time of Muhammad's birth, religious authorities had rededicated the Ka'aba to the god Hubal, imported from the Nabatean Kingdom of present day Jordan. After receiving the revelation and consolidating his forces,

Muhammad destroyed the "pagan" idols and re-rededicated the Ka'aba to the worship of the one true Al-Llah. In this Muslim view, Abraham, the builder of the Ka'aba, was neither pagan, nor Jewish, nor Christian, since his religious observances preceded Moses, the founder of Judaism and Jesus, the charismatic inspiration for Christianity. Abraham's religion was the "original monotheism." Now, several centuries later, Arabs believed they had rediscovered Abraham's original—pre-Jewish, pre-Christian—monotheism. Muhammad ibn Abdullah received the definitive revelation of this religion when he received the Holy Qur'an, the "Recitation," the final revelation of the one true god, Al-Llah, Allah.

Malcolm decided to go to Mecca after a series of events destroyed his faith in Elijah Muhammad and the Nation of Islam. Malcolm had long since become aware of the whispering campaign against him. They whispered that he had gown too big for the good of the Nation, took credit that rightfully belonged to the Messenger of Allah, and wanted to run the Nation. Malcolm claims that he ignored this background noise. He knew how hard he had worked for the Nation. More important, the Messenger knew how hard he had worked and appreciated his selflessness. Did he not go out of his way to give credit to "The Honorable Elijah Muhammad?" Did he not credit the Messenger for raising him from the dead like a Muslim Lazarus? Did he not remind anyone who would listen that Elijah Muhammad deserved all the credit for what Malcolm K. Little had become? Why take the rumors and criticism too seriously? After all, Elijah Muhammad had appointed him as the first and only national minister of the Nation of Islam. (Never again, after Malcolm turned against him, would Elijah Muhammad entrust anyone with the power and authority that Malcolm enjoyed, the authority to act as the Messenger's agent.) The entire country and not merely New York or Philadelphia served as Malcolm's *mimbar* (pulpit). He could do now under an official title what he had been doing with the Messenger's blessing for several years, minister to the Nation of Islam at large.

But the revelation that Elijah Muhammad was a serial lady-killer, an adulterer of the first order shook Malcolm loose from his confidence and complacency. To understand the intensity of Malcolm's reaction, we need to remember who he had been and who he had become. Malcolm spent many years in the sex trade, which deeply affected his view of sex, women, and virtue. He rarely speaks of sex as an act of lovemaking. He rarely speaks of sex, except as an arena of degradation. For Malcolm, sex occurred in illicit situations that degraded and exploited its participants. Sex was a transaction between consumer and service provider mediated by money. Occasionally there was no medium; sex was bartered directly for drugs, cigarettes, food, or any other thing that somebody regarded as worth the exchange. Sex was a hustle. Prostitutes hustled "Johns" for a living and pimps hustled prostitutes. Malcolm inhabited a world, in the street vernacular, of "pimps up, 'hos' down,"[2] and where "Johns" always paid the bill. Malcolm partially supported himself through the "finder's fees" that consumers with unusual appetites paid him for steering them to the appropriate provider of those services. In his relationship with Sophia, he had hustled her and perhaps she had hustled him. Again, sex was a degrading, commercial enterprise. Malcolm's father, a Baptist preacher, a man of god, was not a pimp but according to one of Malcolm's biographers, "papa was a rolling stone." Now, as Malcolm sadly discovered, his surrogate and spiritual father, the Messenger of Allah had committed adultery too. He had done so habitually, without regard for his vocation as a holy man. The man who had pulled him from the mud of his former life wallowed in the mud like the pigs they could not eat. Malcolm went to his aid; however, as Malcolm would soon discover, no good deed goes unpunished. For, when he reached out a helping hand to his fallen master, he got pulled into the very mud from which he sought to rescue the Messenger, only to be smeared with the muddy ingratitude of embarrassed-anger-become-contempt. Was this what Noah felt, "embarrassed-anger-become-contempt" when he cursed his grandson Canaan?

Nobody likes to be caught red-handed. No man and certainly no man of god enjoys being caught with his penis where it does not belong. But Malcolm was a faithful servant, undoubtedly too faithful. So when he initially read the newspaper headlines confirming the rumors he had begun to hear a few years earlier but whose circulation he blamed on the enmity of white devils and Uncle Toms, Malcolm found himself searching the scriptures for something that would help him make sense of these events. He experienced what psychologists call "cognitive dissonance." The rumors and the newspaper headlines did not square with what he believed, wanted to believe, but increasingly could no longer believe. This caused him considerable psychic pain. How could he reconcile, on the one side, his belief that Elijah Muhammad was the Messenger of Allah, the model of rectitude and virtue with, on the other side, credible evidence that the Messenger had committed adultery? Malcolm searched for comforting answers. Perhaps the Messenger's adultery had prophetic significance. Perhaps Elijah Muhammad was like David: both a man after Allah's own heart and an adulterer who had his lover's husband killed. Perhaps he was like Noah who cursed his grandson Canaan to punish his son Ham, who had taken delight in seeing his father naked and drunk. Or perhaps he was like Lot who had sex with his daughters. In the name of Allah, the Compassionate and the Merciful, perish the thought! Malcolm discussed these matters with Elijah Muhammad's son Wallace D. Muhammad.[3] Together they searched the scriptures, the Qur'an and the Bible, for anything that might relieve them of this burdensome knowledge. Unsatisfied with the results, Malcolm took the matter to the Messenger himself.

The Messenger responded to Malcolm's curiosity with a cageyness born of long experience. Malcolm's prurient curiosity displeased the Messenger, especially when the Messenger's explanation did not satisfy him. The Messenger told Malcolm that these events had indeed been prophesied and must be fulfilled. One cannot help but wonder, however, if Malcolm misremembers in a way that, as the lawyers say, prejudices Elijah Muhammad's case. Consider Malcolm's suggestion that the Messenger's behavior might be understood as the fulfillment of prophecy. Now consider the Messenger's response: "'I'm David,' he said, 'When you read about how David took another man's wife, I'm that David. You read about Noah, who got drunk—that's me. You read about Lot, who went and laid up with his own daughters. I have to fulfill all those things.'" How convenient! But given the account that Malcolm wants to tell, is the convenience Elijah's or his? Was Malcolm only trying to inoculate the members of the Nation in the face of the coming epidemic of negative news coverage about the Messenger's adultery? Or was he also fueling the controversy and, perhaps, indulging his own prurient curiosity? If Elijah acted like Noah, did Malcolm act like Ham? Was he a disrespectful voyeur?

A reasonable person might ask these questions. Apparently, many people in the Nation of Islam did ask. While they asked, Malcolm questioned former members of the Nation who reportedly had been involved with the Messenger sexually only to be expelled when they became pregnant and their demand for child support became annoying. If behaving like David, Noah, and Lot were prophecies that the Messenger had to fulfill, their fulfillment was not something that he wanted broadcast to the Nation. This no doubt was an example of his humility!—that "little lamb of a man." But Malcolm did not see humility in this silence. He saw cowardice and evasion. Hence the Messenger's disinterest in the cover story that Malcolm had conceived in which the Messenger's indiscretion became a momentary weakness characteristic of godly men. According to the cover story, the

Messenger's misbehavior had biblical antecedents, was prophesied, and had now been fulfilled. The Messenger was not interested in a cover story but only in covering up his indiscretions. Like a drunken Noah, he displaced the blame for his own bad behavior onto his son. Elijah Muhammad, his family, and security circle considered misdirecting the attention of the Nation of Islam's rank-and-file members by planting the rumor that Malcolm rather than Elijah Muhammad was the womanizer and serial adulterer. Here we see a case of "moral projection" of the most devious sort. Through this defense mechanism, Elijah Muhammad suppresses responsibility for his acts of adultery by imagining that Malcolm was guilty of such behavior. Of course, there is a real possibility that Muhammad's behavior was not an act of projection at all but a cynical, highly self-conscious, and thoroughly manipulative act of public-relations management. By going public with information about Elijah's adultery, Malcolm had started a fire. Elijah and his minions used the most effective technique they could imagine to douse that fire.

On November 22, 1963, in the middle of the adultery controversy, a gunman assassinated President John F. Kennedy. Malcolm had his own moment of indiscretion, speaking on the subject of the president's assassination after Elijah Muhammad had expressly forbidden him from doing so. When reporters offered Malcolm a penny for his thoughts, he remarked that the assassination of Kennedy was a case of "chickens coming home to roost." He added, with a smile, that as an old farm boy, chickens coming home to roost never made him made sad but always made him glad. He remarked that white hatred had not stopped with killing black people such as Patrice Lumumba and Medgar Evers or the killing of South Vietnam president Deim whose assassination, ironically, Kennedy had ordered. On the contrary, white hatred had boomeranged, striking the president dead. Malcolm's critics responded to the statement immediately and intensely. Elijah Muhammad summoned him to a meeting and told him that he had violated the gag order and would be silenced for ninety days. Before Malcolm could speak to his lieutenants, they were informed of his suspension and the news traveled rapidly throughout the Nation of Islam. According to the message, Malcolm would be reinstated within ninety days *if he submitted to the authority of the Elijah Muhammad.* Malcolm says that this proviso made him suspicious since he had clearly submitted, expressed regret for his mistake, and accepted punishment without complaint. In contrast, the message gave Muslims the impression that he had not submitted. A reformed hustler whose skills remained sharp, Malcolm knew he was being hustled. Tailing his suspension, the word "hypo-crite" would soon be uttered by Muslim lips and written in Muslim publications. In the Nation of Islam, this is a death-soliciting term. Malcolm smelled a rat (AMX 346–9).

Three days after his indiscretion the death threats began. The hier-archy of the Nation declared him a dead man and he knew that only one man had the authority to make that declaration, "The Honorable Elijah Muhammad" (AMX 349). Under the pressure of silencing, ban-ishment, the threat of death, and the omnipresent harassment of the FBI, Malcolm took flight. His new Muslim era began as a flight to the training camp of Cassius Clay who was preparing for his heavyweight championship fight against Sonny Liston. This was the first of several hijrahs—that is, acts of flight and refuge-seeking—that would define the rest of Malcolm's life. Visiting Clay, his young friend, on the verge of the biggest fight of both their lives helped to calm Malcolm's troubled mind. It probably did not occur to Malcolm then that his friendship with Cassius Clay (who later adopted the Muslim name Muhammad Ali) would be a casualty of Malcolm's dispute with Elijah Muhammad. Within the Nation of Islam it was time to take sides. Like many people, whether from conviction, fear, or both, Clay chose to side with Elijah Muhammad. But while they were still friends, Malcolm and Clay enjoyed each other's company. While in Clay's camp, Malcolm put the impending fight in its "proper" religious context:

> Cassius Clay being a Muslim, didn't need to be told how white Christianity had dealt with the American black man. " 'This fight is the *truth*,' I told Cassius. 'It's the Cross and the Crescent fight-ing in a prize ring—for the first time. It's a modern Crusade—a Christian and a Muslim fighting each other with television to beam it off Telstar for the whole world to see what happens!' I told Cassius, 'Do you think Allah has brought about all of this intend-ing for you to leave the ring as anything but the champion?' " (AMX 354)

Malcolm continued this minor *jihad* against the *crusading* implications of Floyd Patterson's announcement that as a good Christian, he wanted to fight that Black Muslim Cassius Clay (refusing to acknowledge his Muslim name) and rescue the heavyweight crown from Muslim des-ecration. How ridiculous, Malcolm thought. How sad. Here was a black brainwashed Christian fighting on behalf of the white man who cheered him inside the boxing ring and disdained him as soon as he stepped out. Malcolm remarks that while Patterson's white neighbors loved him as a symbol of black docility, they did not love him as a neighbor. No welcome wagon for his family; rather, his white neighbors drove them out of the neighborhood, forcing him like any other nigger to sell his house (AMX 355–6). Patterson's imagined community, an American, interracial, Christian confraternity ended where the border of the white neighborhood began. Marx says that history repeats itself twice, the first time as tragedy and the second time as farce. The Patterson-Ali affair was a tragifarce. Malcolm's representations notwithstanding, Patterson was a fine human being and we should never forget it. Having acknowledged his virtues, however, the Patterson-Ali affair reminds one in a twisted way of the Jim Jeffries-Jack Johnson fight, when lynching black people rivaled baseball as the national pastime and Jeffries' defeat intensified the search for a "great white hope."

The Clay-Liston fight provided a temporary distraction but the death threats did not stop. Malcolm had a good idea of who was trying to kill him and from which mosques the killers were likely to come. He says that the first direct death order came from New York Mosque 7, his old stomping grounds. A former close assistant gave the order. These facts shook Malcolm awake, alerted him to the depth of the betrayal, disabused him of any thought of reconciliation, and prompted him to protect himself. It was time for a separation: Malcolm psychologically divorced the Nation of Islam and began codifying the terms of the divorce. Given the circumstances, he had three options: Jihad, Hijrah, or Hajj. He decided to do all three: to struggle against forces in the Nation of Islam and in the FBI that would silence him, to flee from their influence, and to make the pilgrimage to the Holy City of Mecca. Malcolm told his sister Ella of his desire to make the Hajj. She took money that she had saved for her own pilgrimage and financed his.

The Hajj is one of the "Five Pillars" of Islam. These Pillars refer to traditional practices that many Muslims regard as basic:

1. *Shahada* (Acknowledgement of Allah): The act of bearing witness. "There is no god but Allah." "Muhammad is the messenger of Allah."
2. *Salat* (Prayer): Worship through five obligatory, daily prayers, plus Qur'anic recitation.
3. *Zakat* (Economic Justice): A 2.5% annual tax on all liquid wealth and interest bearing property. This money is used to ransom captives, relieve the poor, provide hospitality to the wayfarer; in

short, it requires Muslims to share their abundance and increase awareness of community needs.

4. *Sawn* (Fasting): A demanding twenty-nine- or thirty-day fast that occurs during the lunar month of Ramadan. Believers abstain from food, drink, idle talk and behavior, and worldly pleasures, from sunrise to sunset. The purpose is to remind believers (through an empty stomach) of the suffering of the poor and of god's compassion.

5. *Hajj* (Pilgrimage to Mecca): Promotes remembrance and reverence through the ritual reenactment of the founding of the first Muslim community as described in the Qur'an.[4]

Malcolm echoes a common Muslim belief when he asserts that every "orthodox" Muslim who is able should make the Hajj. He clearly accepted a normative conception of "orthodoxy," or right thinking and "heterodoxy," or wrong thinking. He assumes that there is a right and a true way of being a Muslim that is obvious and that any reasonably informed person would recognize. He assumes further that we can easily distinguish this true way of being a Muslim from false ways. He presumes that some authoritative organization or person, a magisterium so to speak, underwrites Muslim orthodoxy and orthopraxis. During his Hijrah from the Nation of Islam, Malcolm constantly uses the adjective "orthodox" to distinguish Sunni Islam from the Nation of Islam. For the first time, he began to distinguish between religious and racial identities, to see Islam as transracial (AMX 3669). Whereas Christianity was a *Herrenvolk* (master race) religion, Sunni Islam was authentically universal. Whereas Christianity provided the ideological justification for enslaving black people during the early period of colonial modernity, Sunni Islam could be their liberator in the contemporary world. Under the star and crescent, black people could join hands with other people around the world, throwing off the yoke of colonialism, white supremacy, and Christian ideology.

Malcolm traveled from the United States in route to Mecca by way of West Germany, with stops in Egypt and Saudi Arabia. His decision to make the Hajj was not spontaneous. He left the United States, fleeing the Nation of Islam's theology, demonology, and ideology. Disenchanted with the Nation of Islam's peripheral role in the black freedom struggle, he fled their conservative, inward-looking politics. Malcolm fled the stress caused by the many death threats he had received and by the constant surveillance and provocations of the FBI. We can presume on the most basic level that he wanted to satisfy the requirements of

Islamic law as he understood it, which among other things called for a
pilgrimage to the Ka'aba where like millions of pilgrims throughout the
Islamic ages he would fulfill the sacred rites. At the Cairo airport, along
with many others, Malcolm officially became a *Muhrim* or pilgrim. He
entered the state of *Ihram*, a spiritually and physically preparatory state
of consecration. Ihram disrupts the pilgrims' ordinary, everyday normality as they enter a qualitatively different space-time demanding a
different kind of deportment. Pilgrims take off their clothes and don
two white towel-like garments. The *Izar* wraps the loins and the *Rida*
drapes the neck and left shoulder, leaving the right shoulder and arm
bare. Pilgrims wear sandals (*na'l*) that expose their ankles to the desert
sun. Malcolm wore a money pouch around his waist to carry his pass-
port and other papers, especially the all-important letter he received
from Dr. Muhammad Shawarbi authorizing his Hajj. The bona fides
of American Muslim converts were suspect. Malcolm would not be
permitted to enter the Holy City without the approval of Dr. Shawarbi.
He took Shawarbi's enthusiastic stamp of approval as a providential sign
from Allah (AMX 368–71).

Every pilgrim dresses the same way. This uniform, simple, even austere attire demonstrates the radical equality of those who submit to Allah.
One could not distinguish king from peasant. This spiritual leveling in
the name of Allah had no exceptions. Malcolm seems especially impressed
by the "powerful personages," as he describes them, who someone was
kind and discreet enough to point out. This must have been a heady
experience. He seems genuinely moved by the pageantry and symbolism: the simple white attire, pilgrims' intermittent chanting "*Labbayka!
Labbayka!*" ("Here I come, O Lord!),", and the din of pilgrims expressing their intention to perform the Hajj. The rainbow of hues packed in
the airplane, all brothers—patriarchy and gender segregation in Islam is
strict—all honoring the same god impressed him. Everyone honored the
other as they stood equally before god. Malcolm describes camaraderie
and fellowship across racial lines as if the experience was completely new.
One cannot help but wonder whether he represses genuine moments
from the past. Is he rewriting his past interactions with white people in
Omaha, Lansing, and Boston to accent, by way of contrast, his experience aboard a pilgrim's flight to Mecca? On arriving at the airport in
Jedda, Malcolm describes a prayer that many of the pilgrims recited: "'I
submit to no one but Thee, O Allah. I submit to no one but Thee. I submit to Thee because Thou hast no partner. All praise and blessings come
from Thee, and Thou art alone in Thy kingdom.'" The essence of the
prayer, Malcolm observes, "is the Oneness of God" (AMX 3713).

In Jedda, Muslim officials detained Malcolm and questioned the authenticity of his conversion. This experience humbles and humiliates him. Humility is a close cousin and the better half of humiliation. Malcolm is humbled by his ignorance of Sunni Islamic rites, his difficulty assuming and sustaining a proper prayer posture, and his inability to speak the language of the Qur'an (AMX 374–86). The contrast between his generosity toward Sunni Islam and hostility toward Christianity in this account is striking. Malcolm constructs Sunni Islam as a "line of flight" from the white supremacy and hypocrisy of American Christendom and the constrictions of the Nation of Islam.

Like many people caught up in the rapture of love or religious fervor (the emotional dynamics are similar), Malcolm seems to lose any ability to make critical judgments in his account of Sunni Islam. In this regard, his conversion mimics his conversion to the Nation of Islam. (I do not mean to discount the difficulty of loving and discerning simultaneously. But blind love, loving without critical discernment led to his troubles with Elijah Muhammad and the Nation of Islam in the first place.) I return to this point later when I consider Malcolm's post-Hajj reflections.

When Malcolm entered the Great Mosque then under construction, which eventually would house the Ka'aba, he describes a feeling of numbness, a common way of describing the sense of awe, awfulness, and awesomeness that many religious people experience in the presence of the "holy." A complex set of rites, the Hajj seems designed to produce such experiences. The first rite that Malcolm describes is tawaf, which he performed with the assistance of a *mutawaf* or guide. While circling the Ka'aba, the pilgrims try to kiss or touch it. However, the great crowd prevented Malcolm from getting close so he raised his hands in reverence and shouted "Takbir! God is Great!" Like many religious rites, the origin of these circuits is unclear and their meaning may have changed over time. But seven is a sacred number in some traditions and the counterclockwise movement may be related to the movement of the sun. Pilgrims perform the second Hajj rite by prostrating themselves twice at the Site of Abraham. Malcolm's guide stood guard lest he be trampled by the crowd of excited pilgrims. The next stop is the Well of Zamzam that Allah revealed to Hagar and Ishmael whom Abraham had selfishly abandoned in the desert. (As is often true in religious narratives, which accent the positive, this story is used to illustrate Allah's care rather than Abraham's cruel indifference to his concubine and their son.) Malcolm and guide drank from the sacred well as Hagar and Ishmael had done. Performing the third rite, they ran between the hills of Safa and Marwa, commemorating Hagar's patience and perseverance in search of water for herself and Abraham's thirsty son. Malcolm does not mention this in his account but when pilgrims passed between Safa and Marwa they often chant "*Lubaika, Allahuma, Lubaika,*" "I obey you Lord, I obey you." The pilgrims then go to the plain of Arafat, where they rest, and then to Mina where in observance of the fourth rite they throw pebbles at three stone pillars that symbolize Shaitan (Satan). For some reason, Malcolm's account of the Hajj ends after the symbolic stoning of the Devil. He does not mention the fifth rite where a sheep or goat is sacrificed before the pilgrims return to the Ka'aba for a farewell tawaf. Malcolm performed the farewell tawaf three times. This rite clearly *affected* him powerfully. After the farewell tawaf, pilgrims distribute the meat of the sacrificed animal among the poor of the ummah. The pilgrimage ends with the sixth and final rite, the Feast of Sacrifice (*Eid al-Adha*), after which pilgrims visit the tomb of the Prophet in Medina. In his account, Malcolm does not mention the sacrifice, the feast, or the minipilgrimage to Muhammad's tomb (AMX 387–8).

Malcolm claims that the Hajj changed his view. He asserted that the Oneness of Allah had removed the disease of whiteness from the minds and behavior of Muslim's who by any measure were white. He saw no difference in sincerity between black and white Muslims. He joyously wrote letters to people he believed would be sympathetic to his changing views. In this emerging view, the "color-blindness of the Muslim world" provided a model for America, if only America could understand Islam's success in eliminating the problem of white supremacy and racial thinking. Malcolm describes how his experiences in the Muslim world transformed his view of white people's capacity for interracial brotherhood. There was no trace of the "white attitude" so characteristic of America. He now believed the capacity for brotherhood was real and the desire of *some* was sincere—white people were not devils by nature (AMX 389–91). Given Islam's transracial success, white American Christianity would do well, were it more receptive of the "Muslim program." Perhaps Islam had the cure for the racial cancer destroying America, an antidote to a looming racial apocalypse. Through the mediation of Islam, perhaps America could be saved from imminent disaster of the sort that brought destruction upon a racist and fascist Germany during World War II.

Malcolm claimed that his time in the Holy Land gave him greater spiritual insight into the American conflict between black and white. His new insight, however, remained remarkably consistent with what he had believed during his twelve years in the Nation of Islam. He argued that the Negro should never be blamed for his racial animosity since he was merely reacting to a four-hundred-year history—slavery, "black codes," antiblack riots, soul murder, and the practice of herding black people into urban ghettos and prisons—of white supremacy. Echoing Lincoln's remarks on the instability of a "house divided," Malcolm spoke about the suicidal nature of this racist path. He hoped that the younger generation of college-educated white people would be discerning enough to see the racial handwriting on the white supremacist wall. Only a turning of their souls, as Plato might describe this kind of radical transformation, to the true, spiritual path exemplified by Islam could ward off an impending racial catastrophe (AMX 392). Thus spoke Malcolm "the Jeremiah" X.[5]

Malcolm's jihad against American-style white supremacy became a jihad on behalf of Islam when he thought about the prospects for Islamic growth around the world. His own experience of the Hajj convinced him that the rate of conversions could be doubled or tripled if its true spirit and pageantry were properly advertised. (Here he recapitulates the same evangelical zeal he exhibited as a younger minister in the Nation of Islam.) He remarks that Arabs did not understand non-Arab psychology or public relations (AMX 396). I suppose that this market language—the language of advertising, consumer psychology, and public relations, or "American-type thinking and reflection," as Malcolm describes it—would come easily to an American Muslim who in a previous life had earned his living in the most predatory market of all, the sex trade, with the crudest and most ostentatious manner of advertising and of consumer preference-testing imaginable. Malcolm was probably unaware of the deleterious effects of markets and their operational values on traditions, especially religious traditions. That Malcolm saw no tension between "trade" and "tradition" should not surprise us. Most Americans do not. His openness to the hidden-hand benevolence of markets speaks volumes about the American, evangelical, and sectarian Christian origins of his religious sensibility. Marx, who described this religious-and-entrepreneurial type in the *Communist Manifesto,* would not be surprised.

Here I return to an earlier point about Malcolm's tendency to live his religious life without critical discernment and I should add his tendency toward infatuation. Shortly after completing the Hajj, Malcolm was a guest of Prince Faisal of Saudi Arabia. He recounts a conversation with the Prince who he describes without any hint of discomfort or ethical-political judgment as the "absolute ruler of Saudi Arabia." According to Malcolm, Faisal condemned the Nation of Islam, described its views as incorrect, and said there was no excuse for holding such views

(AMX 400). For a guy who otherwise was so inquisitive, Malcolm seems blissfully ignorant of Saudi Arabia. Was he unaware of Saudi participation in an African slave trade that preceded, engaged, and existed side by side with the transatlantic slave trade?[6] Granted, Arab slavery was not race-based, but did he not know that many of their slaves were black captives from Ethiopia, Somalia, and Sudan? Some of the black Africans intermarried with Arabs but others were stigmatized as the underclass. Their status partially correlated with phenotype, with what we commonly regard as markers of "race." Even today, dark-skinned Africans are subject to racial bigotry in Arab Gulf countries, a legacy of slavery. The Arabic word for slave, *Abīd,* has both a class and a racial significance. In popular discourse, the "slave" and "black people" connotations of *Abīd* are interchangeable. Even *Zinjī,* ostensibly a more respectful term commonly used to refer to black Africans and African Americans, has pejorative connotations.[7] Malcolm must have been ignorant of these realities. How else can we account for his failure to condemn Saudi racism and slavery? Saudi Arabia did not officially abolish slavery until 1962, ninety-seven years after America abolished slavery and only two years before Malcolm's Hajj. Was he ignorant of Saudi oppression and corruption? What are we to make of his apparently complimentary description of the Prince as the "absolute ruler?" Why would he assume that the Prince could speak authoritatively about Islam? Is this not one more example of an unfortunate tendency to idolize and deify powerful men: his father, Elijah Muhammad, and now the Saudi Prince? To repeat, Malcolm speaks as if there were a grand authority within Islam, a magisterium that determines whether some group is truly Muslim. But there is no such authority. Even if there were an authority, dissidents would contest its claims. Such is the history of religions and nature of traditions. The Islamic bona fides of the Nation of Islam cannot be determined by proclamation or non-controversially since there have always been disagreements about who is inside the House of Islam. Malcolm's "Arabcentrism" serves him poorly. As he basked in the afterglow of his Hajj experience, he did so with a startling lack of insight, blindness born of infatuation.

★   ★   ★

THE FEDERAL BUREAU OF INVESTIGATION, SUBJECT: MALCOLM X_LITTLE. This file (# 100–399321; Section 14; Serials 214–227 report date: 1/20/1965) reveals aspects of Malcolm's jihad against the Nation of Islam. It also provides insight into the circumstances that made his multilevel Hijrah necessary. Malcolm responded to the Nation's vilification of him by vilifying them:

On June 8, 1964, MALCOLM X, in attempting to make arrangements with...Columbia Broadcasting system (CBS) Television, New York City, to provide the full story of the illegitimate children of ELIJAH MUHAMMAD on a film interview, told [FBI deletion] that there are six women involved. MALCOLM said all are former members of MUHAMMAD's secretarial staff who have had illegitimate children with him since 1956 or 1957. According to MALCOLM two of these women have had two children and one of the two women at that time was pregnant with a third child of MUHAMMAD's. MALCOLM claimed that the real reason for the split with the NOI was that when he heard of these indiscretions, he told NOI officials who had in turn told ELIJAH MUHAMMAD in a manner that made it look like he was "stirring up things" instead of trying to resolve them. MALCOLM X told [FBI DELETION] that his life is at stake because he poses a threat to the NOI since public revelation of this information would cause NOI members to desert ELIJAH MUHAMMAD. On the same date [FBI DELETION] received a telephone message for MALCOLM X from an anonymous caller who said "Just tell him he is as good as dead."

★   ★   ★

From Mecca to Medina

By performing the Hajj, Malcolm reoriented his life. Like many sacred acts, it transformed him. He went to Mecca as one person and came back as another. Of course, there is something exaggerated about this account, even if Malcolm prefers it. If the Hajj was a sacred act, it also allowed Malcolm to assert his freedom and declare his independence from the Nation of Islam. Malcolm's Hijrah-become-a-Hajj had become a Jihad against white supremacy and against the Nation of Islam. If white supremacy, whose official representative was the FBI, had always been his enemy, then the Nation of Islam was now his enemy too and would kill him, if it could, before he completed his work. Now, only a half step ahead of the assassin's bullet, Malcolm was determined, in the name of Allah the Merciful and the Compassionate, to do his work the best he could while he could. That work included the propagation of Sunni Islam, which he hoped to accomplish through

Muslim Mosque Incorporated. He also sought following Islamic mandate to establish justice in the world through the creation of a new organization that would be political and secular: the Organization of Afro-American Unity. But this organization would not be established until he returned to the United States.

April–May, 1964. From the Holy City of Mecca Malcolm took flight to Beirut, then to Lagos by way of Cairo, followed in succession by trips to Accra, Monrovia, Dakar, Morocco, and Algeria. Malcolm's Hajj to the Holy Land of Mecca and Hijrah into the motherland of Africa lasted roughly a month. Perhaps this blitzkrieg across the African continent would help prepare him for the lightening-fast battle that he undoubtedly would face when he returned to America where, again, he would cross swords with the FBI and the Nation of Islam. After his Hijrah from Mecca to Medina, the Prophet Muhammad returned triumphantly to Mecca in 630 CE. Would Malcolm's return to America also be triumphant? Would America become his Mecca?

May 21, 1964. Only two days before, Malcolm had observed his 39th birthday while in Algiers. But today he sat aboard Pan American Flight 115, which arrived at New York's Kennedy Airport. Malcolm claims that he found the crush of reporters a curious sight and wondered which celebrity they had come to see. But surely this understates the facts. Malcolm knew only too well that what he said and did made news. It strains credulity to suggest that he did not anticipate the throng of reports or that he had failed to sharpen his scimitar-like tongue in preparation for their hostile questions. The questions came. He answered them. He did so with the skill he had cultivated through frequent practice, turning tendentious questions to his own advantage, saying what he wanted to say rather than what the questions would induce him to say. The reporters asked about violent Negroes—"Negroes with guns." They asked about his "Letter from Mecca." Is it true that he had changed his views? Had he renounced the description of white people as devils? Malcolm gave them what they wanted and perhaps what they did not expect. Yes, he had changed his views. Yes, he had observed Muslims of every race and color worshiping the same god without racial, caste, or class distinctions. Yes, he had been wrong in demonizing all white people, regarding them without exception as devils. But the white problem in America remained serious, not merely a question of civil rights but of human rights. Given the gravity of their circumstances, black people should carry their case before the United Nations and the court of world opinion, including its 750 million "orthodox Muslims." Further, news of black Americans awakening from a long white-Christian-induced sleep gratified millions of black Africans. He remarked that Africans saw Afro-Americans as their long-lost brothers. Referring to Afro-Americans, Malcolm said that Africans *loved us* and even *studied* our freedom struggle! (AMX 414–16).

Malcolm's Hajj experience and conversion to Sunni Islam did not lessen his critique of white supremacy. Nor did it complicate the explicit connection he made between white supremacy and Christianity. He blamed the failure of Negroes to follow him into the fold of "orthodox Islam" on Christian brainwashing. The minds of American Negroes especially the older generation had been soaked in the bloody double standard of Christian justifications of oppression. This same critique underwrites his rejection of love-your-enemy-and-turn-the-other-cheek nonviolence. "What was wrong with that?" he asks, in response to the claim that he advocated arming Negroes. He rejected the usual liberal council that when lynched, burned, bombed, and beaten, Negroes should exercise Christian love and be patient. He disdained those who said go slowly, given the fact that entrenched customs such as white supremacy change slowly. He was suspicious of those who said, "Things are getting better." Malcolm's response to this Christian call for black moderation is as sharp as it is uncompromising and unreconstructed: "Well, I believe it's a crime for anyone who is being brutalized to continue to accept that brutality without doing something to defend himself. If that's how 'Christian' philosophy is interpreted, if that's what Gandhian philosophy teaches, well, then, I will call them criminal philosophies." This critique of the philosophy of nonviolence is as harsh as any he had ever made as a fire-breathing, white-blue-eyed, devil-naming member of the Nation of Islam (AMX 419–22).

Like Nietzsche, whose views he claims he knew but did not respect, Malcolm questions the value of Christianity. Was Christianity not decadent and servile, a slave religion? What good had it done the black man, "America's most fervent Christian?" Has it gotten him anything worth having? "In fact, in the white man's hands, in the white man's interpretation... where has Christianity gotten this *world*?" I find the qualification "in the white man's hands, in the white man's interpretation"—odd. Is he really denying the history of black interpretations of Christianity, interpretations by people such as Vesey, Turner, and Truth? How does he explain the Christian convictions of his own father, or the Catholicism of Marcus Garvey, the man in whose service he claims that his father

died? Is he merely being anachronistic and provocative when he claims
that for a millennium only Islam had power to resist the white man's
Christianity? Surely he speaks in jest—or ignorance—when we recall
that during that same millennium Muslims traded black slaves enthusiastically and for great profit.[8] Malcolm is more persuasive when he cites
the unwillingness to fight racism as the greatest failure of the White
Church. Thus, the church was reaping what it had sown in the form
of the black revolution and the pilgrimage to Islam. Racism is blasphemy. To worship white people, and the very concept of whiteness, as
if they were god is idolatry. As he made these observations "in this year
of grace 1965," Malcolm described the reality of Christian churches
guarded by deacons who stood in the door like George Wallace saying: "segregation today...segregation tomorrow...and segregation
forever!"[9] The message to black would-be worshipers and opponents
of Jim Crow Christianity was clear: *this* house of god did not welcome
them (AMX 424–5).

In a shift of moods both curious and ironic, Malcolm employs the
imagery of Exodus and the religious ideology of African American
Christianity to criticize white American Christianity. He employs
what Theophus Smith calls the "Exodus Configuration," which forms
part of a larger African American tradition of biblical interpretation. It
represents the way that black Christians turned biblical interpretation
toward their own interests in survival and liberation and against the
interests of their masters and oppressors. According to Smith, "In the
Afro-American figural tradition it appears that all corporate liberation efforts can be configured, in the manner of ritual performances,
as dramatic reenactments of Exodus, and their leaders envisioned
as approximate types of Moses."[10] Black people construed Harriet
Tubman, Abraham Lincoln, Marcus Garvey, Martin Luther King, Jr.,
and even Isaac Hayes as Mosaic figures. They imagined America as
Egypt and white people and the American government as Pharaoh.
Black people construed the Civil War, the Emancipation Proclamation,
the great migrations, and the civil rights movement as black liberation
events. They saw analogies between these events and the crossing of
the Red Sea by the ancient Israelites. They transformed Africa, freedom, the North, Canada, Kansas, and even death into the Promised
Land. Psalms 68:31—"Princes shall come out of Egypt, Ethiopia shall
soon stretch out her hands to God"—signified the honored place that
black people held in god's redemptive plan. The religious imagination is complex and dreamlike, permitting all manner of incongruities.
In some versions of the Exodus Configuration, Egypt represents the

Promised Land, or Africa and America represent Egypt, both are implicated in the suffering of African Americans. [11] "Pharaoh" is on both sides—black and white—of the Red Sea.[12] Or drawing on different imagery, America is imagined as the place of black peoples' Babylonian captivity.[13]

I describe Malcolm shift as curious because he code-switches from a blanket and unqualified condemnation of Christianity, the enemy of black people for a thousand years to the use of the Exodus Configuration. This code-switching suggests the possibility of an alternative interpretation of the phrase "in the white man's hands, in the white man's interpretation." Perhaps Malcolm refers to the misinterpretation of the Bible by White Christians. Consider the following:

> I believe that God now is giving the world's so-called "Christian" white society its last opportunity to repent and atone for the crimes of exploiting and enslaving the world's non-white peoples. It is exactly as when God gave Pharaoh a chance to repent. But Pharaoh persisted in his refusal to give justice to those whom he oppressed. And, we know, God finally destroyed Pharaoh. (AMX 426)

Malcolm asks whether white America can atone for her criminal treatment of black people. Upping the rhetorical intensity, he asks: Does she have the capacity to repent? Is she really sorry? He claims that most black people would like to forgive and forget. But forgiveness presupposes atonement. Malcolm doubts that most white Americans are serious about atoning, about turning away from centuries-old behavior, doing justice to black people, repairing relations and making reparations for the damage they have done. Even if white people had the will to atone, can any atonement be adequate to the crime? What about the centuries of unrequited toil that led Jefferson to tremble, Lincoln to affirm the wisdom of pursing civil war, and both to dream of sending black people back to Africa? (AMX 426). These are rhetorical questions to be sure. Nevertheless, they speak to the inadequacy of justice. There is always an irremediable gap between the wrongs that we do or suffer and what we or others do to make it right. Can we ever make it right? Is atonement adequate? Is justice enough? Can reparations repair? These are the kinds of questions that turn some people toward god, the gods, and religion and that turn others away. These questions turned Malcolm from Christianity and toward Islam.

Flecing the Nation and the FBI

After his pilgrimage to Mecca, Malcolm X, now using his Arabic name El-Hajj Malik El-Shabazz, developed a nonessentialist view of racism. He no longer saw racism as an expression of an underlying biological or spiritual essence. The white man, he says, is not inherently evil; his evil is sociological, a result of bad social relations. Since the epiphany in Mecca, Malcolm now recognizes Buddhists Christians, Hindus, Jews, agnostics and even atheists among his dearest friends. He can hardly believe it himself. Why not? After all, his friendships now spanned the ideological spectrum of capitalists and communists, moderates and extremists. He even counted Uncle Toms and white people among his friends (AMX 427, 432). The dramatic requirements of Malcolm's narrative of sudden transformation notwithstanding, these post-Hajj ideological and personal transformations were rooted in the pre-Hajj period. They represent a Hijrah from the religious ideology of the Nation of Islam. Like the Prophet's Hijrah from Mecca to Medina, Malcolm's Hijrah was integrally connected with jihad, with struggling in the cause of Allah.

Like many people who have dedicated their lives to an organization or cause, El-Shabazz had reservations about the Nation of Islam that he repressed. It is hard to be critical of one's savior, especially when one's life has been transformed for the better. It is hard not to idealize—exaggerating virtues, minimizing vices. El-Shabazz had heard unflattering things about the Messenger Elijah Muhammad that he chose to ignore if not forget. For more than a decade, he had encountered Muslims who disagreed with the Nation of Islam and sharply condemned it. But El-Shabazz behaved like a good soldier. Despite his reservations, he saluted the Messenger and obeyed orders until it became clear that the Messenger envied, distrusted, and even feared him. The fact that El-Shabazz interviewed former secretaries whom the press had identified as the mothers of the Messenger's "outside" children only increased his distrust and fear. Even if El-Shabazz was deeply hurt by what they said the Messenger had said—that he was the best minister he had, but was dangerous, and one day would leave him—El-Shabazz, objectively speaking, *was* dangerous. He was in a position to hurt the Messenger, as no one else could by publicizing his adultery and hypocrisy. Can we really accept Malcolm's naïve and self-regarding depiction of himself as a "firefighter" trying to suppress fiery rumors about the Messenger's immoral behavior? Or was there a part of him that wanted to expose the hypocrite, the man who had expelled his brother from the Nation for immorality and who pretended to be the most moral person of all? Is it not reasonable to presume that Malcolm relished his status and felt proud of his accomplishments? Whether Elijah Muhammad deserved credit for making Malcolm a "big man," he had become a big man. Better known and more respected than the Messenger, he had greater personal skills and more charisma. Were he to leave the Nation, he could take many Muslims with him. After all, he had done more than anyone to recruit new members. El-Shabazz could rightly claim credit for the Nation's explosive growth during the past decade. Who could credibly dispute his claim? Further, the economic wealth of the Nation depended on the growth that he inspired. Even more ominous, what if he decided to lead a coup and take control of the Nation? The threat seemed real. Did the Messenger not have good reason to be paranoid? The Honorable Elijah Muhammad had spent the early years of his leadership fleeing those who sought to kill him and seize control of the fledging Nation. Perhaps this was a case of déjà vu.

El-Shabazz's motives in investigating the rumors of the Messenger's adultery were undoubtedly more complex than he claims. Perhaps he was a dutiful son who genuinely wanted to help his surrogate father, the leader of the Lost-Found Nation of Islam in this wilderness of North America, who had found Malcolm when he was lost, cleaned him up, and placed him in a position of leadership. Or, perhaps, as a surrogate son, Malcolm wanted to "kill" the father and possess the Nation. I speculate of course. But my speculative analysis is plausible. How better to account for Malcolm's instantaneous knowledge, despite his public pronouncements to the contrary, that his suspension was not temporary? Malcolm sounds like a man with a guilty conscience.

Malcolm's pre-Hajj formation of Muslim Mosque Incorporated stoked the fires of Elijah Muhammad's anger and fear. How could it have done otherwise? This mosque represented the possibility of a serious schism within the Nation of Islam. Schism was nothing new in the history of the Nation. The same year of Malcolm's suspension, Charles 13X had led a group now called the "Thirteen Percenters: Nation of Earths and Gods" out of the Nation of Islam's fold. But this was a minor schism compared to what Malcolm's formation of Muslim Mosque Incorporated might portend. He had the kind of charisma that might throw the Nation into crisis. What if Malcolm's penchant for Sunni Islam began to peel the Nation of Islam like an onion?

The formation of Muslim Mosque Incorporated was a pre-Hajj flight from the Nation of Islam. In performing the Hajj, during which he formally turned his soul from Masonic-and-nationalistic Islam to Sunni

Islam, El-Shabazz continued his Hijrah from a Janus-faced enemy: the Nation of Islam and the FBI. He took flight from the anti-African sensibility of the "Asiatic" Nation of Islam when he boarded a plane to the African continent. (Back to Africa, to his Garveyite roots: his father would have been proud.) On his return to America, he fled, ideologically, the antiwhite bigotry that characterized his days with the Nation of Islam. By opening himself to the possibility of working with civil rights groups and other antiracist groups, he rose like a black Phoenix from the political conservatism and isolationism of the Nation of Islam. Icarus, the bird-boy with wings of wax who against his father's advice flew too high and too close to the burning sun only to come crashing to the earth on melted wings was now reborn as a Phoenix. But the Nation of Islam wanted to send that red-headed, chipped-tooth Phoenix back to the ashes. There was only one question: How long would this new bird live?

El-Shabazz took flight from those who sought to take his life. He dates this Hijrah from death at three days after his suspension when he first became aware of the death threats and the death squads that shadowed his every move. He knew that Elijah Muhammad envied him intensely for his popularity as a college speaker, and with the national media that behaved, even when it knew better, as if El-Shabazz was the leader of the Nation of Islam. Muhammad envied his skill as a fundraiser, his integrity and incorruptibility. "Malcolm's austere morality, which enhanced his political appeal, was a withering rebuke to the hypocrisy of the Messenger and his entourage. That is, as long as he lived."[14] While they were stealing money from the often poor and hardworking members of the Nation of Islam, much like the black Christian preachers that El-Shabazz criticized harshly, he modeled fiduciary rectitude and responsibility. Like a desert ascetic, he played saint to their money-grubbing sinner. And they resented him. El-Shabazz's response to Elijah's envy, to being followed and threatened with death was predictable. He became cautious, paranoid, and depressed. He also became combative and reckless, and some suggest that he courted death, behaving like a man with a death wish. Was this the same death wish—live fast, die young, catch me grim reaper if you can—that he nurtured as a hustler? Was this a death wish or the desire to live as if death did not matter, where Thanatos serves Eros?

While he and Alex Haley worked to complete the *Autobiography*, El-Shabazz began to speak frequently about the likelihood that he would not live to see its publication. Newspaper articles described his rift with Elijah Muhammad and spoke of threats against his life. The air buzzed with rumors. Inside and outside the Nation of Islam, people speculated about Malcolm's fate. El-Shabazz listened and grew increasingly angry. He wanted to unleash every unflattering thing about Elijah Muhammad that he had repressed. Where he had soft-pedaled, in public statements and even in the *Autobiography*, what he now regarded as the Messenger's religious fakery, phoniness, and immorality, he now wanted to shout from the rooftop. Had he access to their mosques, he would shout it from every "Muslim pulpit" in the Nation of Islam. If only he could to rewrite those portions of the *Autobiography* that cast him as the Messenger's dutiful son, passages that were so sycophantic in their praise of the "Honorable Elijah Muhammad" that they now made the man once called "Detroit Red" blood red with embarrassed anger. El-Shabazz knew Elijah Muhammad. Elijah Muhammad had once been his surrogate father and friend. Malcolm had once called him "savior." Now he admitted to himself what he had known for a long time but had repressed: Elijah Muhammad was not an honorable man. In the epilogue to the *Autobiography*, which I regard as the first biography of Malcolm X, Alex Haley says he was able to persuade El-Shabazz of the folly of revising the *Autobiography* in line with his rapidly evolving views. It is a credit to Haley and a boon to history that he succeeded.

In fleeing the Nation of Islam physically, spiritually, and politically, El-Shabazz strove mightily in the service of Allah. He became a *Mujaddid* (a renewer of the faith) as he struggled against his fear of what the Nation might do to his family, against his fear of death that he denied, and against the FBI, which had dogged his efforts since 1953. His *flight from* and his *fight against* were the same: Hijrah and Jihad.

In the epilogue, Haley provides a harrowing example of the deadly pressure that El-Shabazz faced. On January 28, 1965, El-Shabazz arrived at the Los Angeles Airport where Edward Bradley and Allen Jamal greeted him. They were close friends at a time when he desperately needed good friends. After checking into the Statler-Hilton Hotel, El-Shabazz and his friends encountered a group of six Muslim men whom Bradley recognized. When El-Shabazz rejoined them downstairs after settling into his room, he nearly bumped into this Muslim lynch-mob. Stunned, his face froze. Was it surprise, fear, or both? Even though El-Shabazz realized that he and his companions were in trouble, he did not break his stride. Obviously, the Nation of Islam had him under close surveillance. Their death squads were closing in, tightening the grip they had on his throat. We can only imagine what he thought as his comrades drove away. When he returned to the hotel that evening, there were suspicious and hostile-looking Muslims everywhere. He warned his friends to be careful and ran into the hotel. Later, when he checked out, two carloads of Muslims harassed him and his companions. Already deadly tight, the death grip of the Nation of Islam grew even tighter. This incident occurred in the midst of the Nation's effort, eventually successful, to evict El-Shabazz and his family from their home. In the interim between the court order and the day they would actually move, as El-Shabazz and family slept, a lynch-mob, undoubtedly Muslims, firebombed the house. Malcolm had not insured his home: so complete and naïve was his faith in Elijah Muhammad, so austere his religious observance. Thanks to Allah, the Merciful and the Compassionate, no one was injured. The firebombing occurred on Sunday morning, February 14, 1965. One week later, Malcolm K. Little a.k.a. Malcolm X a.k.a. El-Hajj Malik El-Shabazz would be dead.

In their surveillance and pursuit of El-Shabazz, the Nation of Islam had become like the FBI—the FBI in blackface and red bowtie. But the FBI is the FBI and their talents at surveillance, harassment, and provocation were unmatched. Besides, the Nation had its own problems with the FBI. El-Shabazz knew that the Nation and he were objects of FBI surveillance. The FBI knew that he knew. He refers to the FBI on several occasions. In his most revealing statement, he remarks:

> We were watched. Our telephones were tapped. Still right today, on my telephone, if I said, "I'm going to bomb the Empire State Empire Building." I guarantee you in five minutes it would be surrounded. When I was speaking publicly sometimes I'd guess which were F.B.I. faces in the audience, or other types of agents. Both the police and the F.B.I. intently and persistently visited and questioned us. (AMX 296)

The following observation, confirming El-Shabazz's comments, can be found in his FBI file: "He told them that they would be visited by the Federal Bureau of Investigation (FBI) but that this was only an effort to intimidate them and make them fear to come and hear anything about themselves."[15] In the light of the 9/11 catastrophe of 2001, El-Shabazz's offhanded, tongue-in-cheek comments about bombing the Empire State Building are chillingly ironic. We see, retrospectively, how harassment of the Nation of Islam provides a model of domestic surveillance. Consider the hypernational security state regime to which the September 11 catastrophe gave birth, with its Patriot Acts, semiclandestine acts of torture, and a president who, without a court order, authorized the National Security Agency to engage in widespread spying on American citizens, especially Muslims and people of Arab descent. Muslims and "Arab-looking people" became the Mormons—feared, despised, and persecuted—of twenty-first-century America.

FBI surveillance of El-Shabazz, Malcolm K. Little as he was then called began in 1953 and followed him to the grave in 1965. He became a subject of surveillance when he became a member of the Nation of Islam and his profile within the group began to grow. The FBI had long regarded the Nation of Islam as a subversive group. But their interest in Malcolm K. Little was originally motivated by a letter he wrote in 1950 declaring that he was and had "always been a communist."[16] Malcolm was a shrewd operator who had successfully avoided the draft during World War II and who, in the context of the cold war, knew what buttons to press if he were to further discourage any interest that the draft board might have in one Malcolm K. Little, even if he were confined to a prison cell. Or perhaps he was simply boasting, playing to his Satan persona, and saying what he knew was scandalous. Whatever the reason, the letter came to the attention of the FBI and Malcolm K. Little, now Malcolm X became a subject of surveillance.[17]

Surveillance of Malcolm K. Little began with the Detroit office. The first report piques the reader's interest for a variety of reasons. We learn about the various nicknames and aliases that Malcolm K. Little used on the street, in prison, and after his release: Malachi Shabazz, "Rhythm Red" Little, "Detroit Red" Little, and Jack Carlton. Also interesting is the juxtaposition of the FBI's concern for Malcolm K. Little's possible communist affiliation and their concerns about the "Muslim Cult of Islam," as the FBI then characterized the Nation of Islam.[18] This juxtaposition and even conflation of subversive politics and "bizarre, cultic religion" is crucial to understanding the FBI's surveillance of Malcolm X and the Nation of Islam and Malcolm's reaction. As I indicated earlier, scholarly and popular uses of the term "cult" are very different. For the scholar, a religious cult is a group that centers on a charismatic leader. Any normative characterization of a cult is a separate issue, since its status as a cult carries no prejudgment. In popular usage, a religious cult is a normative term referring to strange, bizarre, dishonest, and otherwise illegitimate forms of religion. Such religions are not entitled to our respect since their religious claims are merely a pretext for politics or commerce or for illegal and immoral activity. The popular language of "cults" is the language of heresy and witchcraft. Cults are "deviant" forms of religion for which people have been imprisoned, banished, mutilated, and killed. Witch-hunting is the prototypical form of this activity where people designated as witches were accused of every deviant behavior imaginable. They ate babies and engaged in sex with the Devil who, given the dominant color symbolism, was often represented as a black man. Bizarre food and bizarre sex—imaging others as eating what we find abominable or engaging in forms of sex that we find perverse—are standard ways of making other people strange and monstrous. Against religious deviants and monsters, all means of persecution—*always construed as self-defense*—are legitimate. Religious deviants are outside the ark of safety, beneath the shield of legal protection, outside the world of moral concern. As purveyors of perversity, license, and licentiousness, "we" can do with them as we will. In the view I am describing, they are not what the "founding fathers" had in mind when they spoke of religious freedom. Their religious eccentricity, in the case of the Nation of Islam, Afro-*Eccentricity*, does not count as "genuine" religion.

Witch-hunting provides the prototype for red-baiting, and not merely in the imagination of Arthur Miller. When the FBI's original concern that Malcolm X might be a communist began to fade, they turned their attention, as they construed it, to his fanatical religion of hate. Indeed, two interrelated aspects of the Nation of Islam seemed to have especially vexed the FBI: their antiwhite demonology and their hostile attitude toward the American government. From a May 4, 1953 file, we get a glimpse of the FBI's knowledge of the theology of the Nation of Islam. According to the file, they "know" that the Muslim Cult of Islam a.k.a Allah's Temple of Islam is a religious cult; that Allah is their god; that Elijah Muhammad is their prophet; that they follow his teachings fanatically; that they advocate disobeying civil laws that conflict with Muslim law; that allegiance should be pledged to Allah alone and not to the American government; that Muslims cannot serve two masters, Allah and the government of the white man and, therefore, they should resist the draft and refuse to serve in the United States Armed Forces; that black people in America are not citizens but slaves; that their slavery will end when they destroy Christians and non-Muslims in the War of Armageddon.[19]

Here you have all the elements for FBI suspicion: an "unpatriotic" and even seditious group whose members hail from a minority group whose very race makes their status as real Americans questionable; a group whose religion is deviant and thus dangerous as evidenced by their draft-dodging refusal to serve their country and their all-round lack of respect for its laws, a group whose theology expresses hostility toward the dominant religious tradition of Christian America, a theology that envisions a violent final conflict between Muslim and Christian. While not mentioned in this report, they were usually described as a group that preached hate against the white race. All police forces by definition are guardians of the status quo. They are conservative, forces of conservation. As the federal police, the FBI clearly saw their task among others as guarding white supremacy and the racial status quo. And here stood a group preaching about white devils who challenged simultaneously both the religious and the racial status quo.

There are frequent references in Malcolm's FBI file to the demonology of the Nation of Islam and to Malcolm's vitriolic sermons in particular:

1. LITTLE spoke on the lines of racial hatred, always referring to the white race as being "the white devils." LITTLE compared EISENHOWER to Pharaoh of Egypt in the biblical days and compared EIJAH MHAMMAD of Chicago, Illinois, as to Moses. He stated that ELIJAH MUHAMMAD is going to lead the " 'black race' out of slavery in the United States as Moses did the Jews" in Egypt.[20]
2. LITTLE stated that there was nothing the FBI could do to stop the spreading of the message that the white man is the devil and the black man is God.[21]
3. According to LITTLE, the Christian preachers are getting paid to deceive the black man by teaching him what the devil (white man) wants him to learn. LITTLE stated that the white man knows that if the black man in North America learned about Islam, then it would be time for the white man to be destroyed.[22]
4. LITTLE spoke about the white race being the "devil." LITTLE claimed that the "white devils" from foreign countries could just walk into the United States and automatically become citizens but the "black men" could be born in the United States and are not treated as citizens.[23]
5. Minister MALCOLM LITTLE was the speaker at the meeting of Temple No. 7...LITTLE spoke along the lines of the so-called religious aspects of the Cult and made comparisons of the "black man's" accomplishments and the evils of the "white devils." LITTLE exhibited a newspaper clipping from the "Washington Post" which contained an article by a Professor O'CONNOR. LITTLE explained that this article by O'CONNOR reflected that Jesus Christ was a black man and LITTLE explained to the group that all the

prophets in the past had been black men and that there never had
been white prophets.[24]
6. LITTLE said that members are "fools" if they put on uniforms of
the "white devil's army."[25]
7. The subject stated that he believes in all the teachings of ELIJAH
MUHAMMAD of Chicago, Illinois, and that ELIJAH MUHAMMAD
was his leader and that he considered ELIJAH MUHAMMAD supe-
rior to all. Subject considered the "Nation of Islam" higher and
greater than the United States government. He claimed that Allah
is God, the supreme being, and that ELIJAH MUHAMMAD is the
greatest prophet of all, being the last and greatest Apostle.[26]

Of course, this unreserved affirmation of Elijah Muhammad and the
Nation of Islam would end less than ten years later when they joined
the FBI in the surveillance and pursuit of Malcolm X. El-Shabazz (my
use of Malcolm and El-Shabazz interchangeably is emblematic a complex transition) had condemned the FBI for suppressing Muslims on
religious grounds. In effect, he charged them with violating the free
exercise clause of the First Amendment, which should have protected
the Nation of Islam from FBI harassment. Ultimately, he claimed, this
suppression was as excessive as ineffective. It only increased interest in
the Nation of Islam and its message of truth, emancipation, and hope.[27]
Now he condemned Elijah Muhammad and the Nation of Islam who
would suppress him because he insisted on being a good Muslim by
holding the Messenger to the same standards of sexual morality that
ordinary Muslims were expected to observe. After his trip to Mecca,
Malcolm distanced himself from the Nation even further by referring
to himself as El-Hajj Malik El-Shabazz. Hijrah and Jihad: El-Shabazz
fled and he fought. He fled the FBI and the Nation of Islam: the former
collected intelligence and harassed him, and provoked enmity between
him and Elijah, while the latter sought to kill him. Along the way he
fought to recreate himself as a Muslim and as a black freedom fighter.
In Islam, politics is a vocation, a sacred duty. Politics *is not* the absence,
"other," or the desecration of *deen* (religion). There are not two worlds—
the world of Caesar and the world of god. While Muslims recognize
a functional distinction between mosque and state, they know that
the religious realm and the political realm are one. Allah commands
Muslims to transform the world by creating a just ummah, a community
that cares for the widowed and the orphaned, for those who are most
vulnerable. El-Shabazz would spend the rest of his short life in pursuit
of a just American ummah. Through Muslim Mosque Incorporated

and the Organization of Afro-American Unity, he engaged in jihad against the forces of white supremacy.[28] He was determined to fight until he died or racism ended and the walls of white supremacy came tumbling down.

Dissident Sons: Malcolm and Wallace

After the flood, Noah became a farmer and planted a vineyard. One day he became drunk on some wine he had made and lay naked in his tent. Ham, the father of Canaan saw that his father was naked and went outside and told his brothers. Shem and Japheth took a robe, held it over their shoulders, walked backward into the tent, and covered their father's naked body. As they did this, they looked the other way so they wouldn't see him naked. When Noah woke up from his drunken stupor, he learned what Ham, his youngest son had done. Then he cursed the descendents of Canaan, the son of Ham... (NLT Genesis 8: 20–25)

Wallace Muhammad and Malcolm X saw *their* father naked, drunk with power and the pleasures that power commands. Elijah had developed some bad habits. He committed adultery habitually and his behavior had become semipublic knowledge, an open secret among those in the know and a scandal among those who were not supposed to know. How would Wallace and Malcolm respond? By discreetly covering Elijah's body while averting their gaze, or would they, indiscreetly, invite others inside his bedroom and make a spectacle of him? Circumstances, including suppressed anger, no longer allowed Malcolm to ignore what he knew: that Elijah Muhammad had fathered several "illegitimate" children. Because of the scandal, disgruntled members were leaving the Nation of Islam, especially the Chicago Temple, the epicenter of the scandal.

Malcolm sought the advice of his young protégé Louis X (the future Louis Farrakhan) who in a twinkling of an eye would become his deadly enemy. He sought the advice of Ella whose part in this drama Malcolm does not mention in the *Autobiography*. Above all, he sought the advice of Wallace D. Muhammad, the Messenger's "seventh son." Other than Elijah Muhammad, Malcolm could think of no member of the family he could trust with this scandalous matter. Malcolm describes Wallace as Elijah Muhammad's "most strongly spiritual son" and the most objective. Exceptionally close, they trusted each other.

In Malcolm's account, Wallace knew instantly the reason for the visit, as if they shared a sixth sense. Before Malcolm spoke, Wallace said: "I know." Malcolm recounts his desperate attempt with Wallace's aid to find scriptural justification for Elijah's infidelity, to mitigate its force in the light of biblical and Qur'anic precedent, anything that would save him from drawing the conclusions he did not want to draw (AMX 342–4). Together they scanned the Qur'an and the Bible looking for documentation of holy men who had fallen short of the mark, sinning or otherwise, engaging in scandalous behavior. There were the stories of David and Bathsheba, Lot and his daughters, Noah and his sons, Moses and the Ethiopian woman. In each case, Malcolm concluded, their good acts outweighed their bad acts. David's valiant act of killing Goliath outweighed his affair with Bathsheba and the murder of her husband. Lot behaved nobly when he acted to save the few good people who lived in Sodom and Gomorrah from god's destructive wrath. This act carried greater moral weight than his incestuous relationship with his daughters. Yes, Noah was a drunk. But he built the ark, preserving the creation from the floodwaters of god's anger. Surely his prudence and obedience outweighed his intemperance. Like David after him, Moses lived a far from perfect life. But he led the Hebrews from their Egyptian house of bondage (AMX 343). Surely liberating a people should carry more weight than the indiscretion of marrying a non-Hebrew woman. Was not Elijah Muhammad even now leading black people from their American house of bondage? As the lives of these biblical patriarchs demonstrated, holy men were not perfect. And is not the perfect (apologies to Voltaire) the enemy of the holy? If we still venerate these patriarchs, a drunken and irresponsible Noah, an incestuous Lot, and a lecherous and murderous David, then why not the Honorable Elijah Muhammad?

Malcolm and Wallace were not merely friends but rivals as well. After serving three years in prison for evading the draft, Wallace attempted to address the 1963 Savior's Day convention only to be blocked by Malcolm. Acting as the head of the Nation in the absence of an ailing Elijah Muhammad, Malcolm refused to give Wallace a platform. Elijah Muhammad's family, Wallace included, did not take kindly to Malcolm's high-handed manner.[29] As the blood kin of the Messenger, Elijah's licit and natural-born children constituted a "royal family." The order of succession would run from father to son and, if Elijah had his way, to his seventh and therefore special son, Wallace Muhammad. From the point of view of many members of the royal family, Malcolm was a usurper, a dangerous pretender to the throne. Such court politics and intrigue notwithstanding, the poor leadership of Elijah Muhammad, especially his incontinence made both Malcolm and Wallace unhappy. Wallace certainly knew his father better than Malcolm and told him that his father would not welcome any interference in his sexual life. Malcolm disregarded Wallace's advice, which led directly to his suspension from the Nation of Islam. Malcolm's comments about the assassination of President Kennedy, as noted earlier, provided Elijah Muhammad with a pretext for suspending his rival. Malcolm pulled Wallace deeper into the mud by informing Elijah Muhammad that he had learned of his sexual improprieties from Wallace. Wallace denied this claim vehemently. Meanwhile, Wallace had his own problems. Because of his own theological and policy differences, Wallace had broken with the Nation and spent a great deal of energy trying to protect himself from deadly reprisal. The death-dealing agents of the Nation of Islam were ubiquitous. Like Malcolm, he feared that he might be assassinated. On August 4, 1964, he asked the FBI and local police for protection from the "punch-your-teeth-out" squads in the Nation of Islam.[30]

According to his biographer Bruce Perry, Malcolm only acted as if he were trying to preserve Elijah Muhammad's reputation. Yes, he and Wallace respected each other sincerely. But they were hardly close. Malcolm's ambition made Wallace wary. Malcolm was too ambitious to be close to anyone, much less his "chief rival for Elijah's favor" and as his successor as leader of the Nation of Islam. Perry claims that Malcolm's public deference to him as Elijah Muhammad's successor did not fool Wallace. "He [Malcolm X] wanted to be the boss." Was Malcolm "insane for leadership" as Elijah Muhammad reputedly said in private?[31] Or does Malcolm's nephew provide a more persuasive account of the relationship between Malcolm and Wallace? According to Rondell Collins, Malcolm and Wallace were close friends.[32] But he also suggests that as early as 1957, members of the Nation of Islam frequently speculated about who would succeed an ailing Elijah Muhammad: Malcolm or Wallace? Such speculation suggests that they had long been viewed as rivals for power. The fact that both men, along with Wallace's brother Akbar Muhammad, disagreed with the policy recommendations of the powerful Chicago faction of the Nation of Islam (the Chicago Mafia) surely intensified the speculation. By this time, the Nation had semidecentralized it power. In addition to the Chicago faction, Elijah Muhammad exercised power from his base in Phoenix, where he convalesced, while New York City provided a power base for Malcolm X. When federal authorities indicted Wallace in 1958 for refusing, at his father's insistence, to register for the military draft, the *Pittsburgh Courier* speculated, given Elijah Muhammad's health problems, that Malcolm might be forced to run the Nation of Islam. Even then, nineteen years before he became head of a reestablished Nation of Islam, the "Charmer" a.k.a. Louis X a.k.a. Louis Farrakhan made a not so subtle bid for power. According to Rondell:

> The commentary [in the *Pittsburgh Courier*] quoted Louis X as saying that if Malcolm was unable to take control, he would do so. This was a gambit by Louis X. He knew that Mr. Muhammad, not Malcolm, was the sick person. Louis was moving cautiously because he was well aware of the fate of others who had opposed Mr. Muhammad.[33]

Given this account, it seems hard not to believe that Malcolm and Wallace were friends and that their friendship was rooted partially in a common perception of the religious deficiencies of the Nation of Islam. They also competed for Elijah Muhammad's attention, affection, and ultimately his power. But Malcolm gazed upon Elijah Muhammad's nakedness with greater aggression and, perhaps, glee than did Wallace. And unlike Wallace, he eventually chose to expose that nakedness to the world.

Nakedness is a trope for weakness, frailty, and vulnerability. Was Malcolm harsh and uncharitable in his reaction to Elijah Muhammad's indiscretions? Perhaps he was but then again, perhaps not. Given what he had overcome in his own life, the asceticism he had cultivated as a bulwark against his own darker inclinations and his willingness to sacrifice family and friends on the altar of the Nation's strict code of sexual deportment, one could predict and justify his harsh reaction to Elijah Muhammad. Was there something gleeful and unseemly in Malcolm's decision to expose rather than cover his father's nakedness as the biblical story suggests was true in the case of Ham and Noah? Or is the true moral of the story that fathers should not expect a higher level of moral deportment from their sons than they demand from themselves? After all, if Ham was a disrespectful voyeur, then Noah was an irresponsible drunk. Whatever the moral, Malcolm's motives were probably mixed. He objected to being muzzled politically, which undermined the effectiveness of the Nation of Islam. Malcolm also had moral objections. If Elijah's sexual weakness disturbed Malcolm, Elijah's hypocrisy disturbed him even more. Elijah's punitive response to Malcolm's suggestion that he atone for his sexual indiscretions disturbed Malcolm most of all. In the end, from Malcolm's perspective, Elijah's failure was religious and moral. Elijah Muhammad was an unrepentant sinner. He would not atone.[34]

He went to Mecca as Malcolm X and returned as El-Hajj Malik El-Shabazz. In the afterglow of the Hajj he wrote letters to family and friends, proclaiming his conversion to Sunni Islam, a conversion that in fact had long been underway. Perhaps he thought about his conversation with Wallace D. Muhammad who had assured him that a Muslim should strive (jihad) to learn as much about Islam as possible (AMX 366). In making the Hajj, Malcolm made the effort. He shared his joy and growing knowledge with the people closest to him: first Betty, second Ella, and then several others.[35] The list included Wallace, who expressed the conviction that only "orthodoxy," a proper understanding of Islam could save the Nation of Islam (AMX 390). (By "proper understanding of Islam," Wallace meant Sunni Islam; his view and Malcolm's view of Shi'a Islam are not clear.) Even before the trip to Mecca, Malcolm and Wallace were dissidents. They knew that their father, metaphorically speaking, was drunk and naked. Now estranged from his father and the Nation he had built, Malcolm responded by building a rival Muslim community that reflected his newly acknowledged Sunni views. With the help of Betty, Ella, Wallace, and a few others, he believed that Muslim Mosque Incorporated could inspire Islamic renewal among African American Muslims.[36]

These developments occurred within the context of Nation of Islam skullduggery and a disinformation campaign by the FBI. "In February 1964 both the *Amsterdam News* (a black newspaper based in Harlem) and the *New York Times* (a white newspaper based in Manhattan) reported that Malcolm might split permanently from the N.O.I."[37] According to Rondell Collins, his mother suggested that the FBI was the likely source of that rumor. Both the FBI and CIA used informants to spread the rumor that Malcolm would form a rival organization of Afro-American Muslims. A second rumor circulating in Harlem described Malcolm as bereft without Elijah Muhammad and trying desperately to return to the Nation. A third rumor had Malcolm driving a hard bargain. He would return to the Nation of Islam only if he and Wallace shared power and the Chicago mob of John Ali, Raymond Sharrieff, and Herbert Muhammad was removed from power. According to Ella, the FBI designed these rumors to incite further animosity between Malcolm and Elijah Muhammad."[38] Their efforts succeeded. The animosity between the two men not only made things more dangerous for Malcolm but for Wallace D. Muhammad as well. Both men were *dissident sons* of the Messenger, who questioned the ways of their father and the direction of the Nation of Islam. In 1964, both found themselves embroiled in bitter controversy with the Nation and with their father, which led to their *excommunication*. While clearly dangerous for Wallace, the excommunication was a death sentence for El-Shabazz.

Several days before his assassination, Malcolm X received a visit in his Chicago hotel room from Wallace Muhammad. Wallace must have smelled the violence in the air and wanted to consult his friend. According to biographer Bruce Perry, Malcolm had good reason to be wary of his former rival. But the past could not be undone; he pushed aside any lingering sibling rivalry he may have felt. Caution was a luxury he could no longer afford. The Messenger's indiscretions demanded a courageous response. Besides, El-Shabazz was angry. Revenge, they say, is a meal best served cold. Malcolm wanted his hot. He told Wallace that he would expose *their* father. "Within a week, Wallace contacted his father and told him that he wished to return to the movement." Perry says that we may never know whether Wallace told Elijah about Malcolm's plans.[39] We may never know whether Wallace knew the details of Malcolm's assassination. What we do know is that Wallace placed an anonymous phone call to Malcolm before his Audubon Ballroom speech warning him of the impending assassination. Malcolm was not available to take the call. Perry remarks in a footnote that "Wallace Muhammad later acknowledged he was concerned that people would hold him partly responsible for what happened that day at the Audubon. After he succeeded his father as titular leader of the Nation of Islam, he lamented, 'I never got a chance to get a hearing before Malcolm X.'"[40]

Nearly thirty years after his death, Wallace referred to articles and editorial cartoons in *Muhammad Speaks* that threaten Malcolm:

> I recall getting some of those papers. And one I remember that stays in my mind is a picture that had Malcolm with horns on his head, and his head had been severed, and they were calling him a Judas. And I recall reading the language of ministers in the paper. I won't say Farrakhan. I know he was one of them but there were other ministers too. And I recall their language. And I said to myself, they trying to get him killed. They want him dead.[41]

The Nation of Islam *excommunicated* Malcolm X and Wallace Muhammad at roughly the same time. *These dissident* sons, one natural-born, the other an "adopted" son, had rejected their father's religiously eccentric and politically conservative vision of Islam. Wallace's objections appear to have been primarily theological. Malcolm's objections were also theological but ethical and political as well. Wallace denies that he tried to influence Malcolm's theology. Perhaps this denial represents a hangover from those deadly times in the early 1960s, when Malcolm had been charged with encouraging Akbar Muhammad—Wallace's older brother—to defect from the Nation. Perhaps Wallace feared being too closely associated with Malcolm. He was no fool. To be publicly associated with Malcolm during that time of crisis when sides were being taken and the assassin's knife sharpened was dangerous, even for the Messenger's seventh son.

While denying that he influenced Malcolm, Wallace acknowledges that Malcolm influenced him. After Elijah Muhammad died, Wallace became the leader of the Nation of Islam. In response to an interviewer's question "Why did you rename the Mosque in New York City after Malcolm Shabazz?" Wallace responded: "Because I felt my own hurt was shared by most of the members in the Nation of Islam. I couldn't accept that Minister Malcolm be written off." He said that with the exception of his father Malcolm X was the greatest minister the Nation had ever produced. He declines as a son might to rank Malcolm higher than his father but Malcolm, he adds, was the most faithful minister that his father ever had.[42] One does not have to be too skillful in reading between the lines of Wallace's obligatory praise of his father to recognize this as simultaneously high prize for Malcolm X and as a veiled rebuke of his father, and of those who assassinated Malcolm, created a climate (as Louis X did) that made the assassination possible, or otherwise turned their back during Malcolm's time of trouble.

If anyone doubts that Malcolm's religious dissent made Wallace's dissent possible, consider Wallace's view of Malcolm Shabazz's influence on the contemporary "reform" movement within African American Islam. If many American Muslims now view Wallace Muhammad as a *Mujaddid*—a renewer of Islam—then Malcolm preceded him in the work of renewal. Malcolm's rough dissent against the "father" made Wallace's smooth dissent possible. According to Wallace, Minister Malcolm initiated the changes that he is now carrying forward. "When I was a young man," Wallace remarks, "Malcolm X was an influence in my life. The thing that distinguished Malcolm X among the ministers was his individuality." Along with his forceful will, Malcolm's individuality attracted new blood into a quasimoribund cult, transforming the Nation of Islam into a dynamic organization. "Malcolm's new thinking, courage and youth," Wallace adds, "attracted most of the young people into following the Honorable Elijah Muhammad and I was one of them."[43] When Malcolm courageously left the Nation, he provided a valuable model for how to leave and how not to leave. Ever observant and concerned about his own safety and future within the Nation, Wallace was a good student.

★   ★   ★

THE FEDERAL BUREAU OF INVESTIGATION, SUBJECT: MALCOLM X_LITTLE. This file (# 100–399321; Section 15; Serials 228–288; report date: 16/2/65) reveals both anger and desperation. The Nation of Islam is tightening its death grip on Malcolm. Any possibility of reconciling with Elijah Muhammad is now past. Malcolm's Hijrah from the Nation of Islam is in full effect:

OAAU held a public rally from 8:15 P.M. to 10:15 P.M., February 15, 1965, at the Audubon ballroom, Broadway and 166th Street, New York City. Approximately six hundred persons were in attendance. There was extensive press coverage of the rally.

Malcolm X talked at length on the firebombs which were thrown into his house in the early morning of February 14, 1965, destroying the house. He was quite angry and upset that the incident had placed his wife and daughters in danger and he angrily accused the NOI of doing it on the direct orders of NOI leader, Elijah Muhammad. He ridiculed the suggestion by the NOI that he set the fire himself and claimed that he knew absolutely nothing about his being evicted from the house on February 15, 1965, based on a court action by the NOI, until he heard it on the radio on February 15, 1965.

★   ★   ★

Last Rites

Malcolm speaks of death:

Every morning when I wake up, now, I regard it as having another borrowed day. In any city, wherever I go, making speeches, holding meetings of my organization, or attending to other business, black men are watching every move I make, awaiting their chance to kill me. I have said publicly many times that I know that they have their orders. Anyone who chooses not to believe what I am saying doesn't know the Muslims in the Nation of Islam. (AMX 438)

In his 1993 "Savior's Day" speech, Louis Farrakhan offers an angry response:

Yeah. I love Elijah Muhammad enough that if you attack him, I would kill you, yesterday, today, and tomorrow. And I'm not a killer. But neither are you. But if someone attack[s] what you love, each one of you in here would become a killer instantaneously. . . . Love casts out fear. We don't give a damn about no white man law when you attack what we love. And frankly it ain't none of your business. What have you got to say about it? Did you teach Malcolm? Did you make Malcolm? Did you clean up Malcolm? Did you put Malcolm out before the world? Was Malcolm your traitor or was he ours? And if we dealt with him like a nation deals with a traitor, what the hell business is it of yours? . . . a nation gotta to be able to deal with its traitors, and cut-throats, and turncoats. The white man deals with his. The Jews deal with theirs. Salman Rushdie wrote a nasty thing about the Prophet and Imam Khomeini put out a death finger on him and it stands today. Its certain paths you don't cross.[44]

El-Hajj Malik El-Shabazz was assassinated on February 21, 1965. Just as he had predicted, the assassins were members or hirelings of the Nation of Islam. They gunned him down in front of Betty who was pregnant with twin daughters, Malikah and Malaak, he would never see. Attallah, Qubilah, and Ilyasah screamed in terror and anguish mimicking the reactions of their mother. Only Gamilah, Betty and El-Shabazz's infant daughter, left behind with friends, was not present.[45] Amidst the ensuing bedlam, Malcolm's life ran out Blood red on the Audubon Ballroom floor.

El-Shabazz's life had been a chronology of changes: youthful-sectarian-Garveyite-"back to Africa"-Christian, become a hustling-drug-abusing-criminal, become Satan, an atheist, become a Nation of Islam Muslim and, finally, a Sunni Muslim. His was a life shaken by a series of spiritual transformations. Not everyone understood the significance of these changes. Perhaps nothing symbolizes this lack of understanding more than the manner in which the body that was El-Shabazz was handled

after his death. On his way to the grave, El-Shabazz was subjected to two
sets of desires, one Christian, the other Muslim, about how his funeral
should be conducted.

In the confusion and grief over his death, most people ignored or for-
got about who El-Shabazz had become. He was a Muslim, a servant of
Allah. But El-Shabazz's fellow Muslims were on guard lest the funeral
be conducted as if he were a Christian. They had good reason to be
concerned. Muslim Mosque Incorporated did not have the facilities
to handle the funeral. Given the enmity between El-Shabazz and the
Nation of Islam, the funeral certainly could not be held in one of their
mosques. The thought of doing so, even if permitted, must have been
intolerable. Besides, Harlem Mosque 7 had been burnt to the ground
apparently by outraged supporters of El-Shabazz. The obvious though
ironic option was to hold his funeral in one of Harlem's many black
churches. Large black churches with the facilities to hold the funeral
did not want to have anything to do with El-Shabazz. And can you
blame them, given his vitriolic condemnation of black brainwashed
Christians and Negro preachers? The Refuge Church of God in Christ
declined. Williams C.M.E. Church declined. Even El-Shabazz's one-
time admirer, the Reverend-and-Congressman Adam Clayton Powell,
Jr. declined a request that the venerable Abyssinia Baptist Church host
the funeral. This black Muslim in a predominately black Christian
world was as controversial in death as he had been in life. Despite such
opposition, one church stepped forward. The funeral would be held
at the Faith Temple, Church of God in Christ. This was the kind of
church from which El-Shabazz had succeeded in "fishing" for many
of the Nation of Islam's new members, reeling them from Christian
waters and into the world of Islam. Now his Afro-*Eccentric* spirit, and
the vitriol with which he proclaimed it, drew a hostile reaction from
all but one of the black churches he had condemned.

These are the particulars on El-Shabazz's death and burial:

1. El-Shabazz was shot multiple times and died on a Sunday.
2. At Betty Shabazz's request, his burial was delayed until the following Saturday.
3. The body that was El-Shabazz was handled by Unity Funeral
   Home of Harlem.
4. In Brooklyn, Sheik Al-Haj Daoud Ahmed Faisal, a Sunni
   Muslim with the Islamic Mission of America said that delaying
   El-Shabazz's funeral service violated the Muslim tradition that
   the sun should not set twice on a believer's body, since the Qur'an

prescribes burial if possible within twenty-four hours. He added that Muslims believe that the soul leaves the body when it has grown cold and that the body comes alive again when buried[46] (AMX 505–6).

5. The body that was El-Shabazz was publicly displayed between 7:10 and 11:00 p.m. on February 23.

6. The inscription on his coffin read "El-Hajj Malik El-Shabazz— May 19, 1925— Feb. 21, 1965."

7. Sheik Ahmed Hassoun, a Sudanese Sunni Muslim prepared the body that was El-Shabazz's for burial according to traditional Muslim funeral rites. His Western clothes were removed. He was washed, anointed with holy oil, and completely draped in a *kafan* (white linen shroud) with only his face exposed. Passages of the Qur'an were read over the mere body he had become. The body that was El-Shabazz was then pronounced ready for burial. Afterwards, the public viewing, a Christian rite that these Muslim preparations had disrupted, resumed (AMX 518).

8. As is traditional among black Christians, the funeral was held with an open casket. However, the lid of the casket obscured any view of Christian objects, the tithe box and candelabra, behind them. The organizers of the funeral concealed these objects in deference to the leader of the Islamic Mission of America who warned that any hint that this was a Christian service would imperil El-Shabazz's soul. Christian rites would make him "a *kafir*, an unbeliever." Already, the public display of El-Shabazz's body had assaulted Muslim sensibilities since, as they understood it, his death was a private matter between Allah and him (AMX 520). Thus an interreligious struggle over El-Shabazz's legacy played out.

9. Omar Osman of the Islamic center of Switzerland and the United States offered the following eulogy: "The highest thing that a Muslim can aspire to is to die on the battlefield and not at his bedside. . . . Those who die on the battlefield are not dead but alive!" (AMX 520). In his view, the jihad that was El-Shabazz's life had ended in a "glorious" death.

10. El-Shabazz was buried with his head facing east, the direction of Mecca (AMX 522). He joined countless black people from the earliest days of the transatlantic slave trade whose last act of facing Mecca—an act performed on their behalf, where in death they were patients and others were their agents—proclaimed their eternal submission to Allah.

Death and burial are the last rite of passage in the life of a religious person. These rites tell us much about how a person lived and what that person meant to those left behind. The interreligious struggle over how El-Shabazz should be "funeralized," to use an African American expression, speaks to the embattled place of Islam in a predominately Christian culture. It also speaks to the concessions made to that culture. Or to put it more positively, it speaks to processes of indigenization that always produce a gap between old and new traditions, between the dogma of orthodoxy and the actual lives of Muslims around the world. Islam emerged within the context of seventh-century Arab culture and bears its imprint like a birth mark. Seventh-century Muslims adopted pre-Islamic notions of how the dead should be treated. To put it crudely, the early Muslim ummah Arabized, that is, indigenized the Revelation from the moment of its reception. If Muslim funeral rites bear the birthmarks of its Arab origins, then we should expect non-Arab funeral rites to become a part of how Muslims in non-Arab cultures commemorate death. El-Shabazz's final rites show the difference between Muslim orthodoxy and actual Muslim praxis. (Again, "orthodoxy" and "orthopraxis" are somebody's notion, and by no means indubitable, unquestionable, or nonrevisable, of right belief and right practice.) Just as African American Muslims found it difficult to observe the Islamic Pillars of salat, Ramadan, and zakat under the conditions of slavery and virtually impossible to perform the Hajj, so El-Shabazz's family and friends had difficulty scripting a "traditional" Muslim rite in mid-twentieth-century America. New circumstances require the invention of new traditions. Malcolm's funeral exemplified the *blue,* improvisational style of black culture. His caretakers did not bury him quickly as the old traditions demanded. They conformed to the prevailing norms in black American culture by displaying the body that was El-Shabazz. The hot desert conditions that made rapid burial normative in the Middle East, and the beliefs that grow around those burial practice as if they were clinging vines, do not obtain in a culture where refrigeration and other modern technologies can delay, indefinitely, the universal horror we experience in the face of bodily putrefaction.

For Malcolm: Ossie's Eulogy, Ella's Pilgrimage

"Here—at this final hour, in this quiet place—Harlem has come to bid farewell to one of its brightest hopes—extinguished now, and gone from us forever." . . . So began Davis' eulogy of this brave, "gallant young champion" of Afro-America. In death, his spirit was unconquered still. "Malcolm," Davis wrote, before the era of gender-inclusive language, "was our manhood, our living, black manhood!" The best that black America has to offer, we honor our best selves by honoring him. Sure, we may have differed with him. But, in consigning his "mortal remains to earth, the common mother of all," we know that Malcolm is no longer a man—"but a seed—which, after the winter of our discontent, will come forth again to meet us." Drawing on the black sermonic tradition, Davis adds: "And we will know him then for what he was and is—a Prince—our own black shining Prince!—who didn't hesitate to die, because he loved us so."[47]

Though Ella Collins led a pilgrimage of three hundred to El-Shabazz's grave, it has not become a site of pilgrimage. It does not hold the symbolic import that the graves of martyrs often hold, especially in Shi'a Islam. No organizations commemorate his status as a saint, as the ascetic and quasimystic that he was. His grave is simple, reflecting the austerity with which he led his postprison life. His gravesite does not attempt to represent him in death in a way that differs from or reverses who he was in life. Perhaps the details of his burial do express the piety[48] of this austere man, who gave up smoking while in prison and never looked back, who reflected the zeal of a new Sunni convert when he expressed the conviction that the Prophet Muhammad would have condemned the nasty habit of smoking had it existed in Arabia during his lifetime (AMX 395). Such was the piety of a man who practiced celibacy for a decade, ate once a day, and lived as if he had taken a priestly vow of poverty. The material poverty of his burial was consistent with the spiritual richness of the life he lived. But, as Orwell said in regard to Mohandas Karamchand Gandhi (Mahatma Gandhi), "Saints should always be judged guilty until proven innocent."[49] They often make other people (especially their families) pay a high price for their saintliness. So it was with Malcolm K. Little a.k.a. Detroit Red a.k.a. Malcolm X a.k.a El-Hajj Malik El-Shabazz.

Before a hail of bullets separated the *rūh* (spirit) from the *nafs* (soul, self, and living body) called El-Shabazz, what did he believe about his final state? We cannot know for sure. But informed speculation is possible. El-Shabazz probably believed that he would "sleep" until the Resurrection of the Dead and the Last Judgment. Until then, he would rest in a peaceful heavenly garden.[50] This "garden," no doubt a metaphor for marvels too wonderful for the human imagination to adequately express,[51] would be his reward for a life well lived. All the austerities he had borne in the cause of Allah would be replaced with a lush and luxurious garden—Paradise.[52] Perhaps he thought these thoughts in the short interval between the bullets that tore through his body and the spirit that left as his blood gathered on the Audubon Ballroom floor.

★   ★   ★

THE FEDERAL BUREAU OF INVESTIGATION, SUBJECT: MALCOLM X_LITTLE. This file (# 100–399321; Section 18; Serials 409–442; report date: 8/9/65) records Malcolm's death and burial. Even in death, Malcolm's life was an object of surveillance by the FBI. Special agents continued to issue reports (file 100–399321, Section 19, Serials 443-; report date 19/4/72) that tracked his influence. The FBI did not close Malcolm's file until 1980. An anonymous agent documents Malcolm's assignation and its aftermath matter-of-factly:

LITTLE, formerly known as MALCOLM X, leader of the MMI, was shot and killed while addressing an OAAU public rally in the Audubon Ballroom on 2/21/65, at New York City. Three members of the NOI were arrested by the NYCPD in connection with the death of MALCOLM X. MALCOLM X was buried in Ferncliff Cemetery, Hartsdale, New York, on 2/27/65.

★   ★   ★

Seven years after this report, the FBI was still vigilant as if Malcolm X, vampire-like, might emerge from his coffin. As the seventh anniversary (May 19, 1972) approached, the Bureau issued a report on "EXTREMIST MATTERS," which urged that the matter be brought to the attention of all agents handling black extremist matters, especially "the black extremist informants":

Because many of today's black revolutionaries regard Malcolm as a hero and a martyr, the possibility exists that the anniversary of his birthday may be marked by them with acts of violence. As an example, last year two NYC police officers were seriously wounded in a machine gun attack by black assailants the night of 5/19. Anonymous letters claiming credit for the attack linked the shooting to "Malcolm's Birthday."

Reverence and Remembrance

In *Passed On: African American Mourning Stories* (2002), Karla Holloway gives a moving account of her visit to Malcolm's modest gravesite. The grave marker, a brass plate attached to a concrete slab, was gone. In its place was a bouquet of withered flowers and a T-shirt emblazoned with Malcolm's prophetic words: " 'It had always stayed in my mind that I would die a violent death. In fact, it runs in my family.' " The intergenerational tragedy Malcolm expressed brought tears to Holloway when she discovered the reason for the missing marker. Engravers were placing "Betty Shabazz," the name of Malcolm's wife, next to his. "This was the summer of her death, which she suffered [ironically] at the hands of her grandson, Malcolm. Her body, but not her name, had already been placed next to his in the grassy, bronzed pathways of Ferncliff."[53]

Epilogue

Surah 1: Al-Fátíha (The Opening)

In the name of Allah, the Most Beneficent, the Most Merciful.
Praise be to Allah, the Cherisher and Sustainer of the worlds;
Most Gracious, Most Merciful;
Master of the Day of Judgment.
Thee do we worship, and Thine aid we seek.
Show us the straight way,
The way of those on whom Thou hast bestowed Thy Grace,
those whose (portion) is not wrath, and who go not astray
    (Qur'an 1:1–7).

PART II

The Spiritual Children of Malcolm X

Darwin describes evolution as descent with modification by means of natural selection. There is no natural selection in matters of the spirit. But there is descent with modification. Spiritual descent operates by a different set of laws, if it can be call law-like at all. Many of its relations of cause and effect remain undiscovered, a mystery to be solved by careful investigation. Lines of descent can never be established beyond doubt and, therefore, are always subject to controversy. There is no DNA evidence in matters of the spirit. Thus experts in discerning spiritual kinship sometimes disagree. And denials of kinship, of ancestry and descent are always possible. Recall Ralph Ellison's eloquent, if nasty (and Ralph could be oh so nasty[1]) denial that Richard Wright was his artistic ancestor and the subtlety with which he distinguished his artistic vision from James Baldwin's in "The World and the Jug." Ellison rebukes Irving Howe for presuming that familiarity, propinquity, and racial affinity are enough to establish artistic descent. In the light of Ellison's example, I am aware of possible objections to my interpretation and have tried to anticipate and respond to them. The final verdict lies with readers. My claims about Malcolm's spiritual legacy are built on the example he set: his Afro-*Eccentric* religious choices, especially his reinterpretation of Jesus, his response to the black freedom struggle, and the way that he "blues" that is, improvises on both, constructing a new identity that circumvents the conventions of the Standard Narrative of Black Religion. Thus, in my Afro-*Eccentric* interpretation, Julius Lester and Jan Willis are the spiritual descendants of Malcolm X.

CHAPTER FOUR

Julius Lester: Blackness and Teshuvah

Biographical Particulars

Julius Lester is a prolific black American writer. He was born in St. Louis, Missouri in 1939 to Reverend W.D. and Julia Lester. His parents and only sibling are deceased. Julius graduated from Fisk University in 1960 on the eve of the student-led sit-in movement. As a folk singer he moved through many circles dominated by civil rights activists and activities. Eventually, he joined the Student Nonviolent Coordinating Committee (SNCC) as a photographer, and became a confidant of Stokely Carmichael. Julius' first published essay is entitled "The Angry Children of Malcolm X" (1966). He achieved notoriety with the publication of *Look Out Whitey, Black Power Gon' Get Your Mama* (1968). In two autobiographies, *All is Well* (1976) and *Lovesong: Becoming a Jew* (1988), he disavowed the views expressed in the earlier book. Julius has been married twice and is the father of five children: two sons and three daughters. His second child's name is "Malcolm Coltrane." From 1971 to 1988, Julius was Professor of Afro-American Studies at the University of Massachusetts at Amherst. After a dispute with members of the Program of Afro-American Studies regarding their alleged anti-Semitism, he accepted a position in the Judaic and Near Eastern Studies Department where he taught until his retirement in 2003.

In this chapter, I treat Julius Lester's life as an attempt to expiate the "sins" of blackness and his revolutionary past. *Teshuvah* is the grand thread unifying the disparate themes of this chapter:

Teshuvah n. Hebrew (teh–shoo–VAH) Repentance. In Judaism, repentance takes many forms and is the subject of many prayers, especially those associated with Yom Kippur. Jewish law says that in order to truly repent, a person must recognize his or her sin, feel remorse, undo any damage done, apologize, and vow never to do it again. As part of the soul searching and *teshuvah* of the High Holy Days, it is customary for Jews to ask their family and friends for forgiveness for any sins, insults, or slights they may have committed against one another over the course of the past year.[1]

The Plunge

1968
Hey, Jew boy, with that yarmulke on your head
You pale-faced Jew boy—I wish you were dead.
I can see you Jew boy—no you can't hide
I got a scoop on you—yeh, you gonna die.
I'm sick of your stuff
Every time I turn 'round—you pushin' my head into
          The Ground (L51)

Julius casts a wary glance toward angry demonstrators from the Jewish Defense League who loudly demand he be fired....

I'm sick of hearing about your suffering in Germany
I'm sick about your escape from tyranny;
I'm sick of seeing in everything I do
About the murder of six million Jews
Hitler's reign lasted for only fifteen years
For that period of time you shed crocodile tears
My suffering lasted for over 400 years, Jew boy
And the white man only let me play with his toys
Jew boy, you took my religion and adopted it for you
But you know that black people were the original
          Hebrews (L 51)

Steve Post a staff member at WBAI in New York City meets Julius outside the station and escorts him inside. Like "Marjorie Waxman, the young switchboard operator" and other Jewish members of the staff, Steve knows that Julius is no anti-Semite. During this time of trouble, several prominent Jews come to his defense. "Robert and Carolyn

Goodman, the parents of Andrew Goodman, who was murdered in Philadelphia, Mississippi, in 1964, and the parents and brother of Michael Schwerner, murdered with Andy, are publicly and privately supportive" (L 57).[2] They too know Julius. And they know that he is no anti-Semite. After all, his role as folk singer and publicist is well known among activists in the freedom movement. So why are fist-shaking members of the Jewish Defense League angrily demonstrating against him? And why are anonymous Jews angry enough to threaten his life?

> When the U.N. made Israel a free independent State
> Little four- and five-year-old boys threw hand grenades
> They hated the black Arabs with all their might
> And you, Jew boy, said it was all right
> Then you came to America, land of the free
> And took over the school system to perpetuate white
>   supremacy
> Guess you know, Jew boy, there's only one reason you
>   made it
> You had a clean white face, colorless, and faded
> I hate you Jew boy, because your hangup was the Torah
> And my only hangup was my color. (L 51–2)

The scope and intensity of the fallout from reading the anti-Semitic poem on radio caught Julius off guard. It left him tired, depressed, and discouraged. Angry, hurt, and confused, this controversy was a liminal passage for Julius. He was betwixt and between the person he had been and the person he would become. Julius was ambivalent. He hated Jews and he loved them. And always, he envied them. The following passage provides a retrospective on his struggle.

1988

I called myself Father, Writer, Teacher, but God did not answer.
Now I know the name by which God calls me. I am Yaakov Daniel ben Avraham v'Sarah.
I have become who I am. I am who I always was. I am no longer deceived by the black face that stares at me from the mirror.
I am a Jew. (L 1)

Oedipus and Atheism

Pre-Liminality is the place, period, and status before the threshold of transformation. "You gon' be a preacher like your daddy!" (L 16)

Julius's earliest memories are not dated by year. What he remembers are the 1940s, summers spent partly with his maternal grandmother in Pine Bluff, Arkansas. She looked like a white woman. Growing up black while looking white, in a white supremacist society, was hard work she would have him know. Julius describes a life of separation, solitude, and silence, a bequest to him through his maternal line. They—grandmother, mother, and he—were a solitary people. But loneliness seems a better word for what he describes as solitude. "We were different, Grandmomma, Momma and me, holding ourselves back from the world and all in it—reserved, polite, formal—acknowledging salutations with the fingertips of white-gloved hands longing for an embrace" (L 7). Julius describes his youthful inability to reach out to other children who stood beyond his gated front yard, constrained by his own sense of being odd. He was not like other kids. His father was a Methodist minister. "[R]obed in a mantle of holiness even before the first diaper was pinned on" his nakedness, Julius was set apart (L 6). He could not do what other kids did such as shoot marbles with the dirty, rough-and-tumble neighborhood boys, catch a Sunday matinee, listen to Muddy Waters play the devil's music on Monday, or play a game of Spades or maybe Gin Rummy on Wednesday. Fenced in by paternal rules, he was also penned by his family's economic independence from white people, the dignity of which his father was determined to protect. His white-looking grandmother and mother corralled him. The father of his grandmother who was also the grandfather of his mother was a white man named Adolph Altschul; a German Jew, he married Julius' maternal great grandmother, a former slave. She is *nameless* in Julius' account (L 6–8). Julius discovered later that his great grandparents never married. No jurisdiction in the South would sanction a marriage between a white man (even a "money-grubbing" Jew) and a black woman. Thus Julius begins a narrative of marginality, eccentricity, and Afro-*Eccentricity* in which his great- grandfather was a Jew in a Jew-hating culture and his mother and grandmother looked like white women in a world that routinely lynched black men for consorting with white women, the suspicion of having done so, or for merely fantasizing. As he puts it elsewhere when describing the terror of the segregated world in which he grew up, "White women are the deepest terror. What a white woman says is truth even when it is a lie" (L 25). This is a not so subtle reference to the twisted landscape of interracial sexual desire and shame, of the alleged "purity" of white women and the "rapist desires" of black men. Long before the lynching of Emmett Till in 1955 seared the awful reality of this ritual of white supremacy into Julius' teenaged memory bank, he was well aware of the danger that white women symbolized.

Born in St. Louis, Missouri, Julius spent his early years in Kansas City, Kansas where his father pastored a local church. He describes his childhood "as heavy and gray" (L 13), denies any memory of laughter, conversation, or the pleasing smell of food cooking on the kitchen stove. Images of church dominate his childhood memories, as if Sunday were the only day of the week. Embarrassed and annoyed, he cannot communicate to his children any sense of the emotional content of his childhood beyond the drudgery of compulsory church attendance and the imposing figure of his father. Julius describes the Reverend Lester as religious but not pious (L 13–14). He does not say explicitly what he means when distinguishing between religion and piety, though he does associate the latter with "family prayer meetings and nightly Bible readings." Conceptually, "religion" and "piety" are close. One might presume that Julius has in mind the popular distinction between reserved and ostentatious behavior, where piety is a kind of sanctimonious performance. According to this view, his father did what religious people *ought* to do without making a big Hollywood-style production of it. Here the absence of ostentation is a measure of authenticity. His father was holy. His holiness did not require an audience, not even a single witness, the validation of somebody saying "Amen."

"In the 1940s," Julius remarks, "a black minister was the recognized and accepted authority in the community—the enforcer of divine law, adjudicator of disputes, provider for the poor, intermediary between the white and the black communities." White people "regarded the black minister as a tribal leader" (L 15). Like his father, Julius is holy. God has chosen him for a special purpose. But who is this god? Is he the god of the perennial philosophy or the god of Abraham, Isaac, and Jacob? Apparently, he is not the god of Julius' father, the Trinitarian god—Father, Son, and Holy Spirit—of the Athanasian Creed. Julius dislikes *that* god and the demands he makes through his representative on earth, the Reverend W. D. Lester. Yet he submits gratefully to his father whose hands he describes as powerful but affectionless. This man is his father, he is this man's son. Like Papa Legba, the Black Atlantic god of the Crossroads, Julius has "One Foot in Heaven" and one on earth. He represents his father who represents god. But he does not like church! And there was much to dislike—the screaming and shouting like "Yes, Lord!," "Thank you, Jesus!" He could never get a conceptual much less an emotional handle on this practice of the Black Church. He found it counterintuitive: it just did not make sense. Why did people scream and shout (obvious signs of distress) if they were happy? And what did Jesus have to do with happiness anyway? Julius did not understand. The old man who "got happy" and ran through the sanctuary muttering "thank you Jesus" must have known something he did not. Surely the woman who got happy and tossed her purse into the choir stand aloft must have had some secret religious knowledge he did not have (L 16–17). Most important of all, Julius was bored.[3] The character Jack in *Jack and the Beanstalk* held more interest and reality for him than the "Holy, Holy, Holy" of Jesus the Christ. Julius' lack of understanding and boredom, he claims, quickly grew into disbelief. One wonders, however, whether disbelief is the right word. As with the six-year-old Malcolm, did Julius have the requisite cognitive maturity; had he even reached the threshold of belief?[4]

Julius pronounces the god of his father dead. But this passive construction is not quite adequate since he claims to have *murdered* his father's god. That god's morality offends Julius who cannot separate it from his father's authority. The "Voynez incident" illustrates Julius' perspective. One night many years ago (Julius claims he was "seven or eight years old") he encountered a girl named Voynez McIntosh at church. The grown-ups were taking care of grown-up business and left Voynez and him to entertain themselves in his father's office. She asked him to read to her from the Bible. He consented but soon grew angry at her cavalier attitude toward the words of the psalmist that, he claims, made him so happy that his "body wanted to jump up and down, dance, turn flips, spin around and around" until he collapsed in laughter. (Julius apparently saw no connection between the giddy ecstasy he describes here and his jaundiced reaction to the "shouting" practices of the Black Church.) Voynez persisted in asking dumb questions, a sure sign that she did not take matters with the holy seriousness they merited. Julius slams the Bible shut in disgust. Suddenly he becomes light-headed, as if he were "high." He experiences a strange sensation as if his head was floating away like a helium-filled balloon. Everything goes black. When Julius revives he is being attended by Doctor Love (this too good to be true!) and by his father who accuses him, without actually saying the words, of fornicating with Voynez on church property. Unable to verbalize his disgust at this possible sacrilege, a sinful defilement of sacred space, Daddy Lester displaces his anger at Julius' budding sexuality onto his irreverent act of angrily slamming the Bible shut. Julius' imaginary sexual sin becomes the sin of treating the Bible sacrilegiously. In his father's eyes, Julius had come of age, having acquired "carnal knowledge." It was not a pleasant experience for father or son. I will give papa Lester the benefit of the doubt. Perhaps he saw something his son could not. Perhaps Julius *had* experienced a sexual awakening, even if he denies, retrospectively, that there was anything sexual about the incident. His exaggerated reaction to Voynez was certainly peculiar, like the prepubescent boy who misperceives his desire as hostility and hits the very girl that he likes. This reaction makes sense for a seven- or eight-year old boy who cannot understand his own budding desire. Perhaps this angry act, of slamming the Bible shut and storming out the room, was Julius' version of a "love tap."

In addition to being put off by his father's strict sexual code, he describes Daddy Lester's god, as "a CPA of morality." Julius expressed scientific objections to his father's god as well. By the time that he entered Fisk University in 1956, he was no longer the young boy who defended the scientific validity of the Bible against the existence of dinosaurs. By then he had concluded that the big bang theory was a more persuasive cosmology than the god hypothesis. Perhaps he had actually sorted through the evidence like a scientist and drawn this conclusion. Maybe he was tempting danger by pulling the lion's tail. Or perhaps he was doing what young men in this culture often do— symbolically murdering their fathers in a competitive bid for independence. But it was not his father that he described as having murdered but the god of his father. After god's death, Julius calls himself an atheist, but like Malcolm X, also the son of a preacher man, he does not have the resolve of a "real" atheist. His new convictions lack courage. He is ill at ease with his act of deicide and begins a spiritual quest. Perhaps these expressions of discontent were his first, exploratory steps along a path toward teshuvah? Julius' spiritual itinerary includes the high textual Hinduism of the Bhagavad Gita, Zen Buddhism, Japanese flower arranging, tea ceremonies, and the art of haiku; Hermann Hesse's fictional portrait of Gautama Buddha (*Siddhartha),* and Aldous Huxley's *The Perennial Philosophy* (L 29). He is especially influenced by the latter book, which provides a popular but dubious theory of religion as a timeless essence beneath the superficiality of historical differences.

College was a volatile period for Julius. He could never quite decide whether he believed or disbelieved or even what it means to say one does. Consider the following: "I dutifully inform Daddy that I believe in God again, but I don't. One believes in what can be known. It is not that I have faith now. I do, but faith is a bridge from the known to the unknown. Belief and faith are not the same as knowing the terror of the Unknown and Unknowable" (L 31–2). Everyone is entitled to their metaphors and poetic expressions. I concede this right to Julius. Nevertheless, it is not clear what he means by distinguishing faith from "knowing the terror of the Unknown and the Unknowable." It is a rhetorical flourish, a distinction without a difference. His capitalization of "unknown" and "unknowable" makes this no less true. It lends his comments an air of pseudoprofundity without telling us much.

Julius Lester's "Just So" Story

A "Just So" story is any story in which events occur as if they were designed to make a certain point. They tend to have a fantastic, fairy-tale quality. They are pat, neat, without loose ends, and full of unbelievable coincidences. While entertaining, these stories are exceedingly didactic though short on evidence as children's stories often are. As a middle-aged adult, Julius Lester becomes a Jew. Thus there *must* have been a series of events from his earliest childhood that foreshadowed his eventual conversion to Judaism. Given this way of thinking, there are no random events. Ostensibly freak occurrences become part of a uniform narrative, whose end, in retrospect is obvious and even necessary. In such narratives one becomes who one always already was in the same way that an oak tree grows majestically from an acorn. Behind everything is a providential design. Rudyard Kipling coined the term "Just So Stories" for a collection of children's stories he wrote such as "How the Camel got his Hump" and "How the Leopard got his Spots." The following excerpts might be called, "How Julius Lester became a Jew."

1. I have become who I am. I am who I always was. (L 1)
   My great grandfather was a Jew, I say to myself. I don't know what that means, not if meaning is confined to words and concepts. But meaning is also feeling and sensation and wonder and questions.... Altschul. I can say it now. Altschul. (L 12)
2. I know the Bible, or at least the Old Testament, my favorite part. (L 14)
3. I hope God is not angry that Jesus is less real to me than the giant in *Jack and the Beanstalk.* (L 17)

4. I love Bach's music more than that of any composer, but my favorite composition is in a thick book Momma bought me. There is no composer's name and I do not know how to pronounce the title because it is in a foreign language. Every day after I finish practicing, I play it over and over. It is not lines or chords; neither does it move, but it does not stand still. It simply is. It is happy and sad at the same time. I play and the beauty becomes pain and then beauty again and in a half-step is inverted into pain once more until beauty and pain wrap around each other like the braids of a girl's hair, and beauty and pain become a piercing that holds me pinioned and I feel old like "In the beginning," old as if I was never born and will never die. The music winds itself around me and wants to take me somewhere, but I am afraid and do not go. When I stop playing there is a painful yeaning in my stomach, a wishing for something I have never had and thus do not know what it is, or a wishing for something which I once had and have forgotten what it was. The name of the composition is *"Kol Nidre."* It is a Hebrew melody. (L 20)

5. I am eight or nine and sit on the floor in the living room before the big Philco console. The news announcer says that Sammy Davis, Jr., has converted to Judaism. "I'm going to do that someday," I say to myself. (L 20)

6. There is another memory:

   Christmas Day, 1951. I am twelve years old. Momma hands me her present. It is big and thick and heavy. A book!...She smiles. "You might want to start by reading the play called *The Merchant of Venice.*"...Why did she suggest that?...Was Momma thinking of her grandfather?...I do not even know what a money-lender or interest is, but I know that Shylock is being mistreated because he is a Jew.

   Shylock. How odd that in him I encounter myself in literature for the first time. It is odd because I did not grow up unaware of black history and literature....Yet in Shylock I see myself as I do not in Du Bois, Johnson, Langston Hughes, Robeson or any other black figure. (L 21–2)

7. I'm not supposed to do this, but...I hear the rabbi say....He walks to the back of the pulpit to where a curtain is closed and draws it aside. "These are the scrolls of our Torah," he says quietly. "...The open curtain reveals an incision in the back wall inside of which are three large cylinders in velvet covers. I stare at them and it is like gazing into a mirror." (L 28)

8. Rhoda Miller, a fellow English major, thrusts a book in my hand and says, "Read this."...The book is called *Exodus*....When I finish, I tell her, "I think I could die for Israel. If any people deserve a country of their own, it's Jews."...What most deeply affects me in the novel...is the love story. Not the one between Ari, the Israeli, and Kitty, the American nurse, but the one between a people and God and a land. I feel a part of that love. (L 29–30)

9. Khalid Tuck-Tuck is a Palestinian who begins each day with an anti-Semitic diatribe....I stare at him coldly...."I wish Hitler had finished what he started!" Tuck explodes, springing from the couch to stand over me....I look up at him. I do not know that I am humming *"Hava Nagila"* until Tuck screams, "I hate that song!" (L 30–1)

10. What I really need to know is: Why do I rage over and mourn for murdered European Jews as I never have for my own people? (L 33)

11. I want to be a cantor. I sit in my tiny furnished room on West End Avenue in the fall of 1961 and yearn to sing Jewish music—as a Jew. When I pass synagogues, I hear melodies of pain and beauty rising toward heaven. (L 37)

Julius is a fine writer. But as a reader I had no great difficulty pulling this "Just So" strand in his narrative. This kind of narrative, I think, is especially attractive to the religious autobiographer. It has, so to speak, a certain "electromagnetic" quality. I am always amazed by the attraction-repulsion effects Julius has on my students. They are attracted by the poetic beauty of his prose and repelled by his identity politics.

Dead Dreams, Deadly Illusions

Julius says that his memory of the civil rights movements is no more vivid than a trip to the outhouse. While purging himself, he experiences a cool breeze on his buttocks, is aware of a man plowing and birds chirping. He is at peace with himself as he experiences the peace of god. Julius finds god simultaneously in the plenitude of nature, amidst literal and symbolic form of shit, and in the monkish solitude of contemplation (L 41). He recounts this "outhouse experience," which is suspiciously similar to Martin Luther's reputed "outhouse revelation" of *sola scriptura* and *sola fides,* after describing his emotional distance from the civil rights movement during his senior year at Fisk University. Fisk was the epicenter of the student movement and Julius at best was a lukewarm fellow traveler. Unlike John Lewis[5] and other students, he would not risk life on freedom rides or in sit-ins. He heard a "higher call." Torn between this call and a desire to participate in the movement, he hung suspended. He describes his paralysis as follows:

> I sit in a back pew, alone, listening to the joyous singing of freedom songs but not loosing [sic] my voice to join the others. I want to belong to the joy of the church, want to be part of the camaraderie shared by those who have been arrested and jailed. I cannot. I must hold myself apart to know what God wants of me, or what I think He wants.

And he adds:

> Is that arrogance, madness or faith? (L 36)

One suspects that Julius has read Kierkegaard's tortured account of the ethics and psychology of faith—*Fear and Trembling, The Concept of Anxiety,* and *Sickness unto Death*—where faith cannot help but appear as madness to the observer and where the subject of faith is never sure of his sanity. The man who had once said that he "could die for Israel," speaking perhaps through the hyperbole of the romantic ideal and the intensity of sexual desire (in making this remark about Israel, his motives were obviously mixed, since he hoped to "get laid" by this good Jewish girl) Julius remarks: "God has not called me to risk my life on a Freedom Ride" (L 36).

Julius is something of a shaman. He appears to have a lot of out-of-body or better yet "out-of-mind" experiences. I am not sure whether this is merely a narrative technique, a way of dramatizing the complexities of memory and the ambivalence of desire, or whether there is something ethically troubling here, a denial of responsibility, an unwillingness to own one's own actions, words, and deeds. These shaman-like experiences occur frequently as when he says, "I did not live the period [the civil rights years] in a way that my memories have documentary value" (L 38), or "My soul did not believe in The Movement" (L 38), or when he says, nevertheless, that "[h]istory claimed me for itself; I became a revolutionary" (L 39), or "Mind conspired with Body to make me believe I was a revolutionary"(L 38–9, 40). On the contrary, "Soul knew otherwise" (L 40). It was as if Julius, reproducing Descartes mind–body dualism, is a soul looking down on his body and its various activities, untouched by the choices that body makes, as if there were a metaphysical chasm and ethical gap between body and soul. This dualistic language is especially curious, given Julius reference in the same passage to Spinoza who criticized such dualism as ardently as he did the spurious freedom that Julius appropriates for himself and denies to his SNCC (Student Nonviolent Coordinating Committee) compatriots. In response to their "Freedom Now!" demands, Julius asks, "Do they really know what freedom is?" Does he? To use Julius' own language, this is a demand for Knowledge of the Unknowable. Can anyone know according to this impossibly high standard? If, as he suggests, the freedom of his SNCC comrades is doggish and domesticated, then I can fairly describe his freedom as disembodied, irresponsible, and dishonest.

To pursue this point further, consider the following passage:

> To be identified personally with words I have written is frightening. I do not assume that a writer is his or her book. Because I can express black anger does not mean I am angry, and it certainly doesn't mean I hate white people. Because I articulate the experiences of many blacks does not mean that I am writing autobiographically. (L 43)

Julius adds that he did not have to suffer the business end of a policeman's night stick, imprisonment, the depravations of a Mississippi plantation, or life as a cotton picker to write about them convincingly. Reading these comments, I imagine Julius saying something like this: "I am a writer and should be accorded the license of the poet. When I write 'we' instead of 'they,' I'm referring to a vicarious experience not an actual one. My metaphors should not be taken literally and my rhetoric should not be read in a flat-footed and uncharitable way. I am a writer, dammit!" Besides, he adds, "I am not even political, even if I am involved in a political movement.... Political writing is a function of Mind. Mind is not me. How can others not know that?" (L 43). Why does Julius claim this privilege of duality, bifurcating a rhetorical self (Mind) and a real self (Soul) while denying that same privilege to others such as former SNCC comrade Stokely Carmichael? Julius claims that Stokely was the Johnny Appleseed of violence; when he spoke, riots happened (L 38). Julius permits no separation between Stokely the rhetor and Stokely the man. The man and the message, the Soul and the Persona are one. If Julius were to have his way, Carmichael's words would stick to him like flies to a dunghill. But regardless of what he writes, Julius seems to think that he ought to come out smelling just fine.

But such irony is too smelly to go without comment. Equally ironic is Julius' reaction to other people's reaction to his first book, *Look Out, Whitey! Black Power Gon' Get Yo Mama!* (1968). Written, he claims, as a humorous account of black anger, the white public received the book without a trace of irony. They collapsed his mood and the angry mood he attributes to the "children of Malcolm X" into an undifferentiated entity, denying his duality as writerly Persona and Soul. They construe Julius as a mouthpiece for "the people" or, as he put it in an earlier autobiography, "a dummy for a revolutionary ventriloquist." "Misperceiving" his attempt to give voice to the black community, they charge him with anti-Semitism. This perception displeases Julius.

Earlier I referred to Julius' penchant for shaman-like, out-of-body experiences where he disarticulates like the leg and thigh bones of a chicken his physicality, rationality, and ethical responsibility. The Ocean Hill-Brownsville controversy also exemplifies this tendency to live out of body while leaving responsibilities behind. More important, it is the pivotal event in my assessment of Julius' account of black Gentile and white Jewish relations, which I claim goad him toward teshuvah.

The controversy involves a conflict between top-down, bureaucratic control and bottom-up, community control of schools.[6] Ocean Hill-Brownsville was a predominately black, Gentile community in Brooklyn, New York. The teachers and their union were predominately white Jews. The demand for community control of the schools quickly led to charges of black anti-Semitism and to countercharges of white racism. This was a year after the year of assassinations, riots, and rage, when Martin Luther King, Jr. and Bobby Kennedy were assassinated and freedom fighters could not help but think of earlier martyrs such as Malcolm X, Medgar Evers, and martyrs less famous. In 1969 Julius hosted a local radio show on WBAI in New York City. He stepped knee-deep into a dunghill of controversy when he had Leslie Campbell, a black teacher and proponent of community control read some of his student's poems on air. One poem was entitled "Anti-Semitism." The poem was self-consciously and unapologetically anti-Semitic; only a person acting on "damaged emotions" would think otherwise. But Julius insisted that the poem be read since it expressed the rage of at least one black child in the face of white teacher hostility to community control. Predictably, the Jewish community reacted with outrage. Several people called Julius an anti-Semite. There were demands that he be fired. The newly emergent militant group, the Jewish Defense League made him a target of intimidation.

Julius' immediate response to the vilification that he received was a long eloquent statement that he read on air. Though I might quibble with portions of the statement, it seems as true now as Julius undoubtedly thought that it was then. The conflict between blacks and Jews is fundamentally a conflict between blacks and whites within a white supremacy society. The Jewishness of the whites and the Christianity of the blacks while relevant is of secondary significance. This seems as true today of black Gentile and white Jewish relations as it was then. This is in no way a denial of black anti-Semitism. Lamentably, blacks share the anti-Semitism of other Gentiles in America and it must be condemned along with the rest. However, to cast black critics of white racist Jews as anti-Semites merits no response. But to cast black anti-Semites as German Nazis in blackface is deeply offensive; historically inaccurate, it offends truth no less than the construction of anti-Israeli Palestinians as Nazis. This sort of rhetoric distorts the truth.

Julius' second response was introspective. Perhaps he was anti-Semitic. Perhaps an unacknowledged reason for airing the anti-Semitic poem was to hurt Jews as he claims they had hurt him. Julius does not explain the specificity of this hurt, how Jews in their Jewishness rather than as white people who happen to be Jews had hurt him. Curiously, he is alternately envious of Jews and apologetic. He feels the need to atone (teshuvah). Looking back at an earlier incarnation of himself that criticized Israel and Zionism, he equates such critique with anti-Semitism. That one could have a principled opposition to a Jewish state and to Zionism (in the same way that one opposes a Christian, Hindu, or Islamic state) never occurs to Julius.[7] In effect, he "flips the script" that Arafat and the PLO wrote in the 1970s when they petitioned the United Nations to equate Zionism with racism. If Zionism cannot be reduced to racism without qualification—and it cannot be—then criticism of Israel and Zionism cannot be reduced to anti-Semitism.

To reiterate, Julius loved and hated Jews, Jewishness, and Judaism. Envy was the vanishing mediator[8] between his love and hatred. As a result of this emotional complexity, Julius is tarred with his own brush. Tar Baby is a venerable figure in black folklore, symbolizing a sticky situation from which it is difficult to extricate oneself. Designed to hurt Brer Fox—the predominantly Jewish, United Federation of Teachers Union whose racism he sought to expose—Julius (Brer Rabbit) Lester become stuck with a tar baby of his own creation. With his angry, envy-driven decision to air the anti-Semitic poem, Julius became the Tar-Baby of anti-Semitism. Two years later, he became a professor of Afro-American Studies at the University of Massachusetts at Amherst.

His professorship was one in a series of important passages. In 1970 his marriage to Joan Steinau ended in divorce. And his daughter, Jody Simone and son, Malcolm Coltrane began a life as the children of divorce. The divorce followed a nearly nine-year career (1960- 68) as a folksinger and photographer, three years (1966–68) as director of Road Islands' Newport Folk Festival, a writing career that began in 1966, and a career as a radio personality that began in 1966 at WBAI-FM, in New York City. He even hosted a television showed called *Free Time* on WNET-TV, in New York City, from 1969 to 1971. Despite the turmoil in his personal life, his professional life revealed variety and wealth. In 1969 he published *To be a Slave,* a Newbery award winner and the first in a series of award-winning books for children and adults.

Vision Quest: Prelude to Conversion

Julius' life appeared to be on track but that is not the portrait that we get in his autobiography. Rather than portrait of a young man as an artist, we get portrait of a young man as spiritually restless. Julius is haunted by the ghosts of his revolutionary past, by his duality and schizophrenia. (He did not merely hear voices but was seduced, dummy-like, into speaking them. Julius was Camus' victim become executioner, an idea that I elaborate in due course.) He appears as precisely the kind of divided, even tortured self that William James in *Varieties of Religious Experience* (1902) describes as a prime candidate for a conversion experience. In the summers of 1973 and 1976, Julius embarks on a two-part vision quest. Like a shaman whose journey takes him to hell in search of a lost soul,[9] Julius set out on a cross–country journey in search of his own lost soul.

The immediate occasion for this journey of self-discovery was an invitation to speak at a conference hosted by the School of Religion at the University of Kansas. During this journey, the state of his soul reveals itself temporally and spatially with every change in geography. His first dated observation is *"July 1–2, Harpers Ferry, West Virginia."* He is there he says to pay respect to John Brown, the fiery abolitionist, the "Old Man," a general in the army of god, to borrow a phrase from Jan Willis.[10] According to Julius, Brown's sense of responsibility before god had a fierce simplicity. His integrity inspired awe. Brown knew that "[l]oving God meant loving the slaves. Being loved by God meant freeing the slaves" (L 74). "Onward Christian soldiers! / Marching as to war." He adds that Brown had the kind of spiritual depth that led him to embrace death as essential to a spiritual new birth and a new birth of freedom. Brown's black-and-white clarity, his certainty in matters of freedom and bondage, life and death do not disturb Julius in the way that the certainties—"Freedom Now!"—of his SNCC comrades did. He offers us no comparative analysis for this disparity in judgment. The ethical difference so far as I can tell hinges on the difference, to put it facetiously, between "god" and "dog." Brown's actions on behalf of slaves were godly, exemplifying divine freedom. In contrast, the activities of black revolutionaries were doggish, tantamount to a dog straining against its master's leash.

From Harper's Ferry, Julius drives through Pennsylvania's Amish country and visits the Ephrata Cloister. He describes this celibate community as the most depressing he had ever seen, which takes up a theme that we encounter throughout the book, namely, the implicit connection that Julius makes between sexual expressivity and spirituality. Like his father's god, the CPA of Morality, this community represses the vitality of the sexual impulse. That sexual repression (sublimation) has its own spirituality does not occur to Julius. On the contrary, the spirituality of abstinence is a foreign idea. Visiting D. H. Lawrence's ranch confirmed this view. A high priest of erotica and sexual freedom, Lawrence had taught Julius to "live—with integrity—in right relationship to the demands of the blood," instinct, and the pagan within us (L 109–10). In Julius' view, spirit cut off from sexual vitality is a moribund spirit.

Shaking the dust from his sandals, Julius drives through Waynesboro, Virginia to Berea, Kentucky, where he reflects on the nature of the monastic life. Monasticism, he remarks, equals holiness and holiness equals Being. Though he does not define Being, one suspects that the theologian Paul Tillich is somewhere in the background of this observation. Julius considers the possibility that a family unit might be a monastery, a place of holiness, a house of Being. After this speculative encounter with monasticism, Julius drives to an actual monastery, the Abbey of Gethsemani. Thomas Merton whom Julius admires once lived and worked there. Julius claims that the monastery's chapel is the first in which he had ever felt god's presence. The Cistercian silence, religion stripped down to its true essence, the unmediated access to god: "Nothing," Julius says, "is more natural than that chapel, those monks and me here with them" (L 77). Julius, it seems, has found a new spiritual home. Deep down where the he that he really is resides, in his telltale heart, Julius is a monk. The Catholic sources of this monkish desire (similar to the Merton-influenced desires of theologian, Howard Thurman and historian, Albert Raboteau) are ignored if not denied in the "Standard Narrative of Black Religion." Catholicism, however, is an important tributary of Julius' Afro-*Eccentric* spirituality.

During his journey across the varied landscapes of American religious history, Julius sees everything through a monastic lens. The restored buildings of an old Shaker community are "another kind of monastery," which contrasts sharply with the "Roofless Church" that he encounters in New Harmony, Indiana. He describes it as "depressingly Protestant" (L 78). Even a pilgrimage to the grave of Paul Tillich cannot raise his spirits. "Everything in New Harmony—the Roofless Church, Tillich's burial site—is a perfect example of religion emanating from the mind" (L, 78). Julius disassociates true religion from mind in the same way that he disassociates his true self from his intellect. Mind is sterile. Emanating from the soul, true religion is passionate and fertile. Curiously, in this neoromantic mood, Julius does not square his distaste for celibacy and what he takes be its energy-sapping spirituality with praise of the monastic life. He does not understand that sexual abstinence is the price one pays for holiness within a monastic order. Repression is the fertilizer if not soil from which the spiritual fruit of the monastic life grows.

On July 14, 1973, Julius spends the night in Nauvoo, Illinois. He notes its Mormon past. Mormons established a settlement there under the leadership of Joseph Smith and Brigham Young. The site of a nascent-autonomous-would-be Mormon republic, it came to a bloody end when scores of Mormons including Smith were murdered by hostile neighbors. The survivors of this anti-Mormon pogrom followed Brigham Young to Utah. But that was yesterday. Today the Protestant ethic and the spirit of capitalism has replaced a spirit of murder as the city of Nauvoo exploits a superficial interest—no blood, no gore, no stories of religious persecution please—in its Mormon past. But even a thriving wine-and-blue cheese industry cannot distract Julius' attention from what he imagines is the sound of "Mormon ghosts moaning." And if this were not depressing enough, Julius considers the many Indian names of the many Indian nations now gone: "Illinois, Iowa, Mississippi, Peoria, Keokuk, Sioux-City—and on and on." He interprets the persistence of the names as a contract with the dead by those who took their lives and stole their land (L 79–80). This act of naming is a kind of backhanded acknowledgment of the magnitude of what had been done to those who are no longer here to speak their own name.

To the list of Indian names without a people, we might add Dakota. While passing through Rapid City, South Dakota, Julius sees a gathering storm on the horizon and questions his decision to visit Wounded Knee. This is how he describes what followed: "There a strange but certain knowing floods my body and a voice says: 'Do not be afraid. The Lord is with you.' I do not know if I am to trust the words. Are they words of wishful thinking? The voice repeats itself: 'The Lord is with you.' I press the accelerator and drive toward the ominous thunderheads" (L 81). How does Julius interpret this experience? He describes the rain as angry, as if it were god's judgment on what had happened here when hundreds of Sioux were terrorized, tortured, and murdered. Driving silently through "the deserted lands of the Oglala Sioux," he dismisses the idea that the storm was merely a coincidence. On the contrary, this was an omen. God was signaling him. But to what end? Julius claims he does not know what purpose god has for his life. "I wish I were an Indian shaman," he says, "a priest of the Great Spirit,[11] accustomed to going off into the hills and being spoken to by God" (L 80–3).

If god spoke to him through the awful sound of thunder and rain, then he also spoke to Julius quietly on the grass-covered battlefield of Little Big Horn. "I am a clump of sagebrush!" he exclaims in what reads like a paraphrase of Ralph Waldo Emerson.[12] And it sounds much like Emerson's religious naturalism too, especially when he adds: "At evening, to hear the wind whistling gently out of the north is to know holiness, all-pervading yet solitary, awesome yet ridiculously ordinary, mysterious but devoid of mystery. This land, this sky are Truth, which is merely the simple recognition of what is and the acceptance of it. I accept and give myself to it" (L 82). Julius does not describe these events, the presence of god in the power of an angry thunderstorm and in the gentle breeze whistling through tall grass, as religious experiences. But that is what they surely were. Where nature is Emerson's cathedral, it is Julius' monastery. This naturalistic impulse that Julius quickly theologizes is another source of his Afro-*Eccentricity*.

From the spiritual heights of the Montana plains, Julius descends to his final destination in Lawrence, Kansas. It is truly a *descent* since the Christian theologians he encounters feel abandoned by god. Julius attributes this feeling to their politicization of Christianity. They think Christians are supposed to redeem the world, want Jesus for president, treat Christianity as if were a caucus of Democrats or Republicans, as if Christianity were synonymous with Caesar. In the erudite musings of these theologians, "Christianity has become a wing of Caesar's Bureau of Propaganda" (L 83). They think that Christianity should rule the world in the same way that Constantine ruled the Roman Empire and then the Christian Church. They forget that god is not our dog, "man's best friend." Nor is god a tool that we can use to manipulate the universe according to our desires. On the contrary, "We are called to live our lives as instruments of god. We are merely human, curls on the waves, clouds that billow at midday and disappear at sunset." GOD ALONE, he says emphatically, is our reason for being, the only justification for our next breath (L 83). Contemporary postliberal theologians (whether Hauerwasian or Radical Orthodox) could not have said it better.

And yet, Julius never tells us who this god is. Is it the Lord YHWH, God the Father, Son, and Holy Spirit, or Allah? Or is it the god of the perennial philosophy? Julius writes as if the identity of god is obvious. His indifference to the identity of god at this stage of his life is an index of his perennialism. The perennial philosophy is the view that a metaphysical substrate underlies all religions. All religions, to use Spinoza's language, are "expressions" of this "substance." In the "West," this substrate is called "God." Across traditions, the advocates of perennialism call this substrate "the transcendent."[13] The idea of "perennial philosophy" was popularized by Aldous Huxley, coined by Leibniz, and is rooted in Aristotelian realism. Even after his conversion, when he affirms YHWH as the unspoken and unspeakable name of god, Julius writes as if this god has no ancestors or peers. He has no interest in exploring the ancestry of YHWH: his local, tribal origins, and the family resemblances he shares with other "El" deities such as the Canaanite god El, the father of the gods and of humankind, or his various transformations through time. To sum up, this god is rooted in the complex religious world of the Ancient Near East and, ultimately, in the history of humanity's religious evolution.[14]

During the summer of 1976 Julius continues his pilgrimage through the spiritual landscapes of America, as if the three-year hiatus between the first and second vision quests was merely a twinkling of the eye. This time he travels through the Indian lands of the west. He marvels at the Snake Dance of the Hopis and makes the following observation: "It is ironic that what is permitted when done by Hopis is condemned when done by poor whites in the mountains of Georgia, Tennessee and Virginia. More startling is that Hopis and poor whites share the same form of religious expression." That there is a superficial similarity between the two is true. But this religious expression signifies differently. If the "Christian Church regards snake handlers as beyond the lunatic fringe," it is not clear that Hopi snake handlers are regarded more highly. They may simply be examples of the exotic, primitive other from whom one expects little, certainly not the standards of a "civilized" white person. As Freud suggests, one does not expect civilized behavior from children, neurotics, and savages.[15] Not expecting much, one judges them according to inferior scale of value. So there is no irony in the disparate treatment of poor, mountain whites and Hopis, if in fact Julius' representation of the difference is accurate. The difference, if it does exist, is legible when read through primitivist lenses.[16] In contrast, there is something ironic about Julius' conclusion, which has the distinct smell of romantic primitivism: "I wonder if it isn't these outcasts from the Christian establishment who keep the faith vital. . . . The Hopi and Christian snake handlers know the living God" (L 107).

Julius is fascinated by the religious significance of the snake, by its diverse symbolic meanings as energy, power, and sexuality. Through the serpentine, undulating bodies of the dancers, he observes, the Snake Dance reconciles the polarities of "earth and sky, passion and reason, cathedral and kiva." And through the magic of the dance, the celibate monk is transformed into a lover (L 107–8). From Hopiland and the Snake Dance, Julius drives to Santo Domingo, New Mexico and the Corn Dance. He marvels at the strenuousness of their worship: the stamina of the dancers, their indifference to perspiration. "They are renewing their covenant," he remarks, "not only with their ancestors but with the Corn God." He doubts that he could meet the demands of this dancing faith. "Such endurance requires an active faith, one which knows it is necessary to dance and chant if the cycle of the seasons is to continue. This is faith beyond reason because the Indians know that the seasons will come and go, each in its time, without their dancing" (L 108). By definition, faith goes beyond evidence, if not reason. What Julius calls faith is more appropriately called reverence and veneration. Through their strenuous celebration, Julius adds, the dancers reject the easy way. They remember what we have forgotten: that god has faith in us. But who is this god of whom he speaks so confidently?

If Julius romanticizes snake-handling Indians and poor whites, he is not always uncritical. A drunken Indian who approaches him and asks for money is a reminder not to romanticize. "Even here," he remarks, "at the center of the world, I am defined by my color." Julius makes this remark because the Indian approaches him, Julius believes, assuming that black people and Indians share a deep, sympathetic connection. Julius is not sympathetic, charging the Indian with reducing his complexity as a black man to skin color, a visible marker of a deep, invisible essence. But Julius does the same with the Indian nations he encounters, reducing them to the then emerging new age stereotype of primitive vitality and spiritual purity. Indians become his noble savages. They provide a weapon to beat back the claims of his native, "depressingly Protestant" religious tradition. Their traditions are his Tahiti, Bali, Mazatlan, and Club-Med, his Ota Benga in a cage.[17] Julius uses them the way tourists and carnival goers have always used the "primitive other." If the Indian whom he encounters imprisons Julius in a cage called "race," then Julius imprisons the Indian in a cage called "primitivism." Neither can see the other in their multifariousness. His expectations disappointed, Julius concludes that the traditions of the Indians, the Snake and Corn Dances, cannot answer the questions posed by his life. The romance of the Corn Dance and the drunken-panhandling-racially essentializing-Indian are two sides of the same reality. He remarks that the miraculous time and space exemplified by the Snake and Corn Dances are rare. Most of the time, we stand outside the magic circle. "Most of us," he adds wryly, "are drunkards looking for a ride home and being turned down by people like me" (L 109). What Julius does not acknowledge is that both his romantic construction of Indians and his cynical conclusions in the face of reality are "flip sides" of his own primitivism. The two sides feed off each other. Disappoint a romantic and you get a cynic.

Looking forward, I wonder if Julius avoids romanticizing Jews and glorifying Judaism. Even worse, does he demonize Arabs, Muslims, and Christians in the way that Malcolm X demonized white devils and Uncle Toms?

Julius' Catholic Interlude

For a liminal moment, Julius "became a Catholic." During this Catholic interlude, he was betwixt and between his childhood African Methodism and his midlife Judaism. While muted in *Lovesong* (1988), his Catholicism is on full display in *All is Well* (1976). It is curious and I think revealing that Julius excludes from *Lovesong* passages that appear in *All is Well*. These passages, referring to "Christ" and "Jesus," occur during the 1973 leg of what I have described as Julius' *vision quest.*

Consider the following: "To confront death is to embrace life. It is to imitate Christ, who knew of his end and when it would be." ... "And I understood why the Bible described the shepherds as being 'sore afraid' when the angels announced the birth of Jesus to them, because I trembled inside, and my fear had nothing to do with the storm." The first sentence occurs in his description of the Shakers, the second a description of his experience at Wounded Knee. Unlike *Lovesong* where every reference to Jesus is negative, these descriptions at worst are neutral. A positive reading does them no violence. This is significant, as I will argue in JULIUS' JEWISH JESUS, since the *Lovesong* narrative seems designed, in a "Just So" sort of way, to minimize the significance of Jesus in the life of a man who claims he always already was (by birth, metaphysics, and desire) a Jew. Indeed, positive references to Christianity as a whole are rare in *Lovesong*. Catholicism, Thomas Merton, and monasticism are notable exceptions. Thus Julius describes the smile of a Catholic nun as godlike. The nuns transcended the antinomy of despair and hope. "They were...as ordinary as dirt and as holy."[18] Throughout a narrative that is unrelentingly hostile to Protestantism, where Protestantism is a metaphor for everything depressing and spiritually dead, Catholicism stands as a possible alternative, a sacred space within which Julius can be or become who he is.

Julius first read Thomas Merton's *Disputed Question* after graduating from college in 1960. Since then a subterranean, Catholic sensibility had begun to grow. Fast-forward six years. SNCC is in turmoil as a result of its decision to expel its white members. Julius is in turmoil over the decision. He commiserates with one of his white friends within the group: she, an ex-Catholic, he, a crypto-Catholic. Fast-forward seven years: now it is Julius and his lover Joanne. She too is Catholic and Julius is glad, for her Catholic heritage, even though she is nonpracticing, allows him to open up to her. Given her Catholicism, Julius knows that she can understand, empathize with, and support him. She can respect the monk that he is. Such was the power of Catholicism.

Joanne accompanied him on his 1973 trip. And now he stood alone on the sacred ground of the Abbey of Gethsemani:

> I return to the monastery and stand before the statue of the Virgin Mary which stands at the center of the quadrangle. I look up into her face and am transfixed, immobilized. I try to move and cannot. During Mass the day before I wasn't able to understand how grown men could be singing about Mary ascending into

heaven, Suddenly, I know it is true! I look at her and think of the Immaculate Conception, and, awe-struck, I whispered: "Why not? Why—*not*? If God is God, then, of course, He could and can do anything He desires. Anything!" (L 86)

This passage sits incongruously within the narrative. Declaring his Catholic love contradicts the anti-Christian narrative that he otherwise constructs so assiduously. It is all the more true when one considers that Julius omits three sentences from the original version of this story in *All is Well*. In that version, after being transfixed by the statute of the Virgin Mary, Julius remarks: "It was a more beautiful feeling than any I have ever known in the arms of a woman." The last sentence, following his emphatic "Anything!" reads: "And that yes, it was true, all of it—the Virgin Birth, the Crucifixion, Resurrection and Assumption! It was true!"[19] It seems odd that Julius does not tarry with and work through the implications of this passage and the earlier version from which it was taken. That it would have complicated if not altered that narrative is clear. Less clear is why Julius decided not to grapple with the complexities and ambiguities of his religious desire. To do so, perhaps would undermine his "Just So" narrative of becoming a Jew. Perhaps the two stories (Catholic love and primordial Jewishness) were in conflict, contesting for primacy like Esau and Jacob in the womb. Perhaps he could not figure out artistically how to represent that conflict. For, in this narrative as opposed to the Jewish one, Julius is a self-described crypto-Catholic, inspired by Thomas Merton and the monastic idea. As he stands awe-struck before the statue of the Virgin Mary, the mother of god, there is no indication that her son leaves him indifferent, that the centrality of Christ leaves him cold, that notions of crucifixion, resurrection, and assumption as Christians typically understand them are incomprehensible if not repugnant. (In this passage, the adult Julius repudiates the child.) Could it be that the art of storytelling in *Lovesong,* with its "Just So" narrative strategy of primordial Jewishness, has gotten in the way of the story being told?

Liminality

The place, period, and status betwixt and between; the border, frontier, and threshold of transformation, conversion, or initiation. Julius remarks: "I cannot go back to who I was, and I do not know who I am becoming." (L 191)

Black, Palestinian, Jew:
Catalysis and Conversion

Throughout *Lovesong*, Julius invokes the suffering of white Jews, which he compares invidiously with the suffering of black Gentiles. He knows such comparisons are ethically problematic but makes them anyway. These comparisons seem to serve several ideological purposes for a man who, at least retrospectively, is narrating the process of becoming a Jew. In a white supremacist society that is also hostile to Jews, Julius seems to manage his aversion to black suffering by accenting the suffering of white Jews. While claiming not to do so, he presents white Jewish suffering as competitive with and as displacing black Gentile suffering. Both claims—blacks Gentiles suffer, white Jews suffer—cannot occupy the same conceptual, ethical, and emotional space. If one voice is raised in protest and lamentation, then the other must be muted. However, the comparative realities of black and Jewish suffering, *in the American context,* are asymmetrical in a way that should trouble the story that Julius wants to tell.[20] He is among the most honest autobiographers I have ever read. Yet there is something dishonest about the complex act of *displacement* (of sympathy and blame) that occurs when he discusses black (Gentile) and (white) Jewish suffering. Something similar is evident in his vignette about the Palestinian student, Khalid Tuck-Tuck. What disappears in Julius' account is history and context. It is as if Tuck-Tuck parachuted out of nowhere, spouting an anti-Semitic diatribe. Julius mentions that Tuck-Tuck is Palestinian but does not say what that means. On the one hand, the word "Palestinian" is historically innocent, ethically and politically indifferent, and even emotionally neutral. On the other hand, it functions in some discursive contexts as a synonym for anti-Semitic. Julius trades on the latter connotation. Thus Tuck-Tuck's anti-Semitic diatribe can be explained without reference to history or qualification by merely citing his Palestinian identity. "Palestinian" functions in Julius' narrative as "Nazi" does. A conversation stopper, it invites us to stop asking critical questions. If you say Palestinian, then nothing else need be said. Julius' personal pursuit of teshuvah and his effort to distance himself from his own anti-Semitic indiscretions have left him ethically and politically blind.

Julius cannot separate his growing attraction to Judaism from an invidious, comparative politics of identity. Black identity must be shown as somehow less compelling than Jewish identity. Julius constructs the following position: While it is wrong to say that blacks have suffered less than Jews, the suffering of Jews is different. This difference is qualitative and thus the "more" of Jewish suffering is reasserted in different terms. Consider the following: "Jews had to wear yellow Stars of David on their clothes to be identified as Jews. My yellow star is my skin. I am alive, however, and Anne Frank is not" (L 33). He adds, "Why do I rage and mourn for murdered European Jews as I never have for my own people?" (L 33). The implications are clear: Julius' proleptical Jewishness has a primordial and metaphysical claim on his loyalty and sentiment. His Jewishness speaks to him from the future and tells him that his blackness is merely a mask of deception. Why construct Jewish identity in polemical opposition to black identity? There is nothing obvious about this construction. Blackness and Jewishness are not antithetical. They are not mutually exclusive. Why does Julius insist on constructing them as if they were? To construe Jewishness as deep and blackness as superficial seems needlessly inflammatory. To construe blackness as aesthetically and epistemically deficient, and even more troubling, as morally deficient, *a lie,* is an act of provocation. Who is Julius trying to provoke and why? I return to this theme in the next few pages, since the relationship between black Gentile, white Jewish, and Palestinian suffering is a large part of his account of becoming a Jew.

Julius claims that his generation of black people is the last to recognize the humanity of white people. As victims of dehumanization, they learned a moral lesson that the 1960s and post-1960s generations did not. They disregarded Camus' advice to avoid the role of executioner. They were victims become executioners since victims are merely executioners too cowardly to sharpen their swords. Julius' comments might have more force were he honest about the source of these sentiments. Consider the following passage that Julius wrote in 1968:

When the three astronauts were killed in February, 1967, black people did not join the nation in mourning. They were white people and were spending money that blacks needed. White folks trying to get to the moon, 'cause it's there. Poverty's here! Now get to that! Malcolm X spoke for all black people when a plane full of Georgians crashed in France: Allah has blessed us. He has destroyed twenty-two of our enemies.

It is clearly written that the victim must become the executioner (emphasis added). The executioner preordains it when all attempts to stop the continual executions fail. To those who point to numbers and say that black people are only ten percent, it must be said as

Brother Malcolm said: "it only takes a spark to light the fuse. We are that spark."[21]

Julius takes Camus' maxim, "neither victims nor executioners,"[22] transforms it into a biblical cadence, *It is clearly written*...and turns it ethically against itself. Later, in the second autobiography, he transfers his own guilt for harboring such sentiments to black people as a group. Displacing his own responsibility as a victim-become-executioner onto others, he never performs teshuvah for his acts.

"By attacking Jews," Julius asserts, "blacks are thinking with damaged emotions. They can no longer perceive their pain." Morally numb, black people lack the courage to face their pain resolutely (L 126–7). They externalize their cowardice by attacking Jews. That Julius had such damaged emotions is no doubt true. He claims that he wanted to hurt Jews the way they hurt him. So we know that he had animus toward Jews. We know that *some* black people share such damaged emotions with him. Whether his animus toward (white) Jews is black peoples' animus writ large is an open question. Julius read a lot of Carl Jung so it seems appropriate to use Jungian categories. Accordingly, why should we not describe the animus that Julius ascribes to black people as, in fact, a manifestation of his own shadow? The anti-Semitic spook that haunts him is he, an earlier incarnation of himself who commissioned the reading of an anti-Semitic poem over the public airways. Whether Julius' emotional problems with Jews are a valid metonym for black people as a whole is a matter of debate. Less debatable is Julius' inability to perceive the pain of Palestinians. Or is the pain of Jews an excuse for ignoring Palestinian pain and denying Jewish guilt? Is this not another product of damaged emotions? Does he not consecrate in the case of Jews, that is, victims becoming executioners, what he harshly condemns in the case of blacks? Does he not owe the reader an explanation for this inconsistency? Or should we conclude that dehumanizing Palestinians is outside the world of moral concern?

Julius seems to battle his own obsessions with blackness through a series of displacements. Notice the following displacement of responsibility for racial hierarchy: "They chose blackness, which did not permit whites to be other than white" (L 126). There is a double displacement: first, primary responsibility for the prison house called racial ideology is displaced from white supremacy to black peoples' obsession with blackness; second, Julius washes his hands of black guilt—"they" and not "us" are guilty. How else are we to interpret his use of the third person "they" rather than the first person "we"? Julius appears to align himself with an aggrieved and put-upon white people whose ability to repent and morally remake themselves (teshuvah) is constrained by the dastardly racial ideology of black people. One does not have to deny the ways in which the call-and-response of white supremacy and the ideology of blackness are mutually reinforcing. But the ideology of blackness is a *defensive response*. The ethical-political difference between call and response cannot be effaced.

"I reread what I have written. I am disturbed. I have written as if I am a Jew" (L 127). Thus spoke Julius, characterizing "The Uses of Suffering," a piece he wrote criticizing the old civil rights leadership for rallying in support of Andrew Young, the U.S. ambassador to the United Nations. It had recently been revealed that Young had met secretly with the PLO, which violated the publicly stated policy of the Carter administration and the U.S. government. There were calls for his resignation and demands that he be fired. Like Wyatt T. Walker, Joseph Lowery, and Jessie Jackson, Young was a veteran of the civil rights movement and a former lieutenant of Martin Luther King, Jr. Walker, Lowery, and Jackson came to their comrade's aid, accusing the Jewish community, according to Julius, of leading the anti-Young effort. Julius was incensed. He had never been a big fan of King,[23] nor it appears was he a fan of his lieutenants. He charged them with self-righteousness, ethnocentric insensitivity, and an arrogant sense of moral superiority. What right did they have to intervene into foreign affairs on the question of Palestinian rights when they had been silent about Jewish rights? Where were they when Jews were being murdered? And when Wyatt T. Walker described Palestinians as "the niggers of the Middle East," Julius was sickened by what he regarded as an obscene claim. "Any pro-Palestinian sympathies I might have," he adds, "had died in Munich where 11 members of the Israeli Olympic team were murdered" (L 128–9).[24]

Julius' anger seems dishonest. It is the kind of anger he perfected no doubt during his black militant phase when his Persona conspired against his Soul and he became "a dummy for a revolutionary ventriloquist." Displaced from its proper object, this anger is designed to distract us and misdirect our ethical judgment. Julius finds the truth of Israeli and Jewish guilt in the dispossession and oppression of Palestinians obscene. It is obscene *and* true. So Julius responds to this obscenity in an obscene manner by taking an act of Palestinian terror at Munich as a synecdoche for the Palestinian cause. Julius reduces the claims of Palestinians writ large to acts of terror (which, however horrible, are sporadic), while ignoring the horror of occupation and Israeli state terrorism against Palestinians. This is strange logic. As if the justice of the antislavery movement could be reduced to Nat Turner's bloody insurrection or John Brown's daring raid on Harper's Ferry or to individual acts of murder by slaves. (By the way, Julius praises John Brown while placing his violence in its proper ethical-political context.) Julius is an accomplished writer but a fuzzy ethical and political thinker.

There is something spooky about Julius' line of reasoning. In effect, he argues that Jews, as victims of the Nazi Holocaust, should have a free hand in dealing with Palestinians. The immorality of this displacement of retributive anger and the moral license it confers is breathtaking. To illustrate this sensibility, note the illogic in the following passage: "Black leadership has shown itself to be morally barren. By its support of the Palestinians, it exemplifies a callousness of spirit to the meaning of the Holocaust, because when six million Jews are killed while the world is indifferent, the right of Israel to exist is unassailable" (L 130). Even if we assume that Julius is right in describing black leaders as hypocritical and morally barren (and given the *full humanity of American blacks* some of them undoubtedly are as he describes), their hypocrisy and immorality does not justify Israeli policies toward Palestinians. The justice of the Palestinian cause does not depend on the virtue of those who criticize the State of Israel. Julius' critique requires black leaders to do *teshuvah* for him, to atone for his transgression against Jews, to expiate *his* guilt for anti-Semitism and assuage *his* conscience through *their* acts of sacrifice. Again, the disproportionate and exaggerated nature of his response and his displacement of blame is understandable (though not justifiable), given the magnitude of his own sense of guilt. Thus where he warned black victims about becoming executioners, he exempts Jews from such critique. All actions by Jews against Palestinians are consecrated as assertions of the rights of the Israeli State. The fact that Jews were victims of the Nazi Holocaust, a German-led crime against humanity and the culmination of a long, Christian-European tradition of Jew-hating, justifies their vicious treatment of Palestinians.

I cannot leave this matter without qualification. Otherwise, how could I account for the following passage?

> I am not responsible for what Israel does as a nation. I have not been to Israel and will probably not go for many years because I do not want to see Jews treating Arabs as blacks were treated in the South [Like Wyatt T. Walker's niggers?]. I do not want to see how racist many Jews can be. I fear that if I go to Israel I will have to write a Hebrew version of *Look Out, Whitey!* (L 177)

Toward Conversion: Julius' Jewish Jesus

Like Malcolm, Julius is the son of a Christian minister. Malcolm's Islamic commitments and Julius' Judaic commitments made them Afro-*Eccentric* in relation to the Standard Narrative. Their emerging religious identities required that they confront the central figure in the Christian tradition: Jesus.

As Julius' interest in Judaism deepened in the late 1970s and his knowledge of Jewish history expanded, he acquired a new perspective on Jesus:

> Now I realize that the so-called Old Testament is the historical and religious record of a people, that it has an integrity of its own separate from the messianic gloss applied by Christianity. That Christianity took the sacred books of Judaism, claimed them as its own and then tried to obliterate Judaism and Jews makes me feel betrayed by my own civilization and parents.
>
> I imagine telling Daddy that his Old Testament is not the story of a people who lacked something because they did not know Jesus but is the story of a people who lacked nothing and therefore did not need Jesus. I imagined telling him that Jesus was a Jew who lived and died a Jew, who never addressed his aphorisms and parables to non-Jews. Jesus belongs to Jewish history, although in a minor and aberrant role. I imagine saying such things to Daddy and the entire universe crumbles, which tells me how much of a child, his child, I remain. (L 142)

Julius succeeds in doing what those who are born Jews or convert to Judaism from a non-Christian religion or convert within a culture that is not dominated by the imagery of Jesus typically need not do. He frees Jesus from his Christian captivity by placing him in his proper historical context as a Jew. Malcolm X had to recover the Muslim Jesus—the Jesus, who always already was a Muslim, never claimed to be Allah, equal to Allah, or associated himself with Allah, the Jesus who always submitted to Allah. Likewise, Julius recovers the Jewish Jesus—the Jesus who never claimed to be the messiah, or the only begotten son of god, and certainly did not claim to be god.

Recovering the Jewish Jesus is crucial to Julius' negotiation of an adult relationship with his father. Negotiation was important, since adopting the traditions of Judaism meant rejecting the faith of his father. So he imagines his new understanding of Jesus as a dialogue with his now deceased father who died on July 31, 1981. Julius was familiar with Freud's portrait of the father as a titanic figure in the life of a child, as the prototype for how the minor and the adult child, through "transference," imagines god. The death of Reverend Lester was an earthquake in Julius' life. In the wake of tidal waves of sadness, there was time for reflection, reminiscing, and taking stock. Like many young people, he chafed under the authority of his father. As a prepubescent boy and as an adolescent, he imagined his father as a man of power, not of love. As a middle-aged adult and now the son of a dead father, he imagines his father in a more generous and exalted way. Julius wants to make peace with him. Were it possible, Julius would tell his father that converting to Judaism does not diminish his love and respect. He would never deny his father's personal, phenotypical, and religious imprint. He would tell his father that he still loves god even if he believes that Jesus is nothing special, merely one rabbi among thousands in the history of Judaism.

Julius thinks about how hard this would be for his father who dedicated his life to bringing people to Jesus while his son, a Jew-in-the-making wrote:

> Why should I give my sins to Jesus? They were my sins. It was my task to mediate them. To give one's sins to Jesus felt like the effort to preserve innocence. "To put oneself under somebody else's cross," Jung wrote, "which has already been carried by him, is certainly easier than to carry your own cross amid the mockery and contempt of the world."
>
> To carry my cross. To lift my stone. To live with the suffering that comes to me, whether as a consequence of my actions or being born black.
>
> To live with the suffering that comes to me because I was born. How do you lift a stone that weeps? You reach down and pick it up. (L 148–9)

It must have been difficult for Reverend Lester to learn toward the end of his life that Julius' church experience had never been what the Reverend might have wished, to learn that Jesus the Christ left Julius as cold as tuna the fish, that Jesus bored him and that Jack in *Jack and the Bean Stalk* was more interesting and had greater reality for Julius than Jesus. Could Julius be right? Did "Christians want Jesus to be president"? Whether this observation is true, Julius had found a way to love his aging father and to honor him in death that did not require him to accept his father's god. Julius had fashioned an Afro-*Eccentric* form of piety and spirituality. He had found a way of honoring his immediate ancestor without his own spiritual pursuits being hamstrung by ancestry, by the choices that his father and his father's father had made.

Black Skin, Foreskin

Recall "Julius Lester's 'Just So Story.'" According to this account, his earliest knowledge that he *is* Jewish occurs as a young boy when he sees the name Altschul on his grandmother's mailbox. His mother tells him that Altschul is his grandmother's maiden name and that his great-grandmother, formerly a slave, had married a white man, a German-Jew named Altschul (L 8–12). But the Jewishness of his great-grandfather did not make Julius Jewish according to Jewish law. Julius knows this but narrates his story in such a way that the discovery of his Jewish ancestry, his preexisting Jewish *being* becomes one of many omens of inevitability in his account of *becoming* a Jew. It is an interesting narrative device, on the same order of importance as his responsibility-denying distinction between Persona and Soul and it merits an equal measure of skepticism and scrutiny.

Other omens of inevitability include his instinctive affinity for the Hebrew melody *Kol Nidre* and Sammy Davis Jr.'s conversion to Judaism, which he initially remembers as occurring when he was a young child rather than the aging adolescent that he was. (Did this false memory, especially the way it played with time, express a desire for authenticity understood as proximity to a sacred origin?) He also remembers reading *The Merchant of Venice* for the first time, his anger at Shylock's mistreatment, his identification with Shylock, and the way this Jewish character revealed his own being, allowing him to encounter himself in a way that he did not in works of black writers (L 20–2). In an entry dated autumn 1958, which follows his reading of Leon Uris' *Exodus* and precedes his description of the Palestinian student Tuck-Tuck, he tells Rhoda Miller "I think I could die for Israel. If any people deserve a country of their own, it's Jews" (L 29). I referred to this passage previously and wish to elaborate briefly. Julius had a crush on Miller. Was his enthusiastic response to *Exodus* a sign of his commitment to Israel, an attempt to seduce Miller, or both? Where does his sexual desire end and political commitment begin? Whatever the answer, Julius' knowledge of the circumstances surrounding the establishment of the

State of Israel gives the lie to his apparent ignorance of the "why" of Tuck-Tuck's rage.

Julius' second narrative of how he became a Jew is more compelling and convincing than his "Just So" narrative. This is how he tells the story:

Winter 1980

I cannot rid myself of the desire to convert. Would I want to if I were not so isolated from blacks now? I don't know. But I do feel lonely and abandoned by my people. If I converted now, I'm afraid I would be doing so only because I am angry at my own people. I know that if Jews did not accept me, I would be devastated. I can only become a Jew when I know that is what God wants of me, when I know that being a Jew is right for me, even if no Jew in the world accepts me. (L 144–5)

December 18, 1981

Why do I want to be a Jew?

The answer is simple: I am tried of feeling guilty for not being in synagogue on Rosh HaShana and Yom Kippur. I am tired of feeling lost on the first night of Passover. I am tired of being jealous when I see Jews going and coming from synagogue. I want my eyes to shine like sky as do those of my Jewish students when they return to class after having gone home for the first night of Passover. (L 160–1)

Julius' decision to convert hangs between his growing contempt for the ideology of blackness, expressed as anger toward black people for what he takes as their abandonment and betrayal of him—ironically, in the wake of charges that he was anti-Semitic—*and* his growing love of Judaism. The mediating term between love and anger is a guilty conscience. Julius has an inconvenient past. At one time, he had been a notorious anti-Semite. Though he never describes himself as an anti-Semite Julius believes that he was widely regarded as such within the Jewish community. How he deals with and repairs (teshuvah) this aspect of his past is relevant to the peculiar harshness of his critique of black people.

When Julius tells his wife excitedly, "I think I'm going to convert to Judaism" (L 160), he is already in the midst of a long process of catechesis and conversion, preparing his mind and heart for life as a Jew. The manner in which he narrates his story mimics the rhythms of the Jewish calendar. Dated entries in his autobiography are interspersed with if not replaced by Jewish ways of reckoning time, by Passover, Shavuot, Rosh HaShana, and Yom Kippur—the highest of the holy days, the Day of Atonement. Julius increasingly thinks through the categories of Jewish sacred time. He approaches Judaism as if it were a magnificent feast. And so it was. It seemed as if all the Jewish holy days were feast days, where communal eating was a sacred act. One by one various elements of his emerging Jewish identity unfolded before him like a multicourse meal. He learned about the meaning and centrality of *Shabbat* (the Sabbath) in Jewish life, the consecration of time by god's chosen people, who set this special time apart by setting aside the concerns of ordinary life. In doing so, they emulated god's act of creation and re-creation. On Shabbat, the seventh day, they rested and remembered. While he struggled with the concept of chosen peoplehood, the notion that god had chosen Jews as the corporate vessel of his revelation, Julius enjoyed his Shabbat meal (L 164–9). "Shabbat dinner," he said with great joy "is a banquet for God." Shabbat was god's beloved. Julius chants a litany of love: " '*Lecha Dodi*,' 'Come My Beloved,' and '*Shalom Aleichem*,' 'Peace to You'" (L 168). The weekly rhythm of Shabbat became the annual celebration of Passover became Shavuot, Rosh HaShana, and Yom Kippur. And on December 18, 1983 Julius Lester officially became a Jew (L 194). Now, as he writes on the first page of *Lovesong*, he knew the name by which god called him: Yaakov Daniel ben Avraham v'Sarah.

Julius' doubts about the compatibility of blackness and Jewishness preceded his conversion. Perhaps he construed his own hostility toward Jews as a hostility that most black people shared. Perhaps he believed that most black people thought with the same damaged emotions that he apparently did. Whatever the case, Julius' doubts were visual and morphological, with a radicalized, somatic-aesthetic quality. These realities led to the following question: How could he become a member of the Jewish people when he did not look like other Jews? (L 191). Other Jews were white. How could he surmount this racial mountain and become a Jew? Abraham had his Mount Moriah and Moses his Mount Sinai; what precedent was there for dealing with the racial mountain of white supremacy? Many American Jews were *Yiddishkeit,* their Jewish identity shaped indelibly by Eastern European culture (L 194). How could Julius ever dream of becoming part of that tradition? In the midst of the conversion process, during the winter of 1982, he describes his fear of entering a Conservative synagogue: "I know no one there, and my blackness burns my skin when I think of walking into a synagogue where I don't know anyone" (L 169). There would be no one there

to vouch for him, to certify his bona fides as a Jew. What if someone challenged his Jewish identity? Under the constraints of American
racial ideology structured by white supremacy, Jewish identity had
been racialized as white since the 1920s. Whatever the official view
within Judaism, the political, policy, and popular view was that Jews
were a white ethnic group, inclusive of observant and nonobservant
Jews. At best, black Jews such as Sammy Davis Jr. were a curiosity.
Ordinarily, they were anomalous, suspect, and not Jewish in its truest
sense.[25] Their Jewishness, to spin Julius' formulation, was a cosmetic
obscuring the reality of their blackness (L 69). In the same way that
Malcolm's American nationality made his Muslim bona fides suspect
in the eyes of Saudi officials in charge of the Hajj, Julius' black skin
was prima facie evidence that he was not a Jew. When you add what
appears to have been an intense sense of guilt for his own anti-Semitism,
the fact that Julius' black skin burned in the presence of white Jews is
understandable. Here we have a peculiar case: white supremacy, Jewish
identity, and a black Jew, formerly accused of anti-Semitism—a volatile
mixture, indeed.

And then there was the problem of Julius' foreskin. There was
nothing he could do about his black skin. If he were to become
a Jew, he would have to find a way of reconciling blackness and
Jewishness. But his foreskin was a different matter. The issue here
was that he *had a foreskin* and had no interest in getting rid of it.
Circumcision was a mitzvah (commandment) he did not wish to
obey. Julius enjoyed the pleasures of sex too much to risk the possibility of a damaged penis and diminished sexual pleasure he feared
might result when his foreskin was lopped off. "Well," he said, "if I
have to choose between being a circumcised Jew and sexual desire,
forget it!"(L 205–6). For a man dogged by his and other people's
doubts about his authenticity, Julius had a real problem. Like his
black skin, his foreskin raised doubts about his Jewishness. Unlike
his black skin, his foreskin was not easily subject to other people's
scrutiny. But Julius entertained the following nightmare scenario:
"of being in the bathroom at a synagogue somewhere and the man
at the next urinal notices that I'm not circumcised and suddenly the
entire congregation rises up and chases me out of the *shul* [syna-
gogue] and down the street, yelling, 'He has a foreskin' " (L 206).
Black skin, foreskin: both are markers of Julius' "inauthenticity."
Black skin is a sign of inauthenticity in the American context where
over time the "Jewish race" was incorporated into the "white race
as an "ethnic group." They were transformed from members of the

"Hebrew race" to members of a common, transethnic white race. (In other words, they were simultaneously given an ethnicity and a new racial identity.)[26] For traditional Jews, a foreskin is a sign of inauthenticity. Julius eventually decides to undergo circumcision. After all, had not the patriarch Abraham undergone this painful rite at a much older age? Julius could not evade this mitzvah. By shedding blood and foreskin, a small act of sacrifice, he reaffirmed the covenant that the Lord YHWH had originally made with Abraham. After this offering of blood and skin and a period of healing, Julius reported happily: "IT WORKS BETTER THAN EVER!!!" (L 218).

Postliminality

I know now who I am. I am a Jew and I am a Lovesong to the God of Abraham, Isaac and Jacob, a Praisesong to the God of Sarah, Rebecca, Rachel and Leah. (L 244)

Julius Lester's Jewish Desire and Ours

Although aware of the existence of other black Jews,[27] Julius writes as if he were the first black convert to Judaism. This says much about the power of his conversion. However, there is nothing unique about his fascination with Jews, Jewishness, and Judaism. Such fascination is as old as the large-scale conversion of black people to Christianity in the early decades of the nineteenth century. According to Yvonne Chireau, a historian of Black Atlantic religion, black people discerned analogies between the Hebrew experience of bondage, emancipation, diaspora, and persecution and their own experience as early as 1790. "These analogies facilitated the various adaptations of Judaism within black religion, including the adaptation of the language and symbols of the Hebrew Scriptures, and the unique formulations of the rituals within Afro-Jewish practices." Owing to "an inherited bicultural heritage or by the appropriation of Jewish accoutrements,"[28] many black people have described themselves as Jews, Hebrews, or Israelites We should not forget that Julius appeals to a bio-bicultural heritage to authenticate his narrative of becoming a Jew. Julius became belatedly what he already was primordially. His conversion, so to speak, was a Socratic act of "reminiscence," as he recovered a pre-existing knowledge that had somehow been lost. Julius' appeal to a preexisting Jewish heritage and Chireau's analysis of that kind of appeal, underscore the significance of Jews, Jewishness, and Judaism in the construction of black American identity. Julius is a latecomer. His sense of newness and originality as a black Jew is merely a manifestation of belatedness.

A *"Reconservadox" Jew*

Regarding his own Judaism, Julius remarks:

> To be chosen by God is to be given enormous responsibility. To be chosen implies that those chosen also choose-or not. It is the element of choice which makes it impossible to speak confidently any longer of Judaism and makes it necessary that we speak, more accurately, of Judaisms. As long as we speak only of Judaism, there will be power struggles over which is the authentic one, and that is a waste of time. There is an unbridgeable gap between what can loosely be called liberal Judaism (Reform, Conservative, and Reconstructionist) and Orthodoxy. Someone raised Reform finds an Orthodox service incomprehensible, and vice versa. The twain cannot meet, and it is time this was acknowledged and the sniping ceased between Orthodoxy and the rest of us.[29]

In *American Judaism* (2004), Jonathan Sarna describes the complexity of American Jewry, which is driven in large measure by America's liberal democratic traditions. America is an engine of difference. Julius' Reconservadox Judaism is artifact and elaboration of liberal democratic, difference-making.

> People laugh when I describe myself as Reconservadox, but I am serious. I prefer services in Hebrew, chanted to traditional melodies. I keep a kosher home. I do not like to drive on the Sabbath but will do so sometimes to go to synagogue. However, I use electricity on the Sabbath and will occasionally engage in a secular activity if it is important enough. That would not include going to the mall, but might include a workshop with an important Tai Chi instructor that I could not avail myself of at another time, Tai Chi being an important part of my health regimen. While I am traditional in my worship, philosophically I am more at home with Reform Judaism's emphasis on the responsibility of each individual Jew to study and choose how to live as a Jew. Christianity has

survived quite well with a multiplicity of denominations. Judaism must also.[30]

That Julius Lester would describe himself as a "Reconservadox" Jew, simultaneously Reformed, Reconstructionist, Conservative, and Orthodox is unexpected but hardly shocking. He is doing what generations of American blacks have done, playing a "blue note" in the melody of American culture. Julius improvises by fashioning the Jewish components of his American inheritance according to his particular needs as a descendant of slaves and as a black person in a white supremacist society.[31] In doing so, he expresses his difference, his Afro-*Eccentricity*.

The Ambivalent Child of Malcolm X

In 1965 Malcolm X was assassinated. In 1967 John Coltrane died. In 1968 Julius' first son was born. The boy's name: Malcolm Coltrane. Malcolm X and Coltrane were icons for members of Julius' generation.[32] A year after the assassination of Malcolm X, a year before the death of John Coltrane, two years before the birth of Malcolm Coltrane, Julius published an essay entitled "The Angry Children of Malcolm X."

Julius mentions Malcolm X infrequently in *Lovesong*. In one case, he is part of a litany of praise and lamentation for casualties and martyrs of the freedom movement. A second reference regards a widespread rumor that Louis Farrakhan was involved in the plot that led to Malcolm's assassination. In a third indirect reference, Malcolm is the object not the subject of the statement. He serves a rhetorical function in a sentence about the joy of spring. The gist of the sentence is that the high cost of car maintenance and repair distracted Julius so much that he would have missed the "Second Coming of Malcolm X"[33] as he had missed the coming of spring in 1976 (L 99). This messianic language, signifying on the Second Coming of Jesus, suggests that the first coming of Malcolm X held considerable significance for Julius.

Remarks he made several years after writing *Lovesong* support this impression: "I do not remember the first time I heard of Malcolm X but I remember clearly the first time I took him seriously." It was winter 1962. Julius worked in the Harlem office of the Welfare Department. For reasons he cannot comprehend, Julius recalls a white supervisor asking him to assist in raising funds for the NAACP (National Association for the Advancement of Colored People). Julius declined, expressing his disregard for "the N-double-A." This is how Julius records what followed: "He looked at me coldly and said, 'What are you? One of those followers of Malcolm X?' The way he said it told me all I needed to know about Malcolm, and I returned his cold stare and said, 'Yes.' Significantly, he treated me with a cool but proper respect after that, something that had been absent before. Such was the power of Malcolm X." Julius does not recall making his way to Harlem Mosque 7 to hear Malcolm speak. But a few blacks employed by the Welfare Department did go to hear Malcolm and gave Julius a summary. "What Malcolm said was fearful to hear, even secondhand. He derided integration and mocked nonviolence. He scorned love and extolled power. He had contempt for everything white and a startling love for everything black. What he preached was hard to embrace. It was even harder to deny."[34] That Julius named his first son Malcolm and entitled his first significant essay *The Angry Children of Malcolm X* is no coincidence. Parts of the essay were republished in *Look Out Whitey! Black Power Gon' Get Your Mama* (1968). Published the same year of Malcolm Coltrane Lester's birth, Julius obviously had Malcolm X on his mind.

His mind appears ambivalent. On the one hand, his comments about white people and white supremacy bite almost as hard and deeply as Malcolm's rhetoric. The tone is similar. While free of the demonizing, white devil rhetoric that characterized Malcolm's language during his Nation of Islam phase, one can hear the same anger in Julius' voice. Though ambivalent toward Malcolm, Julius remarks: "[E]ven dead, he is a man to measure one's self against."[35] Julius is an angry and wary child, both admiring and fearing Malcolm's anger. Consider the following:

> There is still that child in me who senses the violence in how white people talked to his parents in stores, who sees the violence in their eyes, in the set of their mouths, who does not know why he is hated, why so many wish he were dead, that child who knows he didn't do anything to any of them and yet, and yet, I must have because they wouldn't hate me otherwise. (L 75–6)

and

> If you were a child in the 1940s, childhood was a luxury that could get you killed. Education in those all-black schools was a process of being trained—intellectually and emotionally—to survive and persevere. We were not allowed to think that the white world

could defeat us. It would discriminate against us, deny us jobs, force us to live where it wanted us to, lynch us, but defeat us? Never. (L 111)

and

I demand perfection of him [Malcolm Coltrane] now so he will demand perfection of himself later because white people do not care if he lives or dies, do not even care that he is. (L 112)

and

[W]e learned, as we risked our lives, that to change the behavior of white Americans does not transform their souls. They will still believe that by being white they partake of innate and God-endowed superiority. As long as they do, our souls will be the garbage dumps for all they loathe in themselves. (L 68)

On the other hand, Julius had reservations about Malcolm X, especially the untoward consequences of his "violent," anti-white rhetoric and his casual anti-Semitism, a point he made later in a critical piece on Louis Farrakhan, published in *Dissent*.[36] Julius laments the costs, the loss of childhood, and the sacrifice of dreams and desires that the vocation exemplified by Malcolm X demanded:

What do you want? I ask myself again, and enraged, I shout back: I want not to live with the spirits of my slave ancestors needing me to sing the song they couldn't sing. I want not to have the spirits of all the black unborn telling me that I will be their ancestor and that the stone I hew from the mountain and carve into a step will enable them to move on up just a little bit higher. (L 112–13)

In his more reflective moods, Julius wonders who he would be if he were not black, if his life did not dangle "in space, stretched and broken by *the noose of race.*" To have choices is what he cannot imagine (L 112). In his paranoid mood he speaks of being entangled in a *net of blackness* (L 72). In his Orwellian mood he speaks of becoming a liar, a prisoner of *"the black collective"* (L 66). In effect, he becomes a black "Borg," thinking with a single black mind, speaking with a uniform black voice, programmed by the black "Politburo,"[37] the forces of *totalitarian blackness.* In his most polemical mood he remarks—"*Blackness is a cosmetic* obscuring the reality of human existence" (L 69).[38] His most thoughtful mood is captured in the following remark: *"If blackness is synonymous with unthinking and blind loyalty to the race, regardless of what any one of its members do, then I am not black"* (L 208; italics are mine). Julius is one of those rare individuals that every group needs, especially groups that have been subject to chronic degradation whose humanity and equality has been regarded as suspect. He is a gadfly who stings the conscience by biting the group's body politic in the "butt." Julius explores the wounds of blackness not to inflame and reinfect (not most of the time, at any rate); rather, he seeks to expose them to the healing power of air and sunlight. He demands that sore points of the black psyche be examined despite the pain, that the abyss of freedom (in a post–civil rights era) be faced despite the nausea, and that the task of creating new values be accepted despite the terror. Julius is a critic of totalitarian blackness, of black *ressentiment,* of values born of a fearful resentment that dishonor the nobility and sacrifice of the ancestors.[39]

Like Malcolm X,[40] Julius is an iconoclast seeking to break the idols of white supremacy and racial ideology. For both men, the twilight of the idols is at hand. However, there are differences. Malcolm was preoccupied with breaking the hold that the idol of white worship and black self-loathing had on black people. In contrast, Julius is preoc-cupied with the idol of blackness, with resisting the claims of its high priests who demand the kind of sacrifices, obedience, and uniformity that should not be asked, to which no free black person should submit. Thus when fellow black activists asked, angrily, how he could be a black revolutionary and the husband of a white wife, he dismissed them with contempt. "Having grown up in the South," he adds, "where whites decreed who I could and could not marry, I was not going to turn around and give blacks that power."[41] A prison is a prison, even when its builders are black. Black masters are no less despicable than white ones. If you worship it, then blackness is an idol. Julius' pilgrim-age from Christianity-and-Black Nationalism to Judaism was an act of teshuvah. In becoming a Jew, he had to break the twin idols of white supremacy and blackness that held him captive, sought to enslave him, and would seduce, shame, or cajole him into serving false gods.

CHAPTER FIVE

Jan Willis: Duhkha and Enlightenment

Biographical Particulars

Janice Dean Willis is professor of Religious Studies at Wesleyan University. She was born in 1948, in Docena, Alabama to Dorothy and Oram Willis. She has one sister: Sandra Williams. As a fifteen-year-old, she marched with Martin Luther King Jr. during the Birmingham campaign of 1963. Though reared in the Baptist Church, she fell in love with Buddhism while a college student. Jan graduated from Cornell University in 1969. She flirted with the Black Panther Party before pursuing graduate studies at Columbia University. Jan received a Ph.D. in Indic and Buddhist Studies in 1976. Initially, she struggled with her choice to become a Tibetan Buddhist rather than a Black Panther. Jan has never married and has no children. In addition to her scholarly texts, she is the author of an autobiography entitled *Dreaming Me: From Baptist to Buddhist, One Women's Spiritual Journey* (2001). Her mother once told Jan that she reminded her of Malcolm X.

In this chapter, I trace Jan's Afro-*Eccentric* spirit by analyzing her struggle against various forms of *duhkha:*

There is no word in English covering the same ground as duhkha in the sense it is used in Buddhism. The usual translation of "suffering" is too strong and gives the impression that life according to Buddhism is nothing but pain....While duhkha certainly embraces the ordinary meaning of "suffering" it also includes deeper concepts such as impermanence (anitya) and unsatisfactoriness, and may be better left untranslated. The Buddha does not deny happiness in life, although this too is seen as part of duhkha because of its impermanence.[1]

Family Matters

My father meant well, I know. But I also knew that that little girl made me feel dirty when she called me "nigger." There was something in her voice that touched my deepest place and that also seemed to echo other whites' opinion. If *the talk* had to be given, it was already too late for me to hear it. (DM 54, my emphasis)

"The talk" is a painful rite of passage in black families, the necessity of which is declining and we can only hope will eventually disappear. With "the talk" black parents initiate their children into the ways of white folks. They try to provide them with armor against the slings and arrows of white supremacy: the spirit-killing power of contempt, deprecation, and insult—"Hey, where're you going, you *dirty nigger?*" Jan's neighbor, a thin white girl with "stringy white-blonde hair and big bright blue eyes" uttered this insult. From Jan's point of view, "the talk" only reinforced the white girl's negative perception and reinfected the wound that the words had cut into her psyche. But what if Jan's trauma preceded the insult?

Trauma was a family matter. Jan frames her life as a voyage into the "real," a quest for safety and wholeness, a place where she belongs, with a family that loved her—home. Born into a situation of liminality, Jan experienced confusion, doubt, and hurt feelings. But she was not the only person hurting. Doubts about her paternity hurt her father. He wondered, "Is this nearly white-skinned baby girl my child?" His very black skin provided prima facie evidence that she was not. If he was not the father, then who was? Who was his wife's secret lover? How could he have been so blind, oblivious to telltale signs that she was unfaithful? How did she manage to conceal this insult to his manhood? The father of this nearly white baby girl was obviously a white man. If infidelity was the injury, then the "fact" that the father was a white man was the supreme insult in Jim Crow Alabama where the only thing a black man owned was his dignity and even the title to that property was precarious. Daddy Willis, however, had his facts wrong. He, not a white man, had fathered Jan. So imagine the hurt of Jan's mother. To have one's fidelity and integrity questioned under these circumstances, when angry accusations of betrayal, of "sleeping with the enemy," spoil the joy of a new birth (DM 6–7). She faced the prospect of abandonment. When Mary the mother of Jesus was impregnated under mysterious and scandalous circumstances, Joseph, according to the biblical account, was considerate. Dorothy Willis could only wonder whether her husband would be as considerate. If postpartum depression did not affect Dorothy's mental health, then angry accusations of sexual betrayal surely would. This whole affair, the betrayal entailed in the false accusation of betrayal, must have tasted like gall. As Jan puts it, "My mother's hurt and sorrow in all of this cannot be fathomed" (DM 7). Fathomed is the right word. It suggests something deep, murky, and not easily explored. A body of water, perhaps, with powerful undercurrents that are best left undisturbed lest one dredges up what should remain buried.

Though left undisturbed, these currents did not disappear. They flowed across Jan's childhood like a riptide. As a young child, Jan thought that these currents were just as dangerous. Her mother was angry. A frequent object of that anger, Jan could only wonder why her mother called her "evil." Evil is a strong adjective, to be sure. While I can never remember my mother or father using such a hurtful term when referring to me, I can imagine it being in the range of things that a parent under stress might say. Tone and circumstance make all the difference in the world. My purpose here is not to defend Jan's mother but to explain why she might have behaved the way she did. By now, many people understand the mechanism of displaced anger, which usually flows down the family hierarchy. Jan's mother must have been extremely angry at her husband, Oram. Jan, we might say, was the "dog" of her mother's displaced anger. Jan reminded mom of the trauma. Not so much the trauma of a ruptured peritoneum, torn during childbirth, but the trauma of a husband who angrily questioned her fidelity. Of course this is only a hypothesis. There may have been additional reasons for mom's anger.

A chance visit by Jan's maternal grandfather, Alex White, who Oram Willis had apparently never met, alleviated some doubts. His name was certainly descriptive: Alex White's father was a white man and Alex, "half" white, "looked" like a white man. His color explained Jan's light-skinned appearance. This encounter removed her father's doubts but Jan's self-doubt only increased. Her color became a source of duhkha, embarrassing her and causing pain. Did not her mother's friend call her "white gal?" Did not her schoolmates call her "yella gal" and suggest that her father was a white man? Were not these indications that she was not a "normal" black girl? Something about her seemed illegitimate and inauthentic. Jan increasingly became aware of the social meaning of skin color; her color marginalized her. During the civil rights and Black Power eras, her color became "a mark of embarrassment and shame" As an adult she recoiled in horror on discovering that her maternal great-grandfather, Grandfather Alex's father, was a Jewish store owner named Mayer. It was not his Jewishness that offended her but his whiteness. "It was not frustration about which *white* man might have fathered him; it was recognition that *some white man* had. The whole thing," Jan remarks, "turned my stomach" (DM 12). It was miscegenation, "the spectre of white blood," the feeling that one is polluted and dirty that bothered her: "What does one do," she asks, "when the oppressor's blood courses in one's own veins? How could I run away from my own self? How to make peace with such horrific origins? Historically, I was both the victim and the child of rape conceived in terror." The sordid history of slavery and its legacy is inescapable for all Americans, especially for American blacks: "black women unable to fend off white rapists, black men unable to protect their wives and partners. Given such history, the questioning of origins was unavoidable" (DM 11–13).

Like Malcolm, Jan attributes her white ancestry to rape. Neither provides evidence. Though she may very well have been a descendant of a man who was guilty of rape, Jan was certainly not "the child of rape." Jan and Malcolm's hyperbolic rhetoric should be understood as describing the unjust social relations of white supremacy, under which interracial relations both consensual and coercive occurred. They speak of the logic of rape rather than the actuality. Rape should be viewed as a metaphor for white supremacy in the same way that "white slavery" is a metaphor for prostitution. Another interesting similarity between Jan and Malcolm is their "racial marginality". Both were the children of dark-skinned fathers who expressed doubt about the fidelity of their wives and the paternity of their light-skinned children. Their births, in short, were surrounded by doubts, acrimony, and hurt feelings. The circumstances of Jan's birth contributed to a "sense of abysmal isolation and loneliness" (DM 7). Her parents learned to love each other despite this painful episode. With respect to herself and, perhaps, her parents as well, Jan offers the following remark—"Still, there's a funny thing about doubt, anger, and denial once unleashed: in spite of later correction and understanding, they are not so easily relinquished" (DM 10).

Uncertainty about her legitimacy, her parents' love, and her worth, made Jan moody, sensitive, and reflective:

> More than anything else, I wanted my father's love and acceptance. As I grew older, I also wanted to be able to trust and to genuinely love others. To get beyond the pervasive sense of pain and suffering I carried, I knew I would have to find healing, to find that place of belonging that is so basic for us all: feeling at home in our own skins. And so, from my earliest days, my solitary quest became to find a way to accept myself, and to love *me*. (DM 13)

The desire for a father's love is normal and the circumstances Jan describes only intensify the desire. What about a mother's love? Dorothy Willis' relation with Jan seems well within the range of mother–daughter interactions with terms of exasperation and rebuke, *"You must be evil,"* peppering everyday expressions of endearment. In Jan's account, her mother treated her intelligence with suspicion and envy. Or, as Jan puts it: "My father encouraged my intelligence; my mother seemed jealous of it" (DM 26). Jan refers to her mother's "'too much learning is evil' idea" (DM 35). Yet, she says that both parents committed to paying for her college education; further, both had been good students, and neither discouraged her desire to become the "first black woman astronaut" or a theoretical physicist (DM 30, 38). Jan was an anomaly. An anomaly is someone or something that does not fit our expectations. In the Hebrew Bible, certain animals are regarded as anomalous and Jews are forbidden to eat them. In many religious traditions, anomalous people are regarded as sacred, and are set apart as objects of reverence and taboo. Their ambiguous status (both attractive and repulsive) makes us ambivalent toward them. Thus scapegoats who pay for our sins and monsters, whose very monstrosity is a warning from god that something in the social order is awry. Jan confounded the racial and gender expectations of her rural southern community. She was a girl, young, intellectually gifted, and black. Mother's ambivalence, *both pride and envy,* toward daughter's intelligence, is understandable in the dream-deferring Jim Crow South of the late 1950s and early 1960s where the aspirations of black women were limited and their ambitions often crushed. Besides, precocious, inquisitive, smart-mouth children who respond to every "No" with "Why?" can be quite exasperating. A parent is both a teacher and a general. Sometimes parents have the wherewithal to patiently enumerate and explicate a set of reasons supporting their "No." At other times they command and expect to be obeyed, without question; this is what we call authority, a mysterious thing, to be sure. Jan was a conscious if not a conscientious objector to authority. She sees a direct relation between her evil intelligence and her mother's desire that she be saved from the sin of having an inquisitive mind. Church provided an antidote to the poison of the school.

Jan gives a more extensive account of her perception of the Black Church than do Malcolm X and Julius Lester. Nevertheless, there is an interesting thematic similarity between the three around the subject of Black Church spirituality, especially the art of "shouting." Recall Malcolm's account:

> The Gohannases were very religious people. Big Boy and I attended church with them. They were sanctified Holy Rollers now. The preachers and congregations jumped even higher and shouted even louder than the Baptists I had known. They sang at the top of their lungs, and swayed back and forth and cried and moaned and beat on tambourines and chanted. It was spooky, with ghosts and spirituals and "ha'nts" seeming to be in the very atmosphere. (AMX 24)

Now recall Julius' account:

> I do not like church, do not understand why the people shout and "get happy" and scream, "Yes, Lord!," do not understand why one old man "gets happy" and trots around the sanctuary muttering, "Thank you, Jesus! Thank you, Jesus!," do not understand the lady who always throws her pocketbook into the choir loft when she "gets happy." (L 16–17)

Now consider Jan's account:

> Each week the congregation was swept up in a mysterious spiritual frenzy² that began gradually but soon rushed ahead uncontrollably to its cathartic end. Quite simply, nothing scared me more than black women engaged, as good *feeling* Christians, in the activity known as "shouting." (DM 41)

> It always struck me as strange that the phenomena of shouting was [sic] called "getting happy," for it seemed that the acrobatics that we children observed were much more akin to the kind of behavior that warranted straitjackets. People's bodies became stiff as boards. They jerked as if they wanted to bolt and run. They

fought with the ushers, who were there to help them. All this was accompanied by shouts and wails, "Praises to Jesus," and choruses of "Amens" and "Wells!" from the surrounding faithful. Nobody seemed particularly happy to me. (DM 41)

Ushers grabbed for eyeglasses to prevent people from doing themselves harm. In the choir stand, too, someone was getting happy. One and then another. Legs, thighs, garter belts, and underwear. All were seen, as large bodies flapped, and went limp in the ecstasy of the spirit. (DM 44)

Some people just whimpered to themselves (like my mother), and a few tears fell; but they never lost their composure. But sometimes people got hurt. They jumped and fell hard over the smooth wooden pews. High heels got caught and ankles got twisted. People drunk on the spirit. (DM 44)

Like Malcolm and Julius before her, Jan looked askance at the Black Church phenomenon of "getting happy." Her attitude toward it, like theirs, was Afro-*Eccentric*. The notion that this activity defined in some exclusive or even preeminent way what it meant to be religious did not persuade them. They did not accept the notion that being a "real" black person required that one holler and shout. Beyond their aesthetic distaste for "getting happy," they questioned whether these performances were phony rather than genuine. Reservations about the credibility of the performance circumscribed Jan's resistance to Christian discipleship. On the other hand, she responded enthusiastically to the pageantry of the choir as it marched up the aisles and to the sermonic style of the preacher, which she regarded theatrically, as pure performance unburdened by nonaesthetic considerations. These activities did not frighten her as did "getting happy" and the rite of baptism. She regarded with dread the prospect of being dipped in the cold, dark, murky water of the baptismal pool. The uncertainty associated with this passage through water, the prospect of passing from religious childhood to adolescence she found daunting. The prospect of no longer being her mother's spiritual ward and of taking responsibility for own sins, of entering the baptismal water as one person and symbolically emerging as another was a decision that she would rather defer (DM 41–4). Yet, she found herself, despite herself, seduced by the entreaties of the preacher, "Come to Jesus, right now!" (DM 47). Initially, Jan feared even looking at this young man who was not much older than her. If she looked, she might be compelled to give herself to him. Shocked by the electricity of the moment, compelled forward by the kinetic energy of spirit-filled bodies in motion, and seduced, perhaps, by the boyish charms of a sixteen- or seventeen-year-old preacher, she lost control. Or, as Jan describes it: "All around me people were shouting, fainting, and falling out. My mind was reeling; my body felt like jelly. I was hot and cold at the same time, sweating profusely" (DM 46). Jan, it appears, was not immune to her mother's desire that she be saved, the community's expectation that she would be saved, and the seductive power of Protestant revivalism. Jan made her profession of faith before god and the congregation. Baptized by the spirit, the preacher baptized her with water. She entered the water with fear, trembling, and ambivalence and emerged from it with the same.

Despite this before-and-after continuity, she experienced temporarily something she had never experienced and would rarely experience in adolescence and young adulthood, a deep sense of love and communion as the saints of god extended their hands in love: "These hands were wondrous things. They were like *the Holy*[3] opening its arms to me. There was more love there than I had ever felt; and it felt bigger precisely because it was extended not just to me. This love, in a flash, dissolved all fears. These hands took me completely beyond myself" (DM 51, my emphasis). The baptismal experience transformed her affect and emotion. It transported her.

Lions, Panthers, and Snakes

She sat reading a copy of *The Autobiography of Malcolm X* I'd given her. I had come in from outside and was walking across the living room. She looked up from the pages of the book and said to me, "This is exactly how I think of you. And sometimes it worries me.

"What do you mean, Mama? What part are you reading now?"

"Right here," she said, pointing to a passage. "It says Malcolm was straightforward and righteous. That he was dignified, godly, and powerful." (DM 233)

Malcolm X was assassinated in 1965. Later that year, a seventeen-year-old Jan became a first-year student at Cornell University. In 1969, the spirit of the time was partially defined by the legacy of Malcolm X and the publication of Julius Lester's *Look Out Whitey, Black Power Gon' Get Your Mama!* Responding to that spirit, Jan and several other black militant students seized control of the student union building at Cornell University. Willard Straight Hall, or "the Straight," as Jan calls it, is where the Black Student Alliance would press their demands that the University institute a long-demanded Black Studies Program and address resolutely a recent cross burning. From one perspective, Jan appears to have been swept along by a current of events that was larger and stronger than her, unable even if she were willing to dissent from the group, a teenager bending to the pressure of her peers. In this respect, she resembles Julius Lester. And she resembles many people, young and old, facing similar circumstances. From another perspective, Jan was an enthusiast. She was not swept by the current, she drove it: "Come on, June. Get yourself together. We can do this. We must do this!" she said to a comrade overcome by her fear and timidity (DM 118). Jan, the pussycat had become Jan, the lioness.

The students assembled an armory consisting of guns, machetes, broken pool sticks, and anything they thought might serve the cause. If the administration responded to their protest with violence, they were prepared to meet violence with violence. In an effort to organize themselves in a paramilitary fashion, the student protestors established various "ministries." They imitated, no doubt, the Black Panther Party, which among others had its own ministries of information and defense. Owing, one would suspect, to her success in "cooling out" a hysterical June, Jan was named Minister of Women's Safety (DM 119, 121). Curiously, Jan does not describe how the siege ended. What were the terms? Did they achieve any of their ends? Were their chief demands, an adequate response to the cross burning and creation of a Black Studies Program met? Jan does not say. Perhaps this irresolution is emblematic of the times.

Jan's militant phase did not end with the indecisiveness of the student "take over." After graduation, she considered seriously the idea of becoming a Black Panther. By 1969, the Panthers gained fame and notoriety as the most militant wing of the Black Revolution. In the language of the time, they were the "revolutionary vanguard," leaders of the revolutionary pack. They wore uniforms of black berets and black jackets, the color black defining nearly every feature of their attire. Organized as a paramilitary, they carried guns. They also carried copies of the Constitution of the United States and Mao's "Little Red Book." Martin Luther King Jr. was dead and his idea of a nonviolent revolution seemed equally dead. The Birmingham campaign of 1963 must have seemed like ancient history, when as a young teen Jan and her parents had marched with King and against Bull Connor's dogs. But this was 1969. Things were different. King's voice had been silenced by an assassin's bullet. Jan had a decision to make. Should she return to a Tibetan Buddhist monastery in Nepal or join the Black Panthers? Should she, so to speak, pursue the peace of the monastic life or take up a "piece" in support of the revolution? Her situation bore a vague similarity to Julius' situation a few years earlier. Should he join the SNCC and become a revolutionary or pursue an inner compulsion, a persistent desire to become a Catholic monk? Julius became a revolutionary, albeit, as he would later say: a "dummy for a revolutionary ventriloquist." Jan contemplated the same choice. Perhaps "contemplated" is too calm and cerebral a description of her struggle to decide. She agonized night and day. As an intelligent black person, no option seemed more reasonable than joining the party and laying her life on the line in the cause of freedom.

But the heart has reasons of its own. Jan chose the monastery. Her reasons seem compelling. After all, the revolution certainly had its pathologies, especially the problem of male supremacy: "Just as had been the case at Cornell, black women were to keep in the background; they were to be the black man's natural complement, but they were not to take any leadership positions. Yet at Cornell," Jan remarks, "in spite of being a black female, I had 'tasted power'" (DM 127). With these words, Jan echoed Elaine Brown who would eventually become the only black woman to lead the Black Panther Party.[4] As minister of women's safety, Jan was the sole female in a leadership cadre of eight seniors. While she admired the Panthers, she did not want to serve as background, a doormat in a male-dominated gender system. "In a certain sense," she observes, "the power dynamics that operated in society separating blacks and whites were being duplicated here all over again between black men and women" (DM 127).

One wonders whether she protests too much. At the very time that Jan was flirting with the Black Panther Party, Afeni Shakur, the future mother of rapper Tupac Shakur and a leader of the Harlem branch of the Party, was indicted on weapons and conspiracy charges along with other members of the "Panther 21." She was indicted on April 2, 1969, shortly before Jan graduated from Cornell, around the time she considered joining the party. Shakur was one of many women who attained leadership positions in the Party. Further, the party explicitly acknowledged gender injustice in its ranks. Moreover, it did what no other revolutionary group, much less civil rights organization would do by advocating women's liberation *and* gay liberation,[5] and thus attacking the gender system head-on. As in many things, the Black Panther Party was the vanguard of the revolutionary Left. We get a useful perspective from Mumia Abu-Jamal, a former Panther and currently a political prisoner on death row. Drawing on his own wealth of experience, he remarks: "This writer knows of no other instances of radical groups of the period, especially those projected as having a predominately male membership, that had women in the leadership to the extent the Black Panther Party did."[6] Jan broke her engagement with the Panthers. Five years later Elaine Brown replaced Huey P. Newton as leader of the Party.[7] One would be hard-pressed to cite a single example of another revolutionary group that could claim the same, whose gender politics were as progressive as those of the Panthers. Let us be clear. The Black Panthers were guilty of male dominance and gender discrimination. We should not obscure this fact. However, they were more progressive on gender issues than most of their peers. Abu-Jamal adds: "In the ranks and offices of the Black Panther Party, women were more than merely appendages of male ego and power, they were valued and respected comrades who demonstrated daily the truth of the adage, 'A revolutionary has no gender.'"[8] If you are not persuaded by Abu-Jamal, consider Afeni Shakur's response to Jasmine Guy's suggestion that the Panthers "were a bunch of chauvinists":

> *Shakur*: Well, first of all, what it looks like now or what it turned into is not the original ideology of the Panthers. Their belief was that women were *not* to be treated as sex objects. In fact, the party gave me a platform from which to fight sexism. I had leadership ability, and I made use of that. I didn't feel like I was being sexually discriminated against because I *used* the tools they gave me. I spoke up for what I believed in. I spoke up for myself.
>
> *Guy*: Other women in the party were more passive or subservient?
>
> *Shakur*: Look, the women that got used in the party set themselves up to be used. They played pussy games. They used their bodies to get next to the power.[9]

We should resist Shakur's invitation to generalize her experiences. That said, her observations are remarkably similar to Abu-Jamal's experiences: "As for sex, women chose their partners as freely as the men, and many could and did say no."[10]

Considering the observations of Shakur and Abu-Jamal, it is hard not to regard Jan's claims about Panther sexism with some skepticism.

Does this mean that the Panthers created a gender-Nirvana? No, it does not. However, they did succeed, perhaps more than most progressive groups, in mitigating the intensity of the gender-hell.[11] So skepticism is warranted. This is especially true when you compare Jan's reservations about the Panthers with her total silence about male dominance and female subordination in the Christian Church and the Buddhist Sangha.[12] Why does Jan accent the deficiencies of the Panthers, conceal the deficiencies of church and sangha, while ignoring context and comparison? Given the ethical claims they make, should not our expectations be higher in the case of church and sangha? I cannot help but recall Soren Kierkegaard's poignant phrase: "When a baby is to be weaned, the mother blackens her breast."[13] Apparently, in his native Denmark, "blackening" the mother's (white) breast with a substance disagreeable in its dark appearance and bitter taste was a way of discouraging the baby's desire to nurse. The mother's breast is attractive, a source of nourishment and comfort. "How fortunate," the passage continues, "the one who did not need more terrible means to wean the child." Jan appears to be blackening the breast that once nourished her. She emphasizes those aspects of the Panthers that allow her, retrospectively, to explain her resistance to their allure. Through this "more terrible means," she is able to wean herself from the breast of the Panthers, to put a positive "spin" on what she, otherwise, could not help but regard as cowardice. The following account of her decision not to join the Panthers seems more credible. It does not have the retrospective feel of a mother "blackening" her breast:

> I was, and am, a Pisces, always deliberating between choices. I knew that either of these choices [becoming a Black Panther or taking refuge in a Tibetan monastery] would freak out my family. I did not want to worry them, but I had to do something. Amid the revolutionary timbre of the times, I was tossed and pushed along, it seemed inevitably, toward guns and violence. But then, just before taking that fateful step, I bolted. My whole being— mind, body, and soul—bolted. And even though doing so made me feel like a chicken-shit deserter, I had to turn away from it. (DM 128–9)

I do not suggest for a moment that Jan ought to have felt guilty for not becoming a Black Panther. No one had such a duty, even if like Jan they thought so. However, the guilt expressed in her "chicken-shit deserter" self-description might have been intensified by the Afro-*Eccentricity* of her choice to pursue a Buddhist way of life, knowing, as she did, that some people in the black community would regard her decision as frivolous if not bizarre. I read her "guilt" as a kind of "survivor's guilt." She does not repudiate the freedom movement, which she participated in as a high school and as a college student, but she refuses to be swallowed by it.

Throughout the memoir, Jan has a reoccurring dream about lions. Some of the lions are large and magnificent with bloody mouths. Others are miniature, toylike. In one dream sequence, the lions escaped their cages. They made her anxious. Soon they came after her (DM 3–4). And now they were in her house, her bedroom. Jan slept that night under the miniature paw of a miniature lion that would not harm her or let her go (DM 73–4). As if the lion was saying in it wordless kind of way, "Abide with me and I will abide with you." Now she dreams that she is up a tree surround by a pride of bloody-mouth lionesses that scurries with the approach of a great lioness. The lioness beckons and Jan descends the tree. Of her encounter with the lioness, she remarks: "*I feel inexorably drawn to her. I trust her. She stands, motionless, peering at me. A flash of lighting streaks the sky. I recognize it as a sign of power, and I am not afraid. As I come nearer to the lioness I see reflected in her eyes, my own*" (DM 312–13; emphasis in the original). Jan comes to see the world through the eyes of this great lioness. Her chest rumbles. Her head rears. She roars (DM 312–13). Jan did not have the stomach to become a Black Panther but she discovered, nevertheless, that she was lionhearted. As we know, lions frequently rout panthers, chasing them up trees. "I am woman, hear me roar"—this was not merely a 1970s feminist, rhetorical gesture. Jan refers to something more basic: a sense of trust and self-love, which her narrative suggests, were victories against an angry family romance[14] between mommy, daddy, and her.

As for the symbolism of the lions, Jan ties the loose ends neatly with this interpretation:

> During the past years, especially when I began to do family history research in the South, I began to have a series of recurrent dreams about lions. Sometimes frightening, but always awe-inspiring, the lions invaded my dreams and my psyche. They clearly wanted in, though I tried for a time to repress them. I believe the lions are me, myself. Perhaps they are my deepest African self. They are the "me" that I battled ever since leaving Docena and venturing forth into a mostly white world. I believe its time to let the lions come to the fore and to make peace with them. (DM 316–17)

Lions are strong and magnificent. In Buddhism, the lion's roar is the mark of the eloquence and power of the Buddha's speech. His eminent disciples, too, are often referred to as lions. They carry on and embody the Teachings. With the help of some of these lions—especially Lama Yeshe—I have begun to make peace with my own inner lions. (DM 317)

By the end of her narrative, a fearful woman, afraid of lightening, snakes, and Black Panthers, has developed a lion's heart.

The Karma of Blackness

"I am a black woman from the South who teaches Tibetan Buddhism in mostly white elite colleges in the Northeast. I have come a long way since leaving home. It has had its costs" (DM 5). Jan grew up with a deep sense of racial marginality, of not being quite right. She assumes that her feelings mirror those of most black people. It amazes her that black people have maintained their humanity despite a long history of inhumane treatment in this country. "For surely all the signs and signals around us told us otherwise; told us that we were less than human, a people cursed by God to live degraded lives; told us that we were lazy, stupid, and unfit for society" (DM 19). The Ku Klux Klan embodies this inhumane desire to degrade the lives of black people. The psychic terror they inspired in Jan and other black people crippled some and left others with visible and invisible scars. According to Jan, Docena was the "stronghold of the Alabama Ku Klux Klan" and the home of its Grand Wizard. The supreme leader, no doubt, could be seen strutting around a Klan rally like a rooster in a henhouse. Black people, with their spiritual-blues-jazz sensibility, never lost their sense of humor, referring to him mockingly as the Grand Rooster (DM 19). The Ku Klux Klan is the largest and oldest terrorist group in American history. The objects of its terror have expanded and contracted over time but black people have always been its principal targets. The Klan did not exercise its terror against a powerful nation state such as Israel or against the most powerful empire in history—the United States of America. Nor did they operate stealthily like Al-Qaeda. On the contrary, terrorizing the most vulnerable segment of the population, they operated in full view, confident that they had the support of a large cross-section of the community including the churches, courts, and police. Their reign of terror defined normality in American life.

Visibility and invisibility are funny things. If black people were invisible because (mind over matter) white people did not mind and they did not matter, then the Ku Klux Klan was highly visible. Jan recalls a bizarre concave-convex reality of black invisibility and Klan visibility. On the concave side, she notes the absence of black people on television. Whenever a black person was scheduled to appear, just before they *would have appeared*, a message would appear on the screen—"Trouble along the cable." Heavy-handed censorship by local television stations meant that Nat King Cole or Sammy Davis Jr. would not be seen on the Ed Sullivan show or wherever they were scheduled to appear. Black celebrities were kept out of sight and the desires and aspirations of black people, which they represented, were kept out of mind. On the convex side, television broadcasts of Ku Klux Klan conventions were common. These were not CBS, Edward R. Morrow exposés or a Mike Wallace-generated hit-piece. The purpose of these broadcasts was to support a grand ole institution not to condemn it. "We Southern television viewers," Jan remarks, "were treated to two- and three-day-long spectacles that reminded us that the Ku Klux Klan was strong; that white supremacists were all-powerful and fully in control. It would have seemed that such racism tied into the airwaves of the media would have been impossible, to say nothing of illegal. But I am a witness" (DM 63). Shameless displays of power by the Klan, hateful white people throwing blinding acid into the eyes of black children, the lynching of fourteen-year-old Emmett Till in Money, Mississippi, Eugene "Bull" Connor's vicious dogs, the bombed-out Sixteenth Street Baptist Church, soaked in the blood and covered with the body parts of four little black girls—this was the Alabama, the America of Jan's childhood. The church bombing precipitated Jan's participation in the famous Birmingham campaign of 1963. A fifteen-year-old sophomore at Westfield High, she joined a cadre of children who answered King's controversial call for a children's campaign against the segregationist power structure of Birmingham. This campaign reminded observers of the Children's Crusade against Muslim "occupation" of the Holy Land. It expressed the desperation of the Movement's leaders. Malcolm X was hardly the only critic of this desperate tactic. But as the cliché goes, desperate times require desperate measures. Neither desperate nor fearless, Jan answered the call. The vicious dogs of segregation did not bite her, nor did its brutal cops beat or arrest her. But she saw people bitten, beaten, and arrested. Like countless, ordinary, courageous, and anonymous black people and a few nonblack people, she willingly presented her body as a living sacrifice, holy and acceptable, for the cause of black freedom. During this conflict, King wrote "Letter from a Birmingham Jail" (DM 57–61). We have no evidence that Jan read King's letter at the time. We wonder whether she agreed then or in retrospect with the following sentiment expressed in the letter:

> I have almost reached the regrettable conclusion that the Negro's great stumbling block in the stride toward freedom is not the white Citizen's Councilor or the Ku Klux Klanner, but the white moderate who is more devoted to "order" than justice; who prefers a negative peace which is the absence of tension to a positive peace which is the presence of justice; who constantly says, "I agree with you in the goal you seek, but I can't agree with your methods of direct action": who paternalistically feels that he can set the timetable for another man's freedom; who lives by the myth of time and who constantly advised the Negro to wait until a "more convenient season." Shallow understanding from people of good will is more frustrating than absolute misunderstanding from people of ill will. Lukewarm acceptance is much more bewildering than outright rejection.[15]

Here I make a sharp transition from King to Karma. Perhaps the transition is not so sharp since we have been talking about the suffering (duhkha) of black people and thus the question of merit. I know that there are alternative ways of understanding Buddhism. However, where the experts disagree, the nonexpert is free to choose among the disputants and the conflicting views they advocate. I shall take no position on the dispute between devotees and/or scholars on how Buddhism is best understood. Rather, I cite a passage from David Brazier's *The New Buddhism* (2001) that informs my interpretation of Jan's memoir, especially her view of karma. I should note two things: first, while an influential interpreter of the Buddhist tradition, Brazier is not an academic scholar; second, I am suspicious of the concept of "authenticity" that he advocates. My reliance on Brazier should be understood in the light of these provisos.

Drawing on the work of the "Critical Buddhists," a reformed movement dedicated to retrieving what its advocates regard as Buddhism's "authentic core," Brazier offers the following:

> Dependent origination is the basic Buddhist teaching and it has implications. These include, first, the teaching of nonself or *anatma*. Critical Buddhism is an *anatmavada*. Buddhist ethics are

not, they assert, about retiring from the world in order to rediscover your original enlightenment, they are about acting unselfishly in the world. They include, secondly, a strong and particular emphasis upon karma. *Karma is to be seen as implying responsibility for one's actions in this life. It is not to be seen as implying that all the disparities of this life are really all right because they just reflect good and bad deeds in previous existences* (my emphasis).

Thirdly, dependent origination is to be seen as the primary teaching and the concept of *sunyata* (emptiness) is to be seen within the context of dependent origination, not the other way around. . . . Fourthly, in the context of dependent origination, nirvana is not to be seen as a transmundane, ultimate, absolute or anything of that kind. It is to be seen as a change in life resulting from understanding.[16]

Karma is a theory of causation: because this happed that happened. Jan does not mention karma very often. The one instance I found suggests that she accepts the "boomerang" version of karma; the notion, as one of her black students put it, that "what goes around comes around." Given her student's background, this formulation probably relates to the biblical notion of "sowing the wind and reaping the whirlwind." In this view, karma is not merely a theory of physical causation but a theory of moral causation as well: because you did this in this life or in a previous one, you suffer this or reap the benefits of that. While not mentioning karma specifically, Jan gives us reason to believe that she accepts this view. Karma is part of a conceptual ensemble that includes reincarnation, a concept that Jan initially rejected. But a car accident in the South of France and a revelation at a Tibetan monastery in Nepal changed her view.

The car accident occurred during the summer of 1969, after Jan had decided not to join the Black Panthers. Along with her friends Randy Fingerhut and Randy's boyfriend Robbie, she had decided to travel to India by land. While in the South of France, they were involved in a head-on crash. Jan was pinned in the wreckage, suffered a mild head injury, and briefly lost consciousness. Confused scenes from her life played before her mind's eye like a bad movie. Almost as suddenly as the accident, her skepticism about reincarnation began to dissolve, washed away by the imminence of death. She could have died and this fact appears to have concentrated her mind and clarified her beliefs, forcing her to look beyond her poker face skepticism and to reveal her true hand. What she discovered when she looked closely is that she did believe in reincarnation. How else could she explain her love of Irish folk music, her instinctive desire to dance to its rhythms? Perhaps she had been Irish in a previous life. After all, both the Irish and black people had long histories of oppression and suffering at the hands of English oppressors (DM 135–7). Following her accident, Jan's Tibetan hosts in Nepal reinforced her newfound belief in reincarnation when they informed her that she had been a Tibetan in a previous life. In fact, she had been one of Tibet's earliest Buddhists. This explained the instinctive affinity that Tibetans had for her. That she, an American black woman, was interested in Tibetan Buddhism did not surprise them. They recognized her. They knew who she *really* was.[17] The "spot of blonde" in her hair explained her interest in Buddhism. It showed that she had been blessed by Trisong Detsen, King of Tibet after the completion of the Samyas Monastery. She had helped to build this great monastery, the first in Tibet, toward the end of eighth century AD. The blonde spot was a mark of distinction, the result of the barley flour sprinkled on the heads of the monastery builders by a grateful king (DM 174–8).

Prior to her accident and her Nepal experience, Jan surely had occasion to reflect on her love of Irish folk music and her "spot of blonde." A scientifically oriented thinker from an early age, she presumably was well acquainted with the concept of recessive genes. Why did this explanation of her "spot of blonde" or an ontogenetic explanation, such as exposure to some agent of mutation when she was an infant, lose its appeal? Why are chance and the vagaries of taste insufficient explanations of her love of Irish music? If reincarnation explains her love of Irish music why not her love of Dvořák and Rimsky-Korsakov whose symphonies she loved as a young girl? (DM 28). Why is reincarnation a compelling explanation in one case but not in the other? Obviously, I find the logic of Jan's explanations curious. They do not appear to address the reasons for her previous disbelief, namely, the inconsistency between the concept of reincarnation and the concept of *sunyata*, the absence of an essential, independent self. If this kind of self does not exist, then how can karma follow a self through a series of lives? How can a self, devoid of inherent existence, be reborn at all? If it is not a "self" that is reborn but a "karma formation,"[18] why speak at all of reincarnation, which presupposes some sort of spiritual essence, some sort of identity that travels through time? This is a philosophical problem for Buddhism of the same order as the Christian notion of *homoousion* (the notion that Jesus and god are the same substance), which underwrites the conclusion that Jesus, as a human being, is metaphysically unique. This is a claim, I should add, that theologians have never addressed satisfactorily, much less persuasively. Jan does not answer difficult questions posed by the concept of reincarnation, difficulties she once acknowledged and critically scrutinized as a physicist-in-the making and would-be Wittgensteinian philosopher.

Given her account of black suffering (duhkha), she can only ignore these questions by embracing a vicious (as opposed to a virtuous) inconsistency. Consider the following: "It is the trauma of slavery that haunts African Americans in the deepest recesses of our souls. This is the chief issue for us, the issue that must be dealt with head-on—not denied, not forgotten, not suppressed." Denial or suppression of this trauma, she remarks, only hurts black people more deeply, causing them to embrace limiting, disparaging, and repugnant views of themselves. "We as a people," she adds, "cannot move forward until we have grappled in a serious way with all the negative effects of this trauma" (DM 160). The fact of blackness, as Frantz Fanon put it, cannot be evaded. Born as a black woman in a white supremacist society, Jan suffered "rejection for no good reason." As a smart, quick-tongued girl, she found herself at odds with family and community expectations. A youthful dreaminess and melancholy followed her through childhood and adolescence (DM 232). "Even as a small child," she remarks, "I had wondered how I had come to be a member of this particular family. Though for the most part, I felt cared for, I puzzled over why I had been born into a black family in a place where racism was a palpable feature of the environment. What was I supposed to learn from the experience?" (DM 243). Jan is clearly preoccupied with the duhkha of black people and her suffering *as a black person* in particular. How could she not be? But her preoccupation makes sense only if she rejects the idea that suffering is recompense, a kind of impersonal retribution for bad acts in prior lives.

Curiously, Jan never explores the relationship between black suffering and the notion of karma. In Christian theological terms, what she needs is a theodicy. But Buddhism has no need of theodicy—it has karma; perhaps she needs a "karma of blackness." The question she needs to consider, to put it colloquially, is "Why do black people catch so much hell?" She comes close to posing this question but then turns away. I find her evasion unsatisfactory. To think about black people and karma is also to think about caste. Some Buddhist versions of karma are nearly indistinguishable from Hindu notions of karma, which are integrally connected to the caste system. The word "caste" is a Portuguese-derived term for the Sanskrit word *varna*. Varna means "color." On some interpretations, varna is a psychospiritual term, signifying various degrees of attainment. According to other interpretations, varna is a social-racial term rooted in the conquest of the indigenous, darker-skinned inhabitants of the Indian subcontinent by lighter-skinned Indo-Iranian invaders (*circa* 1500–200 BC). These invaders solidified their conquest and organized society by caste. They relegated the vanquished, darker-skinned inhabitants to the lowest orders of society. Caste is a system of privilege and privation, of advantage and disadvantage. Caste privilege is a form of capital that has powerful transgenerational effects. Likewise caste privation (the absence of capital) is reproduced across generations. To put it succinctly, caste is the presence or absence of economic capital reinforced by social, political, and symbolic capital. According to Brazier, Buddhism was a revolt against the caste system. It embodied a critique of the Hindu notion of reincarnation as the transmigration (metempsychosis) of atman, the eternal self, the rebirth of which underwrote the caste system.

Jan is aware of superficial similarities between caste and white supremacy. She describes her own sense of humiliation, her inability to escape what resembled a white supremacist social order during her first trip to India. "Madame, what caste are you?" A Punjabi Sikh, the owner of a dry-foods stand posed this question. Surprised and offended, Jan responded defensively: "I am American. We don't have castes in America" (DM 97–8). In retrospect, the apparent absurdity of what she had uttered defensively without thinking struck her with great force. Her denials notwithstanding, she had to confront the "reality" of caste in India and in America. Contrary to claims "by some prominent African Americans that India is a wondrous land of brown-skinned rulers and people without discrimination," India's caste system, like America's system of white supremacy, is "a color-and racially-based form of social and economic discrimination" (DM 98–9).

Like Jan, a number of scholars have drawn on the caste system to illuminate white supremacy. Jan moves directly from ancient forms of color symbolism to the ideology of racial identity structured by white supremacy. In his monumental study, *Caste, Class, and Race* (1947), Oliver Cromwell Cox, a critic of capitalism and its colonial, imperialist, and white supremacist modalities, calls this enterprise and its underlying assumptions into question. The mistake quite simply is this: "The writers who use modern ideas of race for the purpose of explaining the origin of the caste system make an uncritical transfer of modern thought to an age which did not know it. The early Indo-Aryans could no more have thought in modern terms of race prejudice than they could have invented the airplane."[19] While somatic-aesthetic differences, specifically skin color may have been a part of Aryan-Dravidian conflict, the caste system itself does not correspond to differences in skin color; it is not a two-caste, black and white, Aryan and Dravidian system. Furthermore, the caste system may be older than the encounter between the Aryans and the Dravidians. Moreover, he criticizes the "Aryan thesis": we do not know in terms of gross morphology whether the Aryans were "white." Aryan is a linguistic not a "racial" classification.[20] To illustrate this point, consider English. Most English speakers are neither British nor American in nationality nor phenotypically white. "'Sudra' is not synonymous with 'Dravidian.'"[21] Jan cites "varnish" as a cognate of varna, which suggests that "color" is the exclusive or dominant meaning. In addition to color, varna has several denotations, including appearance, caste, exterior, kind, species, and "jati." Jati refers to "the form of existence determined by birth, position, rank, family, descent, kind."[22]

According to Cox, spurious arguments for the racial origin of caste, which tend to deny the evolution of the caste system, have a circular logic:

> Theorists begin by comparing the origin of caste with the modern black-white pattern of race relationship. An identification of the phenomena having been made, they proceed to establish their racial theory of caste; then they return forthwith to identify present-day race relationship with caste. In the meantime, they remain oblivious of the ongoing caste system as we know it in India. Therefore *their* origin of caste, and not that of caste in action, becomes the standard. In other words, they must assume race relations today to be caste relations only as they conceive of the latter in their origination.[23]

The upshot of Cox's analysis is that while both caste and race (white supremacy) are forms of social hierarchy, they are profoundly different. A comparative analysis of the two shows that the latter is not rooted in the former or vice versa. Socially and metaphysically, they belong to different conceptual universes.

If I have spent what appears to be an inordinate amount of time on Cox's analysis of caste, it has everything to do with Jan's understanding of Buddhism as anticaste. I have no doubt that Buddhism is anticaste, the repudiation of the India's distinctive system of hierarchy being a foundational act of Buddhism as a social movement. Nor do I doubt that Buddhism has many resources for black people burdened by the historical reality of white supremacy. Whatever its founding gestures, Buddhism does not exist in a vacuum. It is part of particular social structures and cultural systems and has evolved in tandem with them. Invidious forms of hierarchy are part of every sociocultural system. Over time, some forms of Buddhism have evolved in such a way that their notions of karma and reincarnation are virtually indistinguishable from Hindu notions based on caste. This notion of karma cuts in the direction of fate rather than freedom, explaining why things necessarily and justifiably are the way they are. According to this view, if black people suffer racial subordination in this life, then they must have done something to merit such suffering in previous lives. There is no evidence that Jan accepts this fatalistic view of the specificity of black people's duhkha. However, the notions of karma and reincarnation that she appears to accept (recall the story about her previous life as a Tibetan and her role in building the first monastery) logically entail just such a fatalistic conclusion. If we are to avoid such a conclusion, then Jan is obliged to refute the equation between black suffering and karma as merit. To put it bluntly, "Is karma a backward-looking system of moral accounting that justifies what is on the basis of what was?" or "Is karma a forward-looking system of cause and effect, a compassion-driven concern for the effects of current actions, here and now?" To sharpen this blunt statement, is black suffering the effect of a cause called white supremacy or the consequence of previous bad acts by black people?

In his critique of the Black Theological Project, William R. Jones asks a provocative question, "Is God a White Racist?"[24] This question, he argues, is the logical consequence of claims that black theologians make about the nature of god: that blacks are god's chosen people; that black people are god's suffering servants; that god is black; that god is good; that god is a cosufferer with black people in the work of liberation; that black people are not guilty of prior sin for which their current suffering is deserved punishment.[25] When these claims are coupled with the fact that black people suffer disproportionately, then the idea of divine racism emerges as the unacknowledged threshold issue for black theologians. On pain of contradiction, they must explain why god is not a white racist. I argue analogically that Jan's notions of karma and reincarnation pose a similar question for her, namely, "Do black people suffer because they deserve it?" This question is the logical consequence of claims that Jan makes about the nature of black suffering. From her own testimony, we can distill the following claims: first, white supremacy is evil; second, slavery was its most monstrous embodiment; third, the legacy of slavery—"black codes," Jim Crow, stigma, and humiliation—is horrible. Black people cannot move forward until they directly confront this trauma. I claim that Jan needs to clarify the relation between karma and reincarnation. Failing such clarification, she is subject to the Buddhist equivalent of the charge of divine racism, let us call it "karmic racism," which is the notion that something in the universe, a nonhuman agency explains why black people catch so much hell—that is, suffer unjustly and disproportionately.

Jan's Buddhist Jesus

Since I did not consider myself to be overly religious, it still strikes me as strange that wherever that Greyhound traveled, a clear vision of Jesus glided along, just outside my window. I can only assume that I must have prayed during those long hours—prayed for safety, for food, for a welcoming place. And my prayers were answered: I was not traveling alone. Jesus floated there, with me. And whenever I doubted or felt particularly afraid, I had only to glance to the window to see that He was still there, riding the wind currents, a holographic epiphany, life-size, reclining, gently smiling Jesus.

My mother and I, it was said, had been born with cauls over our eyes. This meant we saw things that other human beings did not. My mother told tales of having seen men grow as tall as trees right before her eyes and then suddenly disappear. But I always thought these stories were like those my grandmother Jennie told about "hants," the spirits of long-dead folk who returned to guide the living or, as she often said, to tell the living something important, like where gold was buried. But I did not normally have such visions. Nor had I ever seen any portrayal of Jesus that looked like this one, with His body lying down, His head supported by His right hand. Later, I would see this exact position on depictions of the Buddha's passing away, his so-called Complete Nirvana posture. But then, I knew nothing about Buddhism. I only knew that Jesus rode with me on that first bus ride to Cornell and that His gently smiling eyes comforted me throughout that journey. (DM 76)

Malcolm had his Muslim Jesus, Julius his Jewish Jesus, and Jan has her Buddhist Jesus. Each was reared as a Christian: Malcolm in a Baptist-Seventh Day Adventist-Pentecostal milieu, Julius as a Methodist, and Jan as a Baptist. Each became disenchanted with their native traditions at an early age. Malcolm claims that even as a six-year-old, he was already suspicious of the claim that Jesus was divine. Julius says that the character Jack in "Jack and the Beanstalk" had greater reality for him than Jesus. Jan's description of the place of Jesus in her life is more expansive and conventionally Christian than are the descriptions of Malcolm and Julius. Jesus is her companion, a spiritual presence and a comforter during times of anxiety (duhkha). Jesus is someone that she can see with the naked eye, and to whom she can pray. Jesus is not a stumbling block as he is for Malcolm and Julius. If we accept his account, Jesus represented a cognitive problem for the six-year-old Malcolm, the kind of problem that bedeviled liberal Christians who could not accept miraculous depictions of Jesus, which violated their Newtonian views of the universe. For the Muslim Malcolm, the Christian Jesus was a blue-eyed devil, the point man for white supremacy. But when properly understood, Jesus was a black man, a good Muslim, and the third greatest prophet of Islam. For the youthful Julius, Jesus was a bore. In contrast, the adult Julius and Jewish convert, regards Jesus as an aberrant Jew (from the perspective of Rabbinic Judaism, he is almost irrelevant when compared to his contemporary, Rabbi Hillel) whom Christians used in a perverse way against Jews. And, before his Jewish conversion, Julius was a crypto-Catholic awe-struck before a statue of the Virgin Mary. Jan does not share the reservations of Malcolm and Julius. On the contrary, Jesus is a stepping-stone to the Buddha. In the hands of a skillful Buddhist, Jesus becomes a bridge to the Dharma: Jesus is a strategy, one of the "skillful ways" of bringing people reared in a Christian milieu to a fuller knowledge of the Buddha Dharma. As we shall see, during crises, Jan conflates Jesus and Buddha. There appears to be no conflict between the two. Jesus and Buddha are complimentary as Jan's reference to the similarity between Jesus in a position of repose and the Buddha's Complete Nirvana posture underscores.

A self-proclaimed "Baptist-Buddhist," Jan is part of a Buddhist-Christian dialogue. While often unorganized, participants have institutionalized this dialogue with conferences and journals. More than a hundred books devoted to the topic have been published. To illustrate Jan's Christian-Buddhist synthesis, consider the views of Heinrich Dumoulin and Elizabeth West, dialogue participants chosen at random. According Dumoulin, the goal of the dialogue is mutual understanding, cooperation, and promotion of the common good of humankind. This dialogue has various levels of superficiality and depth. The goal of the first level is basic communication. When successful, it leads to cordial social interactions, acquiring knowledge of the other's system of values, encountering the actual practices of the other, and to "mutual understanding based on deep religious experience." The dialogue achieves its greatest significance on this experiential level.[26] Speaking from the Christian side of the dialogue, Dumoulin rejects mutual transformation—where each side crosses over into the other, dislocating and reconfiguring their assumptions and categories—as a goal. Dialogue promotes understanding by clarifying differences. Simultaneously, he seems intent on translating Buddhist concepts using Christian categories. He is interested in the ways that Buddhism complements rather than challenges Christianity, the way they "fuse" rather than "fission." In contrast, Jan speaks, simultaneously, from both sides of the dialogue. Her dual position provides an interesting perspective. Whether she is interested in dislocating and reconfiguring categories remains to be seen. But I would be surprised if she did what Dumoulin does, which is to fit Buddhism into a Christian bed of Procrustes. He cuts Buddhism to fit by using Christian concepts such the Absolute, the Eternal, the Personal, and the Transcendent.[27] Dumoulin seems interested only where dialogue confirms his Christian assumptions. Though deep, mutual, boundary-bending transformation need not be a goal of dialogue, it is an irremediable possibility. On the other hand, dialogue can clarify and rigidify boundaries, creating new energies, intensities, and passions around differences.

Elizabeth West is also a Christian participant in the Buddhist-Christian dialogue. Like Dumoulin, she defines "deep dialogue" as that which occurs on "the level of practice and experience rather than belief and doctrine."[28] But her commitment seems qualitatively different. Whereas Dumoulin searches for a comprehensive theology to illuminate what each party brings to the dialogue, West manages to resist the urge. She takes seriously the absence of the kind of metaphysical speculation characteristic of Christian theology in the sayings, sermons, and stories attributed to the Shakyamuni Buddha. West knows that this absence is meaningful. Therefore, she focuses on practice rather than theory: nothing illustrates the possibilities of dialogue better that the Buddhist Noble Eightfold Path and the Christian Beatitudes. Table 5.1 illustrates her comparative scheme.

As the subtitle of her book, *The Eightfold Path of Jesus Revisited with Buddhist Insights,* suggests, West emphasizes specific behaviors that lead to what Buddhists call enlightenment and what Christians call blessedness. Metaphysical considerations—dependent origination, karma,

Table 5.1   Comparison between the Noble Eightfold Path and the Christian Beatitudes

The Noble Eightfold Path	The Eight Beatitudes
Balanced View; Right Seeing; Right View	Blessed Are the Poor in Spirit; Theirs Is the Kingdom of Heaven
Right Intention, True Intention	Blessed Are Those Who Mourn; They Shall Be Comforted
Right Speech	Blessed Are the Gentle; They Shall Inherit the Earth
Right Action	Blessed Are Those Who Hunger and Thirst for What Is Right; They Shall Be Satisfied
Right Livelihood	Blessed Are the Merciful; They Shall Have Mercy Shown to Them
Right Effort or Energy	Blessed Are the Pure in Heart; They Shall See God
Right Mindfulness	Blessed Are the Peacemakers; They Shall Be Called the Children of God
Right Samadhi (A Difficult Word to Translate. It Can Be Rendered as Concentration, but Contemplation Feels Truer to the Essential Meaning.)[a]	Blessed Are Those Who Are Persecuted in the Cause of Right; Theirs Is the Kingdom of Heaven

[a] West, 55–6.

and no-self versus creation, providence, and the immortal soul, are secondary considerations, subservient to the liberating practices of the Noble Eightfold Path and the Beatitudes. They help us understand why metaphysical principles are less important than belief-embedding practices, that is, *habitual acts*. If this metaphysical-practical distinction is correct, then the Eightfold Path and the Beatitudes may also be a great way of approaching Jan's perspective as a Baptist-Buddhist.

Jan is a Tibetan Buddhist. So the views of her spiritual leader, the Dalai Lama might be relevant to our discussion of her self-description as a Baptist-Buddhist. From the Buddhist side of the dialogue the Dalai Lama appears to agree with Dumoulin: dialogue is a matter of finding practical harmonies as opposed to seeking conceptual understandings that might lead to mutual transformation. If the point is to change our behavior, what difference do conceptual differences make? The following Tibetan expression captures the Dalai Lama's resistance to dialogue as conceptual transformation: "Don't try to put a yak's head on a sheep's body." He augments this pastoral advice with the following remark, "Nagarjuna, a famous second-century Indian master, stated in one of his philosophical writings that if one was determined to equate two things, one could find points of similarity between any-thing! Carried to the extreme, the whole realm of existence would turn into a single entity, just one thing."[29] The Dalai Lama made this state-ment in response to people who called themselves Christian-Buddhists. Consider his comment in the light of Jan's description of a panic attack that she experienced when she learned that her mother had fallen gravely ill and that her death was imminent:

> I peered at my Tibetan *mala*—my prayer beads—lying on the table. Then I put my hands together.
> "God, please help my mother," I thought. But the words did not ring true. I felt like I needed first to apologize for not having called His name more often. I switched next to Jesus, thinking that he was probably the best intercessor. Again, I first apologized. It was not that I didn't believe in Them, or in Him, for to Christians the two are one and the same; it was just that I was not used to this form of prayer. I thought next of Lama Yeshe and Lama Zopa. Calling them clearly to mind, I prayed, "Please, help my mother now!" Next the Buddha of compassion came to mind and I began saying his mantra, *Om mani padme hum, Om mani padme hum, Om mani padme hum.* The two traditions, Baptist and Buddhist, began to clash in my mind. I felt flushed. I was scared; nothing was clearer than that. Now, when there needed to be some clarity, when I needed to know what to do, I was stuck, almost frantic. My mother was probably dying. What should I be praying for? (DM 279–80)

In the words of the Dalai Lama, is Jan trying to put a yak's head on a sheep's body when she describes herself as a Baptist-Buddhist? Contrary to Nagarjuna's advice, is she trying to equate things that are wholly dis-similar? I do not think so. The hyphen between Baptist and Buddhist is pregnant with difference. Jan does not synthesize Christianity and Buddhism, translating one tradition in terms of the other or mutually translating each tradition. I take her as suggesting something much more difficult and radical. She is asserting the simultaneity of her Christianity and her Buddhism. She is a Buddhist most of the time. Under ordinary circumstances her practices conform to the Noble Eightfold Path and their underlying metaphysical presuppositions. Christianity modifies her primary commitment to the Buddha, the Dharma, and the Sangha the way an adjective modifies a noun. But under extraordinary cir-cumstances, she finds her self, simultaneously if not equally, in two different conceptual worlds, Buddhist and Christian, which work in concert on the practical level without becoming one conceptually. Is this schizophrenia? If Jan is hearing voices, they are not telling her, as the perennial philosophy would, that deep down Buddhism and Christianity are the same. Jan does not deny the deep metaphysical differences; she ignores them. The logic of her faith, if that is the right word, is no longer a disjunctive "either/or" but a conjunctive "both/ and." This is not syncretism. She proclaims herself a Buddhist and a Christian, which, conceptually, is no more (or less) objectionable than the claim that Jesus is wholly god and wholly man.

As a college student, Jan studied the Christian philosopher Soren Kierkegaard who criticizes what he regards as the phony faith of most Christians. Anyone can say that they believe, or can say this or that is true. But if you want to know what someone *really* believes, what they *really* think is true, look to those things for which they are willing to die or kill—like Abraham on Mount Moriah who, hearing a voice that no one else could hear, and the authenticity of which they would have probably doubted, prepared to sacrifice his son Isaac at god's command. Observe how people behave under the threat of death. Given the reality of her mother's death and the prospect of her own death aboard a plane she thought would crash, Jan becomes a Baptist-Buddhist. Buddha joins hands with Jesus, as she prays in hope and fear to both (DM 310).

Some people accept her Baptist-Buddhist self-description with equanimity, if not enthusiasm. In contrast,

[m]any others, who've had occasion—or taken the license—to comment on it, have stridently voiced disdain and disapproval: "Either you believe in Christ, our Lord, as your sole and only savior, or you're lost!" A young, well-educated, and articulate black man who was visiting Wesleyan once told me exactly this. To this vociferous attack by a newly reborn Christian, and others like it, I can only say, "Well, I trust that Jesus Himself is more understanding and compassionate." The Jesus I knew from the Gospel stories was the Jesus who had ministered to women, to the poor and downtrodden; and He was the Jesus I knew personally, because, He had ridden with me on that bus ride to Cornell. Moreover, it seems to me that those who see a disjuncture in my being a Baptist-Buddhist haven't spent any amount of time reflecting on what, or who, a Buddha really is—or a Christ, for that matter. As always, in matters of faith and of the heart, a little concrete experience and

practice usually takes one higher, while at the same time sets one on firmer ground. (DM 311)

Despite the negative response of people such as the "young, well-educated, and articulate black man," who had recently converted to Christianity, Jan has become who she is. She acknowledges the truth claims on her that both Baptists and Buddhists make. More important, neither tradition is a destination. They are maps for the journey called life (DM 311). Maps, as a wise man once said, are not territory. And "going to the territory" is sometimes an uncanny ride. Through an eccentric, Afro-*Eccentric* act of improvisation, Jan has mapped out the territory for herself. In doing so, she *blues* the Standard Narrative of Black Religion. She plays a Baptist note in a Buddhist tune, bluing the melody of one tradition even as she does the same to the other. Jan creates something new. She makes the black Baptist Church contemplative. She makes Buddhism "swing," as she orchestrates a Buddha-Jesus tune that has never been heard.

What Would Buddha Say?

"What do those Buddhist monks have that our own Baptist Church can't provide?" (DM 244). Jan puts this question in the mouths of her parents who were alarmed by her decision to study in India and what they recognized as her growing interest in Buddhism. One could imagine them saying, "What will become of her Christian faith?" and "What will happen to her eternal soul?" Jan never addresses her parents' question directly. But we can distill an answer from the self-portrait she provides by looking to her own account of why she became a Buddhist.

Jan suffered from doubt and suspicion surrounding her paternity, racial marginality and insecurity, racial fear that took on a free-floating quality in her life, and intense anger rooted in this gendered and racial family drama. The circumstances surrounding her birth included her father's doubts, her mother's emotional pain, and the bitterness that cut between them like a knife. Earlier, I described her light-skinned racial marginality, which factored in her father's doubts and led black children and adults to derisively call her "white gal." Further, her intelligence led some black people and many white people to question her racial and gender authenticity. Jan presented an anomaly. As I remarked earlier, anomalies do not fit our neat categories. They make us uncomfortable.

They make us think unconventional thoughts that raise questions about our identity and the way we live. In a white supremacist society, blacks are responsible for not making white people uncomfortable, especially by not asserting their equality and demanding justice. In a male-dominated society, women are expected to defer to male leadership and authority, which in part means not asserting their independence or appearing to be too intelligent. Intelligence is a "hard" and "sharp" virtue and women should be "smooth," "soft" and, to put it crudely, "wet." Jan violated these expectations.

The reactions of others made her insecure and angry. There are striking examples of her anger throughout the memoir. Consider the white school superintendent who visited her segregated elementary school and responded to her intelligence and ambition in the condescending and smarmy way that characterized official representatives of Jim Crow. Jan was cast as a minstrel girl, performing her curious intelligence for the amusement of the superintendent. This official was her "Mr. Ostrowski." You may recall Malcolm X's high school English teacher, Mr. Ostrowski, who told Malcolm that he had too much ambition and that becoming a lawyer was not "a realistic goal for a nigger."[30] What is so disturbing about this advice is the pretense of concern for Malcolm's well-being, a concern that he might hurt himself by overreaching. This concern for a black person, expressed as a condescending pity is the only kind of concern that a white person in the white knuckled-grip of white supremacy could imagine. Mr. Ostrowski expresses contempt for a black boy who has the temerity to reach high, whose ambition threatens a Jim Crow system that would relegate him to a subordinate status. In both cases, the intelligence and ambition of black children were regarded as a joke. Jan reacted with hate to the white superintendent and this new-fangled "coon show." With the "guess who's coming to dinner" incident at the home of her white friend Robbie, her hatred grew murderous. Robby and his girlfriend Randy invited Jan to attend his parent's house party. Her presence shocked his parents and their guests so much that they fell into an embarrassed and embarrassing silence. Jan reacted immediately and viscerally. That heightened, hypersense of visibility and vulnerability that black people feel in these situations sent Jan into a murderous rage. Here it would be good to hear Jan's own voice: "For the whole of two days my body quivered. I was sick with rage. My heart, I was sure, was going to explode. My head was all crazy. I was feverish and had chills at the same time. I could not eat. I could not sit or lie still. My mind turned around a single thought: murder, slaughter" (DM 111). Jan's rage might appear extreme to the uninitiated. But for those who are familiar with the intensity of this kind of racial shame, which is usually one of many such events, this response is not so extreme. Murder *seems* like a reasonable response to this kind of dishonor. Jan raged against a familiar white gaze that reduced her to an object of anxiety, a black, two-legged problem. The silence of Robbie's parents and their guests said it all; what could *these white people* possibly have to say to someone such as her? She was a curio, a circus freak.

Incidents such as her "guess who's coming to dinner" experience may seem small. As she observes, however, "[t]here is an immensity of pain and harmfulness in the little things" (DM 236). This general claim applies in particular to three cases involving, respectively, a jewelry store clerk, bank clerk, and a clerk at a Ramada Inn who was coldly disposed toward black people. When she asked to see some cigarette lighters the jewelry store clerk responded: "We only have expensive cigarette lighters here!" (DM 235). The implication that she could not afford their lighters angered Jan. The clerks' underlying assumption that "black" equals poor was not merely an empirical judgment but metaphysical. *This is what black people are.* The clerk's intellectual laziness blocked any possibility that Jan might be an exception to what the clerk took to be the rule. Jan responded with inaudible, inarticulate, and muted rage. When that rage found words, it spewed forth volcanically as curses, imprecations, and vitriol: "You racist piece of white shit! Don't you know that I could buy you if I wanted to? That I could pay your measly salary three times over on only half of my own? But seeing a black person you assume, you presume, you poor distorted excuse for a human being" (DM 235). Dynamically, the bank and hotel incidents were similar. The bank clerk behaved too familiarly, as whites under Jim Crow tended to, treating Jan's sister as if she were a servant, or a younger person, referring to her by her first name rather than addressing her as Mrs. Williams. There was the added insult of placing the money on the counter rather than in her hand, as if her blackness might rub off. At the hotel, Jan and her nephews jumped into the pool and the white children crawled out. Along with white women lounging on the deck, they abandoned the pool area to these unwelcome guests. This incident occurred in the context of a hotel that made it clear by its niggardly service and gruff manner that Jan and her family were not welcome (DM 235–8).

The last example of Jan's anger that I shall consider relates to her genealogical research and the "utility of spit." This incident, one of "the little things" that happen to black people daily, comprises an iceberg of such incidents for which the "guess who's coming to dinner" incident that threw Jan into a murderous rage was merely the tip. Alex Haley's genealogical research inspired Jan to investigate her genealogy. As you may recall, Haley cowrote *The Autobiography of Malcolm X.* Later he published *Roots* in which he traced his ancestry back to an African man of the Mandingo people, named Kunta Kinte. A television miniseries based on the book made him a minor celebrity. Haley and Jan were friends. With his example in mind she went to work. Like a good historian, she began with what she knew and went to the archives. She says that the research carried her to exhilarating heights and abysmal depths. The deepest abyss of all was slavery. Like most black people, she had slave ancestors on both the maternal and paternal sides of her genealogical tree. She recounts the sadness of encountering records of ancestors long dead who were torn from their families and sold, sometimes repeatedly, often on a whim but usually to pay a debt. She recalls newly freed slaves who affirmed their humanity and dignity by renaming themselves: "Person," "Worthy," and "Self." Within the context of her research, she had an *extraordinary "experience,"*[31] which recalls Malcolm X's apparition of the Asiatic man and Julius Lester's encounter at Wounded Knee. Provoked by the very melancholy of the land where her ancestors had lived and died at the command of their masters, she describes her experience as follows: "Often, in the shadows of evening's dusk, I thought I saw groups of huddled slaves silently waiting to cross a river or creek. [Was this the Underground Railroad? Were these some of the "many thousands gone"?] Sometimes the shadows congregated under some large oak. I felt these figures communing with me, saying, 'Yes, we are here.' With my heart, I recognized and greeted them" (DM 244–5, 248–50).

Becky James, the local historian of Marengo County, Alabama, provided a particularly galling source for Jan's anger. James had information that Jan needed. For four years Jan had sought James' help in piecing together her family genealogy. During that time, according to Jan, James held that information close to her breast, waiting patiently for the moment when she could drop it like a bomb. Jan discovered that her maternal great-grandfather was a white man named Gaius Whitfield. She does not say whether he was a slave master or not. I suspect that he was not but his father undoubtedly had owned slaves. Jan discovered further that two of her eight ancestral lines traced back "directly to white slave owners, or to white men who lived more recently." The Wakefield line was one of those slave-owning lines. Jan discovered what many black people know theoretically, if vaguely, that among their ancestors are white slave masters, the very people who held their black ancestors in bondage. (Sadder still, Jan seems unaware of black slave masters in the ancestral woodpile: in America and, of course, in Africa.) Jan describes James' satisfaction in being the bearer of this bad news. As if to rub it in, she attributes Jan's intelligence to her great-grandfather—a white man. How else to explain her obvious intelligence and academic success? Jan's parting image of Becky James is of "a devil licking her chops" (DM 251).

But rather than actively remembering this incident and the devilish imagery of Becky James and thus cultivating the deep-seated hatred that she felt, Lama Pema suggested that she spit:

> "You should just think of this lady like spit." Not quite sure I had heard him correctly, I asked, "Like *spit?*"
> "Yes, like *spit!*" Then he motioned with his mouth in imitation of spitting. "If someone spits, you know, on the ground, it would be silly for that person to stand there and contemplate that spit, or wish to suck the spit back into his mouth. You just spit, and you go on. So, think of the meeting with this lady and the bad emotions that came out of it as spit. Spit it out, and keep going!" (DM 255)

To paraphrase Nietzsche's aphorism from *The Advantages and Disadvantages of History for Life,* one must know when to remember and when to spit.

Depending on which theory of the emotions one subscribes to, there are two basic emotions, desire and fear. All other emotions are rooted in these two. Even if one does not accept the theory of basic and secondary emotions: Jan's anger is clearly rooted in her fear. Among other things, she fears snakes, lightening, the Klan, and violence; external violence to be sure, and, perhaps, her own latent capacity for violence. I have spoken of her fear of snakes, an instinctive, atavistic fear, which produced a desire to flee or to kill. Think of the reflexive response that many people have when they encounter a spider, mosquito, or fly. Some of us kill them on general principle or, I should say, on instinct. Jan did not wish to kill snakes so much as to have others kill them for her, whether her childhood neighbor Dot Chambers or her Nepali yardman, Lakshman. She wanted snakes dispatched as quickly as possible. Once she commanded Lakshman to kill a snake that had entered the house. She remarks that this deadly and hateful disposition toward a living creature is unbecoming of a Buddhist or Christian. "But," she adds, "I did want to kill that snake just as, when a child of three, I had wanted to kill Dot Chambers. Today, I know that what I *really* wanted to kill was the overwhelming fear that rose up and crippled me." In Jan's Freudian language, the snake was merely a displaced substitute for her real fear. Jan's hatred rooted in her fear leads to two additional emotions: shame and guilt (DM 23–4). Shame is about being inadequate (as a woman, black person, Christian, or Buddhist?) and the fear of exposure, that one's inadequacy is subject to someone's gaze, if only the "little man" or "little woman," as it might be, in one's head, one's inner self, cultural superego, or the "they." Guilt is the knowledge that one has violated a legal or ethical precept (such as killing a sentient being) that one has done something wrong.

Curiously, Jan never considers the symbolic meaning of snakes and how that may have factored in her fear. Jan is not a "cradle Buddhist" but a Western "convert." In the West, two interpretations of the symbolic meaning of snakes, one Christian the other Freudian compete for dominance. In the Christian interpretation, the snake is Satan's archetype, embodying temptation and deception. Snakes are anomalous, having neither legs nor arms, neither wings nor fins. "Lowdown and dirty," the snake slithers on its belly, and is associated, literally and figuratively, with slime. Snakes and humans have a natural antipathy toward each other. The snake is evil. According to the Freudian interpretation, in contrast, the snake is a phallic symbol (for Freud, in contrast to Lacan, the phallus is the penis), a symbol of sexual desire. Given the dominant chain of Christian associations, Jan's claim that her disposition toward snakes is unbecoming of a Christian merits some skepticism. Given her reticence to speak about her sexual life, a "sin" in this age of confession and self-revelation, we might wonder about the relevance of the Freudian interpretation of the snake as an icon of repressed sexual desire. Even without this speculation there is good reason to assume that Jan's cultural context both Christian and Freudian reinforces her instinctive, reflexive, and atavistic fear of snakes. Nor should we forget that she offers her own quasi-Christian, quasi-Freudian interpretation of her deadly fear. According to this interpretation, her fear of snakes symbolizes multiple sources fear, woven together into a single object by the dreamwork of condensation and displacement.

Jan describes her fear of lightening. It is unreasonable and it outruns any calculation of probability or citation of empirical evidence. Yet, there is a kind of symbolic logic to her fear. Lightening struck her as personal and intentional. So she took it personally. When it thundered and the lightening flashed, god was doing his work. Jan feared that she was the target of that work. To borrow a line from Emily Dickinson, Jan's life "closed twice before its close"[32] when as a child, the lightening struck her house. Death knocked at the door and roared through the house as if it were a SWAT team exercising a raid. Popping, cracking with sudden bursts of illumination, the lightening overwhelmed the house's electrical system and threw its residents into a chaotic scramble of p-jays and flying bed linen. "We dropped to the floor," she remarks, "huddled in fear while God, with a vengeance continued His work" (DM 256–8). Her grandmother tried to comfort the children in the peculiar way that adults do when she said that there was nothing as mere humans that they could do: "'The Lawd's working now!'" One could imagine Jan responding sarcastically, "Thanks god!" But even she was too frightened for sarcasm. Besides, she may have been hit. Even now she cannot be sure that she was not struck or that god's finger did not deal her at least a glancing blow on that chaotic night. That her fear was genuine and lifelong, there is no doubt. Later, in therapy, she discovered a new interpretation of her fear. Her dread when watching the movie *The Chamber,* where a young, naïve, white northern lawyer drove to a southern Ku Klux Klan camp meeting, was similar to what she felt during an electrical storm. Then she made a key association between the lightening and, as she describes it, "the flaming embers I had seen fly up into the night sky when, as a young girl, the Klan had burned a cross in front of our house.... I could at last make sense of things." She connected the embers from the cross burning to all the encounters she had experienced with hate-filled people and the dangers they posed for her family to every lightening storm she had ever experienced (DM 259–60, 265–6).

Snakes, lightening, the Ku Klux Klan, "hey, white gal, who's your daddy?" the smarmy, white school superintendent, the "guess who's coming to dinner" incident, the "little things," genealogical research, Becky James, and spit—these make up the hydra-headed source of Jan's fear and anger. Much fear, much anger. It is no coincidence that Jan flirted with the Black Panther Party. She was an angry woman. In underscoring this point, I draw a beeline from her childhood encounter with the Ku Klux Klan to her later seduction by the Panthers. The racist violence of the Klan, the storm troopers of white supremacy would be met by the revolutionary force of the Panthers. Never again would she experience the kind of helpless terror that she did when she huddled in her home with mother, sister, and grandmother against the assault of the Klan. Then she had thought about grabbing her father's

shotgun but fear froze her in place. According to her current interpretation, she did not *really* want to hurt anyone. Instead, she wanted
to talk to the Klan, to persuade them that she and they were equally
human, that violence was not necessary and that there was a better way.
I do not doubt that she felt this way. However, I doubt that her sentiments were pure or that her desire for nonviolent dialogue displaced
her desire to grab a gun and pull the trigger. Our motives are usually
an ambivalent mixture. Considering her explosive reaction to lesser
slights, acts of violence, violations, and injustices, it is hard to sustain an
argument for pure motives. In my interpretation, her attraction to the
Panthers, while partly explicable in terms of the revolutionary tenor of
the time, roots, nevertheless, in a lifetime of terrifying and humiliating
experiences that made her as ripe as a Docena, Alabama peach. Jan had
good reasons for her anger.

   Jan's fear-rooted anger provides the first answer to the question,
"What do those Buddhist monks have that our own Baptist churches
can't provide?" As I understand it, Jan's answer holds that Buddhism
provides a better theory of duhkha, of the unsatisfactoriness of life.
Given her own suffering, she finds Buddhism especially attractive.
Jan does not make a negative argument by describing Christianity as
deficient. Speaking positively about Buddhism's virtues, she claims
that it diagnoses and treats her problems (duhkha) more effectively.
Considering her own claim, she should not have been surprised when
black students crowded her Buddhism courses. Could their experiences really be that different from hers? Apparently, the answer was
"no." They found her eccentricity, her Afro-*Eccentric* spirituality
compelling.

   In her inaugural lecture at the University of Santa Cruz, Jan noted
that "Buddha" is a title not a proper name, which "*is given to anyone
who has 'awakened to' and 'understood' (the term's literal meaning) the true
nature of reality.*" To be awake is to exhibit selfless compassion for all
beings (humans, gods, and animals) still bound in duhkha. She remarks
that the number of people who will, are, or have awakened to the
truth of the Buddha Dharma is countless. Only people can become
Buddha; gods and animals need not apply. Thus Buddha refers to a class
of persons and not merely to a sixth-century man named Siddhartha
Gautama. Born a prince, Siddhartha abandoned everything in pursuit
of enlightenment. He spent his "post-enlightenment" life teaching two
things: duhkha—"the suffering inherent in our continual, unsatisfactory circling through the unhappy states of birth, sickness, old age,
death, and rebirth"—and its cessation. He preached the end of duhkha

through a meticulous analysis of its causes. Jan offers the following summary:

> The most succinct formulation of the Buddha' doctrine was provided in the very first sermon he delivered. That First Sermon set forth the Four Noble Truths of Buddhism, namely:
>
> 1. There is suffering.
> 2. There is a cause of suffering.
> 3. There is the cessation of suffering.
> 4. There is a path leading to the cessation of suffering.
>
> As footnotes to each of these Truths, we are enjoined to understand fully the first, find and eliminate the second, realize directly the third, and practice the fourth. Far from being a pessimistic tradition, Buddhism offers the promise of freeing ourselves and others from suffering. (DM 1923)

If suffering is the preeminent consideration of Buddhism, and American black people have suffered disproportionately, then it should come as no surprise that the Buddhist message, encapsulated in the Four Noble Truths, would resonate among black people. The black students who flocked to Jan's class inhabited the same world she did. The ways they suffered no doubt were similar to hers. Even if we discount the allure of the exotic, of that which is different, unfamiliar, and thus attractive in a romantic sort of way (romantic Orientalism), the message had much to recommend it. There are several reasons why the Buddhist account of duhkha (sleepwalking) and *nibbana* (enlightenment) may have been more attractive than, or at least competitive with the Christian account of sin and salvation. Buddhism did not carry the cultural baggage that Christianity did. There was no powerful, cultural-theological myth such as the "curse of Ham" (actually Noah's cursed the descendants of his grandson Canaan) that justified the enslavement and subordinate status of black people. Undoubtedly, Jan's students were just as ignorant as most Americans of Buddhism's complicity with various forms of oppression and injustice such as Zen Buddhists' complicity with the Empire of Japan. Buddhism came to America as a set of principles and practices shorn of their historical and cultural specificity in Asian societies. (Like "traveling theory," religious traditions travel best when disembedded from the cultures that produced them.) With this cultural stumbling block removed, the potential universality of Buddhist principles and practices could emerge. The notion that duhkha has a cause, that it can cease, and that there is a path toward its cessation makes suffering legible and not mysterious or locked inside the inscrutable will of god. This account of the unsatisfactory character of life places agency and responsibility in human hands. For many black people, this account of suffering, bondage, and liberation might be especially attractive.

All "religious" traditions (and we acknowledge that religion is an inadequate concept) must come to terms with the relations among, animals, gods, humans, and other beings—ghosts, monsters, and demons. In qualitative terms, they must explain the relations among animality, humanity, and divinity. Buddhism's distinctive explanation might attract blacks since it liberates humans from subjection to god and the gods, the burden of exercising dominion over animals, and the many forms of duhkha (unsatisfactoriness, frustration, and suffering) that flow from both. Given the Afro-*Eccentric*, Baptist–Buddhist spirituality she had forged, Jan might have offered these explanations in response to the question posed by her parents: "What do those Buddhist monks have that our own Baptist churches can't provide?" To put it in a fashionable if colloquial way, this account of Buddhism's allure is what a Buddha might say.

CHAPTER SIX

"Bluing" the Standard Narrative

Each of the autobiographers became who they are because on some level they could not tolerate who they were. Their radical transformations occurred at the intersection of religious commitment, racial identification, and the allure of black freedom struggle; the polar demands of religion, race, and politics sometimes pulling them in antagonistic directions. Common markers of their passage to the persons they became included the world-shaking death of a parent, the troubling relationship between ancestry and rape, the meaning of Jewish ancestry under the conditions of white supremacy and in a society that defined Jews as white; the terror of the Ku Klux Klan; the relations between holiness, enlightenment, and diet, and opposition to Jim Crow—in summary, they are bound by their struggle through the dark passages of American life.

Black Religion is a consequent not an antecedent—primordial—reality, an artifact not an essence. Produced by people identified as "Negro," "colored," "black," or "African American," Black Religion emerged from a violent intercultural encounter under the conditions of conquest, slavery, and white supremacy. Black people transformed the traditions they encountered by "bluing the note" and producing a sound that was recognizable but different. The autobiographers "blacken" Islam, Judaism, and Buddhism by "bluing" them. In the process, they simultaneously transform our understanding of those traditions and our notion of what it means to be a black person. In my view, Black Religion is an act of improvisation; it is also a provocation. The life-narratives of the autobiographers reveal this double work. If the Black Church improvises—riffs—on the white Protestant Church, then Malcolm, Julius, and Jan riff on the Standard Narrative. They blue the note by swinging in double time.

I shall now reconsider the questions concerning Black Religion that I posed in chapter 1: What is its nature and scope? What is the relation between religious commitment and racial identity? How do Malcolm, Julius, and Jan emplot their Afro-*Eccentric* narratives of Black Religion?

1. None of the autobiographers directly addresses the question of Black Religion's nature and scope. However, during his Nation of Islam phase, Malcolm comes closest with his claim that Islam is the black man's religion. In addressing this question, he provides an alternative, if not incongruous Asiatic-centered account of Black Religion and identity. This directly challenges the Standard Narrative. Eventually, Malcolm qualified this view but does not appear to have abandoned it. In contrast, Julius appears to accept the Standard Narrative: Black Religion is the Black Protestant Church. Whatever else it may be, Black Religion is antithetical to Judaism. As he understands it, Jewish identity is deep and black identity is cosmetic. Jewishness speaks truly; blackness deceives. Judaism frees him from the authoritarian extremes of black solidarity and from the Christianity that encodes this pathology; it enables him to construct an Afro-*Eccentric* identity. In contrast, Jan melds black Baptist Christianity and Tibetan Buddhism, which suggests a basic compatibility on the level of practice, despite deep metaphysical difference. In this view, Black Religion is a radical form of openness to the otherness of the other; in this case, the otherness of Buddhism. Her improvisational version of Buddhism comprehends the *duhkha* of racial identification. Such identification expresses a form of unsatisfactoriness. However, racial solidarity might be a "skillful means" that Buddhists can use to overcome the *duhkha* of white supremacy and racial hierarchy. On the question of scope, Jan provides the most radical answer, and the answer most compatible with my artifactual and nonessentialist view. She sees Black Religion as continuous but not coterminous with "the" Black Protestant Church. Traditions are not hermetically sealed; they borrow, interpenetrate, and mutually transform. Each autobiographer is aware of the ways that Black Religion is a reaction to the white nationalism of the American Church and nation-state. None expresses awareness of Afro-diasporic religions such as Vodun, Santeria, and Candomble. However, I doubt that any of them would exclude these traditions from the scope of Black Religion. On the other hand, I am not sure they would be as explicit as I am in affirming the potential "blueness" and, therefore, "blackness" of virtually any tradition. In short, to be "black" is to be "blue."

2. Each autobiographer acknowledges a relationship between religion and race. To the question "Is religion constitutive of Black identity formation?" Malcolm's answer appears to be "Yes." At least he held this view during his Nation of Islam phase. He seems to have accepted the "primitivist view," which holds that blacks have a genius for religion similar to their purported genius for music, dance, and bodily expressivity. (As I noted in the chapter 1, Du Bois' *The Souls of Black Folks* provides the canonical formulation of this view.) When this natural genius expressed itself poorly, blacks became brainwashed Christians. When expressed well, they became Muslims. (I have found no evidence that Malcolm ever renounced this view. However, the practical realities of the black freedom struggle, to which he was fiercely committed, forced him to work with black Christians. Further, he befriended black Christians throughout his life, even while denouncing them as brainwashed.) The relationship between religion and race seems to trouble Julius the most, in large part because he assumes that Jewish equals white. Given this assumption, he has difficulty distinguishing his affirmation of Jewishness from an invidious critique of blackness. If Malcolm sees black Christians as defective black people, then Julius sees blackness as a defect that deceives those who subscribe to it and obscures what is really real such as his hard-won knowledge that he is a Jew. In contrast, Jan does not construct an invidious relation between religion and racial solidarity or religion and black mental health. One can be both black and "other." In this regard, Jan realizes the promise of Afro-*Eccentricity* to a degree that Malcolm and Julius do not.

3. By writing about their own lives, the autobiographers have become historians of the self, so to speak. Every history has a plot and each autobiographer emplots her narrative in particular ways. As the hero in a story whose tragic end he anticipates, Malcolm emplots his narrative as a tragiromance. In this story, he triumphs over his baser instincts, overreaches, and is betrayed. He is both Icarus and Caesar. Malcolm combines a radical critique of white supremacy with a conservative ideology of culture and racial solidarity, which is hostile to gender equality and fails to recognize the otherness within the racial self, what those in the tradition of Ralph Ellison describe as the "blackness of whiteness" and "whiteness of blackness." Malcolm's dominant narrative trope is metaphor; specifically, the couplet: white devil-Uncle Tom. Malcolm tells a grand story about the depredations of the former and the complicities of the latter. In the process, he sings the praises of Islam and blames black brainwashed Christians, especially their clergy for complicity with white supremacy. In contrast, Julius' dominant

trope is irony. Things are never what they seem. It is as if he presents his first-person narrative from a third-person point of view, emphasizing the gap between the first and the third, the Persona and the Soul. Julius' narrative reads like a grand comedy, full of misadventures and incongruous elements. It also reads as a satire of true believers such as his former comrades in the SNCC, especially Stokely Carmichael and of Malcolm X—their spiritual father and his. His judgments, now liberal, now conservative appear as if they are transideological but this very vacillation *is* Julius' ideology. He is revolted by and revolts against racial identification, against the ideology of white supremacy that oppresses and against the ideology of blackness, which reimprisons black people while claiming to liberate them. Like Julius, Jan emplots her narrative as comedy. But there is nothing satirical about it. The satirical attitude has a jaundiced if not misanthropic presentation, with demonizing (Julius cannot resist the temptation) as a standard technique. The demonizing rhetoric (white devils and Uncle Toms) that characterizes Malcolm's narrative and that colors Julius' narrative (blackness as superficial, if not a lie) is largely absent from Jan's account. As a Baptist-Buddhist, she celebrates the incongruous elements of life. Recall the "young, well-educated, and articulate black man" who told her, "Either you believe in Christ, our Lord, as your sole savior, or you're lost!" (D 311). Jan does not agree. She reconciles what he finds irreconcilable. Ideologically, Jan's narrative sounds liberal. Her dominant trope is synecdoche, which expresses a dialogical, if not "democratic" relationship between her Buddhist and Baptist selves.

Coda: My Point of View as an Author

In chapter 1, I described some of the problems that confront religion scholars, especially the relation between tutored and untutored habits of belief. This Coda is a meditation on the Black Church experience that captures, so to speak, the phenomenology of my perception. Along the way, I offer idiosyncratic reflections on creed. I explore, in short, the assumptions, motives, and methods, the forms of inquiry and evidence that shape my perspective as the author of this book.

★   ★   ★

> Those who hold to the notion that there is a definite kind of experience which is itself religious, by that very fact make out of it something specific, as a kind of experience that is marked off from experience as aesthetic, scientific, moral, political; from experience as companionship and friendship. But "religious" as a quality of experience signifies something that may belong to all these experiences. It is the polar opposite of some type of experience that can exist by itself.
>
> John Dewey[1]

If noisy demonstration and quiet meditation are polar religious dispositions, then I tend toward the latter. I am very emotional, emotional in the way that women are stereotypically said to be emotional. My eyes tear easily, my voice trembles and sounds as if something is breaking—but—I do not have a Pentecostal or charismatic bone in my body. Emotional but not Pentecostal: my religion does not make me want to shout. Though not immune to charisma, I am suspicious of it. Feeling without thinking is blind. The charismatic authority of the preacher is resistant to reasons. It is monarchical, antirepublican, antidemocratic (in their philosophical rather than partisan meanings), and too often operates, as kings do, by decree and acclamation. Thus my anti-Pentecostalism is both instinctual and a carefully cultivated, robust republicanism. I despise the very idea of royalty. Whether profane or sacred, whether their kingdom is state, church, or heaven, I do not like kings. My disposition makes me unusual in the Black Church where a neo-Pentecostalism dominates, making the loudness of one's celebration and the ostentation of one's gestures an index of authentic Christianity. In that context, I am an oddball, a misfit, a coldwater fish in a hot tub. I stick out like a sore thumb, a "hard on," an inflamed pimple on someone's ass. Yet, like shoes that are too big or, more to the point, like a monk at a bacchanal this misfit is who I am. Undoubtedly, there is hyperbole in this description. My fellow congregants might say that I exaggerate and that their objective observations of me do not confirm my subjective self-description. Their observations, no doubt, would be true. Nevertheless, this description does capture my subjective relation to myself as a participant in the worship services of the Black Church. It is subjectively true.

★   ★   ★

> There is such a thing as faith in intelligence becoming religious in quality—a fact that perhaps explains the efforts of some religionists to disparage the possibilities of intelligence as a force. They properly feel such faith to be a dangerous rival.
>
> John Dewey[2]

"If you're been saved, you oughta feel somethin', you oughta shout sometime!" The preacher regards me with the anxiety of a comedian "hung out to dry" by a tough audience: they are not laughing, Bill is not shouting. Something is obviously wrong. I should be "filled with the spirit" and "getting happy," but I am not. The preacher is observant. He knows when a "dog won't hunt" and when a sermonic tactic "won't preach" and so he tries another tactic, a conjuring trick that preachers use when they run out of anything to say: he makes fun of my "ejumacation." This is a time-honored tactic in the Black Church where the college-educated do not predominate and intellectual inquiry is not the ideological norm. Former vice president Spiro Agnew has nothing on the Black Church when it comes to suspicion of intellectuals.

The *Anti-Intellectualism in American Life* (1963) that Richard Hofstadler wrote about lives and thrives in the Black Church. "Egg heads" and "pointy headed" intellectuals are suspect in a religious context that posits an inverse relationship between knowledge and faith. After all, does scripture not say that god uses the base things of the world to confound the wise? The preacher circles me intently like a great bird of prey, reconnoitering, poking, prodding, and looking for an opening, a way to attack. Soon he tires of the hunt, concludes that Bill is a tough case, "special" in the condescending way that we describe others as special. As in the nature programs that one sees on television, the preacher loses interest in the prey.

I live on the border of the Black Church, in a twilight zone of sacred space and profane space, in a permanent liminality. There is much in the church that makes me nauseous; my stomach can tolerate the church only in small homeopathic doses. Too much church poisons. But in small doses, it provides medicine for my soul. Better than psychotherapy, drugs, or sex, it is certainly better than anybody's chicken soup! The church both poisons and cures. I am a witness to its seductive powers and affects. Thus I am bound to the church and to its double work of poisoning and curing by a many-stranded cable of ambivalence: in the church but not of it, of the church but spending most of my time on the threshold of entering or leaving. Yet, sometimes I find it necessary to be there. The church is a beautiful, sublime, ugly, and grotesque work of art. To riff on Lerone Bennett Jr.'s description of black peoples' attitude toward America, I love the church with a love that is full of hate and hate the church with a hate that is full of love.[3] Love and hate: for me, it does not get any better or worse.

★   ★   ★

> Religion and poetry are identical in essence, and differ merely in the way in which they attach to practical affairs. Poetry is called religion when it intervenes in life, and religion, when it merely supervenes upon life, is seen to be nothing but poetry.
>
> George Santayana[4]

As Pierce and Dewey knew, propositional beliefs are overrated. Beliefs are important when they produce habitual forms of behavior. Whether a Jerry Falwell or a Christopher Hitchens, fundamentalists of all kinds, those who idealize, absolutize, or otherwise reduce a religious tradition to a text do not understand this fact. In *The Problem of Christianity*

(1913), Josiah Royce poses a famous question: "In what sense, if any, can the modern man consistently be, in creed, a Christian?"[5] To a remarkable degree, is my answer, if the thoroughly "artistic," arti-factual, and artificial nature of the Christian creed is acknowledged. Creeds are products of the human imagination: "true fictions" that sometimes help us flourish. If this is true, then prayer, to use Santayana's language is a "soliloquy," the act of whispering in our own ears. As Hamlet might have said, "To pray or not to pray that is the question." I am deeply moved by prayer as a form of spiritual discipline. (Don't get nervous. "Spirit" is wholly natural, a capacity of the body, arising, like all human capacities, from the evolutionary history of our spe-cies. There is nothing spooky about it, anymore than energy is matter's ghost.) The blue notes especially move me. To paraphrase Emerson, sometimes a cry, shout, or moan is better than a thesis, sermon, or explication of sacred doctrine. During prayer I enter deeply into myself through intense concentration, surveying and making judgments about my character. My ego diminishes as my empathy with others expands, as their cries and pain become mine and mine become theirs. I do not pray—where prayer is understood as praising, beseeching, or confess-ing to a superhuman Other—but I do meditate, fast, and offer libations to the "spirits." And I try very hard, with modest success, to live with compassion for others.

Religion overlaps and transacts with various domains of spirit. This domain includes art, drugs, sports, and violence, experiences that grab, lift, and transport us to another place. Sex occupies a huge part of the spiritual terrain. Sexuality is both a rich source of religious metaphors and an object of religious anxiety, regulation, and taboo. Sex and vio-lence are two forms of spirit that religious traditions try desperately to repress, co-opt, or otherwise master. In that light, I suggest that the extensive moralization of sex epitomized by the notion of "lusting in one's heart" (as opposed to the ethical-prudential regulation of sex) is absurd. My sexual ethic is minimalist, containing only two principal moral "oughts": (1) there ought to be mutuality and (2) there ought to be an appropriate, minimal age of consent. All other principles are derivative.[6] Like sex, violence is so seductive that the sexualization of violence (think Janjuweed and Abu Ghraib, or any gross asymmetry of power) is a major problem. As some observers—Girard, Fanon, and the author of the biblical *Apocalypse*—suggest, violence is a cleansing and therapeutic power. I believe that the desire for violent decontamina-tion and therapy is irremediable. The gods love blood. They demand and consecrate violence; patriotism celebrates violence, and it fuels our entertainment, revealing, perhaps, our deep fantasies. Though usually evil, violence is occasionally a tragic necessity. To put this ugly truth in the crudest terms, some people—"us" and/or "them," on relatively rare but unavoidable occasions—must be killed. Some people (and goods) must be crushed so others can thrive. There is no noncontroversial way to kill; injustices will occur, regret is irremediable. This is the human condition.

Though we may disagree about its contours and details, religion encompasses activities in which people express their very best qualities and their very worse. *Religion is adverbial; it intensifies our propensities to do both good and evil.* Its ethical and political importance is manifest. That students are curious about the commitments of their professors, especially in religion studies should not surprise us. With good reason, students assume that our commitments are relevant to what we teach and how we teach it. I respond to such questions evasively. When that does not work, I explain that a "belief" is *a disposition to act in particular ways; beliefs disconnected from behaviors are empty.* Were I to describe my religious commitments in creedal terms, I would begin with the following qualification: I have "naïve" or first-order views and views about my views that are "sophisticated," second-order, or metaphilosophical. In my metaphilosophical view, creeds are artifacts of the human imagination; its most cherished objects have no independent reality. As a naïve believer, I'm a Unitarian Christian. I belong to the repressed, underside of Christianity, to a side—there are many Christianities—that lost. Arius and his descendants whom the dominant church calls "heretics" are my coreligionists. This is my dominant mood. But there are other moods as well where the Trinitarian God whispers in my ear. How crazy is that? Like Montanus, I hear the Holy Spirit speaking directly to me, qualifying, resignifying, and even superseding anything written in a sacred text or anything that my church or tradition might hold as true. Why bow and scrape before a sacred text, written thousands of years ago, when god speaks directly to you, here and now? In my arrogant-Emersonian view, god speaks to me now the way he spoke to Abraham then. How crazy is that? And sometimes I hear the voices of three hundred and sixty five gods, one for every day of the year. After all, didn't Emerson say that the days are gods? How crazy is that?

To put a finer point on things, I believe in god and in nature, which are the same reality under different descriptions. I believe in the devil and all his demonic minions. As a jurist might say, they are "on all fours" with god and human nature. (*Stated otherwise, god and devil—the Dao and Nirvana, for that matter—are products of the human imagination.*)

I believe in Allah, the Cosmic Buddha, the Christian god, Damballah, Eshu-Elegbara, the Great Rainbow Serpent, Olorun, Vishnu and all his avatars. I believe in the Hebrew god identified by the Tetragrammaton YHWH and in any other god or goddess in whom anyone has ever believed. I believe they are the same, *that is,* they are our collective "will and idea," objective manifestations of our highest or lowest subjectivity, our idealized father image transferred writ large onto the cosmos as "Big Daddy," or the primordial, prelinguistic "memory" of mother, our first object-relation and love-object. In short, the gods are creatures and we are their creators. As wonderful characters in a tragicomedy that we write, gods are our national, ethnic, racial, gender, and other group identities and loyalties *deified.* Gods are the phenomenology of our deepest hopes and greatest fears, our darkest resentment and most heartfelt gratitude. They are the way that our best and worst qualities appear to us, as if they were objective, external, and other than us. By creating gods, we give our acts—of exalting and debasing, explaining and mystifying, rewarding and punishing, terrorizing and comforting—cosmic support. If only flatfooted, neo-atheists acquired an arch by understanding this fact, then they would be able to walk around this issue more deftly, understanding that the gods—the "many" and the "one"—are the "cunning of our imagination." The gods give life charm, beauty, goodness, and joy. They also make life disgusting, ugly, bad, and sorrowful. We create the gods and they eat us alive. Like metaphor, such cunning is irremediable. Accordingly, gods are our ideals "alive and kicking" and at the point of death, at the extremes of good and evil, but mainly in the moderate and mediocre middle. Gods are the way that our natural environs, earth and sky, appear to us. Gods are a mirror into which we look darkly. Gods are US. We create gods (the "one" and the "many," the "one true god" and all the "false" gods) just as surely as birds build nests, bees make honey, and spiders spin webs of beauty and death. Adaptation, beauty, and death: my philosophy of religion in a nutshell.

Above all, I believe in Earth, the Great Cannibal-Mother Goddess[7] who gives us life and takes it away.

★ ★ ★

Of course, acknowledgement that we do not know what we do not know is a necessity of all intellectual integrity.... We doubt in order than we may find out, not because some inaccessible supernatural lurks behind whatever *we* can know.

The things in civilization we most prize are not of ourselves. They exist by the grace of things and sufferings of the continuous human community in which we are a link. Ours is the responsibility of conserving, transmitting, rectifying and expanding the heritage of values we have receive that those who come after us may receive it more solid and secure, more widely accessible and generously shared than we have received it. Here are all the elements of a religious faith that shall not be confined to sect, class, or race. Such a faith has always been implicitly the common faith of mankind. It remains to make it explicit and militant.

John Dewey[8]

Religion—abstracting from the many religions—provides a place to nest. (Gods—nasty, naughty, and nice—are imaginary companions in the nest.) Religion is a grand conceptual and behavioral tool, an adaptation that helps us cope with anxieties around mortality and morbidity, expressing our deepest hopes and fears in the face of impermanence, ignorance, and irremediable insecurity. But religion is more than that. A school of virtue and of vice, it has become a way of life, inspiring art, science, and ethics, genocidal warfare, and playfulness. Though counterintuitive, one might think of the art and artifice of religion by analogy to the automobile, which as a tool for getting us from one place to another in a time-efficient manner has ramified into a way of life, informing the way we play, inspiring our art-aesthetic, art-technological, even our art-legal and commercial imaginations. Humans are "artists" by nature. We imagine and create. We survive through our talents as artificers: manipulating our environments, adjusting as we must to realities that resist our efforts. In this technical sense (of art, artifice, and "artificial"), humans are "religious by nature."

"Gods"
THOUGHT of the infinite—the All!
Be thou my God.

Lover divine and perfect Comrade,
Waiting content, invisible yet, but certain,
Be thou my God.

Thou, thou, the Ideal Man,
Fair, able, beautiful, content, and loving,
Complete in body and dilate in spirit,
Be thou my God.

O Death, (for Life has served its turn,)
Opener and usher to the heavenly mansion,
Be thou my God.

Aught, aught of mightiest, best I see, conceive, or know,
(To break the stagnant tie—thee, thee to free, O soul,)
Be thou my God.

All great ideas, the races' aspirations,
All heroisms, deeds of rapt enthusiasts,
Be ye my Gods.

Or Time and Space,
Or shape of Earth divine and wondrous,
Or some fair shape I viewing, worship,
Or lustrous orb of sun or star by night,
Be ye my Gods.
(Walt Whitman, *Leaves of Grass*)

[E]very god has a devil for a father.
(Friedrich Nietzsche)[9]

Plus a woman and a man for grandparents!
(William David Hart)

NOTES

One Afro-*Eccentricity* and Autobiography

1. Jan's birth name is Janice Dean Willis. She goes by "Jan," which I use throughout the text.
2. Both Rorty and Derrida criticize the claim that the subject (including the autobiographer) has a privileged access to his own thoughts. See R. Rorty, *Philosophy and the Mirror of Nature* (Princeton, NJ: Princeton University Press, 1981) and J. Derrida, *Writing and Difference,* trans. Alan Bass (Chicago: University of Chicago Press, 1980).
3. J. Olney, *Metaphors of Self: The Meaning of Autobiography* (Princeton University Press, 1972), 37.
4. R. White, "Autobiography against Itself," *Philosophy Today* 35, no. 3/4 (1991): 297.
5. P. Ricoeur, "Narrative Identity," trans. Mark S. Muldoon. *Philosophy Today* (Spring 1991): 73.
6. Ricoeur, 80.
7. R. Porter and H. R. Wolf, *The Voice within: Reading and Writing Autobiography* (New York: Alfred Knopf, 1973), 4–5.
8. H. L. Gates, ed., *Bearing Witness: Selections from African-American Autobiography in the Twentieth Century* (New York: Pantheon, 1991), 4.
9. J. D. Barbour, "Character and Characterization in Religious Autobiography" *Journal of the American Academy of Religion* 55, no. 2 (2001): 307–27.
10. Barbour, 306.
11. Barbour, 309.
12. Barbour, 310–11.
13. Barbour, 312.
14. Barbour, 313.
15. Barbour, 314.
16. Barbour, 314, 316.
17. J. Willis, *Dreaming Me: From Baptist to Buddhist, One Woman's Spiritual Journey* (New York: Riverhead, 2001), 165.
18. Barbour, 313, 316.
19. Barbour, 317–18.
20. Barbour, 324.
21. T. Parsons, ed., *Max Weber: The Theory of Social and Economic Organizations* (New York: Free Press, 1964), 154.
22. W. E. B. DuBois, *The Souls of Black Folks* (New York: W. W. Norton & Company, 1999), 123–9.
23. C. West, *Prophesy Deliverance!* (Philadelphia: Westminster Press), 5–6.
24. DuBois, 123–9.

206 Notes

25. W. E. B. DuBois, *The Negro Church: Report of a Social Study Made under the Direction of Atlanta University; together with the proceedings of the Eighth Conference for the Study of the Negro Problems* (Atlanta: Atlanta University Press, 1903).

26. Two rich studies—A. Raboteau, *Slave Religion: The Invisible Institution in the Antebellum South* (New York: Oxford University Press, 1978) and T. Smith, *Conjuring Culture: Biblical Formations of Black America* (New York: Oxford University Press, 1994)—exceed the limitations of the Standard Narrative.

27. See B. Lincoln, "Theses on Method," *Method & Theory in the Study of Religion* 8 (1996): 225–7.

28. N. J. Delong-Bas, *Wahhabi Islam: From Revival and Reform to Globanl Jihad* (New York: Oxford University Press, 2004), 260.

29. D. Gallen and C. Carson, *Malcolm X: The FBI File* (New York: Carroll & Graf Publishers, 1991), 30.

30. See *Black Protest Thought in the Twentieth Century*, ed. A. Meier, E. Rudwick, and F. L. Broderick (Indianapolis: Bobbs-Merrill, 1971), 469–84.

Part One   The Spiritual Journey of Malcolm X

1. The first three quotations are from G. Breitman, ed. *Malcolm X Speaks: Selected Statements* (New York: Grove Weidenfeld, 1965), 7–8, 126, 148. The fourth quote is from B. Perry, ed. *Malcolm X: The Last Speeches* (New York: Pathfinder Press, 1989), 156.

Two   Jahiliyyah and Jihad

1. See R. J. Rickford, *Betty Shabazz* (Naperville, IL: Sourcebooks, 2003), 14.

2. In his *Autobiography*, Malcolm X describes his father as a Baptist minister and a dedicated organizer for Marcus Garvey's Universal Negro Improvement Association (AMX 3). There is a lot of disagreement on this point. See Jan Carew, *Ghosts in Our Blood: With Malcolm X in Africa, England, and the Caribbean* (Chicago: Lawrence Hill Books, 1994), x. Also see L. A. DeCaro, *On the Side of My People: A Religious Life of Malcolm X* (New York: New York University Press, 1996).

3. S. Freud, *Future of an Illusion,* trans. James Strachey (New York: W. W. Norton, 1961), 24.

4. B. Perry, *Malcolm X: The Life of a Man Who Changed Black America* (Barrytown, NY: Station Hill Press, 1991), 3, 5–6. In his semihagiography of his uncle, *Seventh Child: A Family Memoir of Malcolm X* (Secaucus, NJ: Carol Publishing Group, 1998), R. P. Collins, the son of Malcolm's older half sister Ella, does not mention his grandfather's abuse; nor does Malcolm's third daughter, Ilyasah Shabazz. See I. Shabazz, *Growing Up X: A Memoir by the Daughter of Malcolm X* (New York: One World/Ballantine, 2002).

5. Perry, 8, 11. Perry's biography is controversial. For two strong critiques, see L. A. DeCaro, 298–9 and Bill Yousman, "Who Owns Identity? Malcolm X, Representation, and the Struggle over Meaning," *Communication Quarterly* 49 (2001): 1–18. http: //web4.infotrac (last accessed on December 24, 2007). I agree with the critics of Perry as far as his jaundiced reading of Malcolm's significance is concerned. He seems hell-bent on undermining Malcolm's importance as a political figure and gives scant attention to his religious significance. In this regard I think that Perry is an unreliable guide. On the other hand, the scope of his research and his often insightful analyses cannot be denied. I rely on Perry for biographical information and psychological insights not for ethical-political analysis.

6. When I first wrote this Freudian, primal horde account of Malcolm's relation to his father, I was not aware of a similar account by Eugene Victor Wolfenstein. See E. V. Wolfenstein,

The Victims of Democracy: Malcolm X and the Black Revolution (Berkeley: University of California Press, 1981), 94–6.

7. S. Freud, *Totem and Taboo,* trans. A. A. Brill (New York: Vintage Books, 1918), 170–1, 181–9.

8. Perry, 12–13.

9. Perry, 13.

10. DeCaro tries to impugn the legitimacy of Earl Little's Baptist faith by suggesting that it was merely cover for his Garveyism. I disagree. The complex relations between New Yoruba traditions of Orisha worship, such as Santeria, and Catholicism is a better model for understanding the relation between black Christianity and the religion of Garveyism. Here as elsewhere in his account, DeCaro's evangelical, pseudoscholarly notion of "orthodoxy" undermines his analysis. See DeCaro, *On the Side of My People: A Religious Life of Malcolm X,* chapter 4: "Early Life and Religious Training."

11. After Earl's death, she would join a splinter group (sect) of the Adventist church known as the Seventh Day Church of God. See Perry, 21.

12. Perry, 12.

13. Object Relations is a psychoanalytic theory that privileges relationships over instinctual drives. This theory holds that "the early formation and differentiation of psychological structures (inner images of the self and the other, or object)" are crucial to the development of self and that these inner structures are evident in interpersonal relations. The mother is an especially important "object" within this theory. A healthy object relationship with the mother, specifically, with her breast is the basis of all relationships. See M. St. Clair, *Object Relations and Self-Psychology: An Introduction* (Belmont, CA: Wadsworth, 1986), 2, 10, 42, 74.

14. Carew, x.

15. Carew, *ix.*

16. Carew, 6.

17. Color appears to have been a major issue in Malcolm's life. According to Perry, he appears to have been racially marginal: "A loner, he mixed infrequently with pupils of either race." In Lansing, blacks were no more accepting of him than whites had been in Mason. I think that Perry's interpretation betrays his relative ignorance of color dynamics among black Americans. Malcolm's light skin color was as likely a badge of pride and source of envy as a cause of marginality. See Perry, 4–5, 16, 32, 40.

18. Perry, 24.

19. Perry, 18.

20. Perry, 31.

21. See DeCaro, 67–8.

22. See Cornel West, *Prophetic Fragments* (Trenton, NJ: Africa World Press, 1990), 43.

23. There are significant differences between historical memory, which relatively speaking is disciplined, orderly, and logical and autobiographical memory, which is not. See D. C. Rubin, ed., *Remembering Our Past: Studies in Autobiographical Memory* (New York: Cambridge University Press, 1995).

24. Indeed, Louis X a.k.a. Louis Farrakhan had written a popular Nation of Islam song in 1958 entitled: "White Man's Heaven is a Black Man's Hell." See V. L. White, Jr., *Inside the Nation of Islam* (Gainesville: University of Florida, 2001), 40.

25. See A. H. Fauset, *Black Gods of the Metropolis* (Philadelphia: University of Pennsylvania Press, 2001) and H. Brotz, *Black Jews of Harlem* (Knopf Publishing Group, 1998).

26. Like other sectarian forms of religion, Christian, Islamic, and Jewish, Pentecostalism emerged in the big city, among the lower socioeconomic classes. "Sect" like "cult" is a technical term in religion study; used properly, it is neither normative nor invidious. To call a group sectarian or cultic is only to say, respectively, that it has splintered from another religious group or that it, like the primitive Jesus movement, has a charismatic leader at its

center. Many readers of Malcolm's autobiography do not properly distinguish between the scholarly and the popular uses of these terms, especially "cult," which in popular usage carries an invidious significance. Pentecostalism has long since transcended its early status as a sect, and is now, perhaps, both institutionally and transinstitutionally, the most important movement within Christianity worldwide.

27. Conjure is the residual presence of the "African sacred cosmos" in the cultural practices of black Americans.

28. According to Perry: "Neither Ella nor Earl was as dark as Malcolm claimed. His insistence that they were was indicative of the way he equated blackness with the strength his light-skinned mother had lacked." Perry, 42.

29. Perry, 70.

30. DeCaro, 71.

31. Perry, 87.

32. Perry, 50.

33. DeCaro, 71. In his earlier, more comprehensive, but thoroughly controversial biography, Bruce Perry takes Malcolm's claim of having been run out of Harlem at face value. He suggests that it was Malcolm who had trouble acknowledging this fact. See Perry, 89.

34. Transcribed from The American Experience, "Malcolm X: Make It Plain" part I. (© 1994 WGBH, Boston, MA and Blackside. Distributed by PBS VIDEO).

35. Fanon refers to Hegel's famous "master-slave" dialectic as well as his account of self-consciousness and the role that mutual recognition plays in the process. Fanon questions the adequacy of the account and its inability to account for the psychopathological depths of white supremacy. See G. W. F. Hegel, *Hegel's Phenomenology of Spirit* (New York: Oxford University Press, 1977), 111–19.

36. F. Fanon, *Black Skin, White Masks* (New York: Grove Press, 1967), 63.

37. Malcolm's relationship with Sophia occurred in the 1940s. By the late 1940s, lynching was nowhere near the cataclysm it had been when [Ida B.] Wells had begun her antilynching campaign. See P. Dray, *At the Hands of Persons Unknown: The Lynching of Black America* (New York: The Modern Library, 2003), 406.

38. See S. Cotta, *Why Violence? A Philosophical Interpretation* (Gainesville: University Press of Florida, 1985), 59.

39. My comments have nothing to do with whom Malcolm ought to have desired or loved. We desire whom we desire and love whom we love. My comments go to the construction of his desires and his level of self-knowledge.

40. Perry, 77–8. Perry writes: "Like a prostitute, he sold himself, as if the best he had to offer was his body" (83.). This aspect of Perry's analysis seems to especially vex DeCaro, 65.

41. See http://www.afro-netizen.com/2005/05/malcolm_x_gay_b.html, http://www.guardian.co.uk/g2/story/0,3604,1486997,00.html, http://www.marclamonthill.com/mlhblog/?p=424 (last accessed on December 27, 2007).

42. The gun was not loaded, AMX, 478.

43. C. Cullen, *The Black Christ and Other Poems* (New York: Harper & Brothers, 1929), 83.

44. W. R. Jones, *Is God a White Racist?: A Preamble to Black Theology* (Boston: Beacon Press, 1998), 28–36.

45. Cullen, 84.

46. DeCaro, 78.

47. R. L. Wilken, *The Christians as the Romans Saw Them* (New Haven: Yale University Press, 1984), 53, 55–6, 58–62, 66, 201.

48. R. King, *Orientalism and Religion* (London: Routledge, 1999), 35–9.

49. "Accuser" is one of Satan's names.

50. Malcolm was imprisoned for six and a half years: February 1946 to August 1952. Why he claims eleven years of incarceration is unclear.

51. DeCaro, 78.

52. For a similar view, see V. Harvey, *Feuerbach and the Interpretation of Religion* (Cambridge University Press, 1995).

53. G. E. Kessler, *Studying Religion: An Introduction through Cases* (Boston: McGraw-Hill Higher Education, 2003), 86, 89.

54. C. Holmes, "Women: Witnesses and Witches," *Past & Present*, no. 140 (1993): 45–78.

55. For Fanon's comments on the Devil as a black man, see F. Fanon, *Black Skin, White Masks* (New York: Grove Press, 1967), 146, 167, 188–190.

56. J. B. Russell, *Satan: The Early Christian Tradition* (Ithaca: Cornell University Press, 1981), 40, 45, 62, 170, 173, 190.

57. R. E. Hall, "Cutaneo-Chroma (skin color) as Post-Colonial Hierarchy: A Global Strategy for Conflict Resolution," IFE PsychologIA 9, no. 3 (2001): 139–152.

58. M. Rudwin, *The Devil in Legend and Literature* (La Salle, IL: Open Court Publishing Company, 1931), 45. Rudwin quotes a passage from Anatole's autobiography in which his daughter describes the Devil as a nigger (119). Also see Teresa of Avila who describes the Devil as a "hideous little Negro." See *The Life of Saint Teresa of Avila by Herself* (London: Penguin Books, 1957), 222.

59. The demonization of black people is not only a white problem but is also multiracial. See R. E. Hall, 139–152.

60. See T. Harris, *Exorcising Blackness: Historical and Literary Lynching and Burning Rituals* (Bloomington: Indiana University Press, 1984) and O. Patterson, *Rituals of Blood: Consequences of Slavery in Two American Centuries* (Washington, DC: Civitas/CounterPoint, 1998).

61. Malcolm's Nation of Islam demonology is heir to the Jewish and Christian traditions of demonization that E. Pagels describes in *The Origins of Satan* (New York: Random House, 1995).

62. C. H. Johnson, ed., *God Struck Me Dead: Religious Conversion Experiences and Autobiographies of Ex-slaves* (Philadelphia: Pilgrims' Press, 1969), 59.

63. See W. Proudfoot, *Religious Experience* (Berkeley: University of California Press, 1985), 122–4, 188, 224–5.

64. See M. C. Taylor, ed. *Critical Terms for Religious Studies* (Chicago: University of Chicago Press, 1998), 334.

65. Taylor, 335.

66. T. K. Beal, *Religion and its Monsters* (New York: Routledge, 2002), 17.

67. Taylor, 337.

68. Taylor, 338.

69. J. S. Strong, *The Buddha: A Short Biography* (Oxford, UK: Oneworld, 2001), 52–4, 60, 63, 65–6. Also see K. Armstrong, *Buddha* (New York: Penguin Putnam, 2001), 66–97, and R. A. Mitchell, *The Buddha: His Life Retold* (New York: Paragon House, 1989), 32–47.

70. Strong, 67–76.

71. J. Esposito, *Islam: The Straight Path* (New York: Oxford University Press, 1991), 8.

72. Watt, Montgomery W., *Islamic Philosophy and Theology* (Edinburgh: Edinburgh University Press, 1985), 10.

73. The muezzin calls Muslims to prayer.

74. According to Perry, Malcolm claimed to trust Betty 75 percent. Perry, 190.

75. See J. Cone, *A Black Theology of Liberation* (Philadelphia: J. B. Lipincott, 1970), 199.

76. T. Khalidi, *The Muslim Jesus* (Cambridge, MA: Harvard University Press, 2001), 9–14.

77. Khalidi, 26, 34.

78. Transcribed from The American Experience, "Malcolm X: Make It Plain" part I. (© 1994 WGBH, Boston, MA and Blackside. Distributed by PBS VIDEO).

79. Gallen and Carson, 243.

Three   *Hijrah* and *Hajj*

1. S. H. Nasa, *Islamic Spirituality: Foundations* (New York: Crossroad, 1987), 120.
2. "Ho" is Black English for "whore." However, anyone who gets used is a "ho" and those who use them are hustlers, pimps, or players.
3. While each man respected the other, Wallace and Malcolm were as much rivals as friends. See Perry, 365.
4. See J. L. Esposito, ed., *The Oxford History of Islam* (New York: Oxford University Press, 1999), 77–86.
5. For a description of this tradition of using Biblical figures and metaphors in appealing for justice for black people, see D. Howard-Pitney's *Afro-American Jeremiad* (Philadelphia: Temple University Press, 1993).
6. According to Perry, Malcolm knew about the slave-trading history of Arabs. Indeed, he had used this knowledge to deflect criticism of the Nation of Islam by Arab Muslims. He charged that Arab Muslims were just as guilty of enslaving black people as European Christians. We must assume that he ignored Muslim complicity in the slave trade for strategic reasons. See Perry, 268. For an informative account of Arab-Islamic slave trading, see Ronald Segal's *Islam's Black Slaves* (New York: Farrar, Strauss and Giroux, 2001).
7. C. Fluehr-Lobban, *Islamic Society in Practice* (Gainesville: University of Gainesville Press, 1994), 101–2.
8. See R. Segal, *Islam's Black Slaves: The Other Black Diaspora* (Hill and Wang, 2002).
9. See http://www.archives.state.al.us/govs_list/inauguralspeech.html (last accessed on December 27, 2007), George Wallace's 1963 gubernatorial, inaugural address
10. Theophus Smith, *Conjuring Culture: Biblical Formations of Black Identity* (New York: Oxford University Press, 1994), 67.
11. Smith, 58, 62–3, 65–6.
12. See *David Walker's Appeal* (New York: Farrar, Straus and Giroux, 1995).
13. Smith, 238–40.
14. Perry, 214, 225.
15. Gallen and Carson, 125.
16. Gallen and Carson, 95.
17. The State Department, CIA, and various military agencies also place Malcolm under surveillance. See Perry, 324–5.
18. Gallen and Carson, 97.
19. Gallen and Carson, 100.
20. http://foia.fbi.gov/malcolmx/malcolmx1.pdf, 35.
21. http://foia.fbi.gov/malcolmx/malcolmx1.pdf, 72.
22. http://foia.fbi.gov/malcolmx/malcolmx1.pdf, 69–70.
23. http://foia.fbi.gov/malcolmx/malcolmx1.pdf, 36.
24. http://foia.fbi.gov/malcolmx/malcolmx1.pdf, 38.
25. http://foia.fbi.gov/malcolmx/malcolmx1.pdf, 39.
26. http://foia.fbi.gov/malcolmx/malcolmx1.pdf, 42 (last accessed on December 27, 2007).
27. Gallen and Carson, 225.
28. E. E. Curtis, *Islam in Black America* (Albany: State University of New York Press, 2002), 103–4, claims that Malcolm was not successful in integrating his religious commitments as a Muslim with his political commitments as a Pan-Africanist.
29. Curtis, 110–11.
30. Curtis, 111.
31. Perry, 233–4.
32. Rondell P. Collins, *Seventh Child: A Family Memoir of Malcolm X* (Secaucus, NJ: Carol Publishing, 1998), 135.

33. Collins, 136.
34. If we have any doubts about the strictness of Malcolm's religious commitments, consider the following: "As an Islamic leader, Malcolm's personal routine was uncompromising. For example, his dietary regimen rigidly followed Elijah's laws; he ate only one meal a day, fasted several times during the month, and did not chew gum or eat snacks between meals. His views on entertainment, women, and general sporting activities had also changed from the days when he was a thief, pimp, and dope user. He refused to go to dances and parties, frowned on sporting events as activities only for the enjoyment of whites, and perceived women as liars who used their bodies to exploit men of leadership. His views were fixed and extreme. Nonetheless, he expected all Muslims, especially in Boston, to adhere to his views. Malcolm's uniqueness made him an exotic and strange figure among people in the black community. However, it was Malcolm's social, political, and religious language that caused the greatest stir." See V. L. White, Jr., *Inside the Nation of Islam* (Gainesville: University of Florida, 2001), 36–7.
35. Collins, 160.
36. Collins, 160.
37. Collins, 162.
38. Collins, 162–3.
39. Bruce, 344.
40. Perry, 365.
41. Transcribed from The American Experience, "Malcolm X: Make It Plain" part I. (© 1994 WGBH, Boston, MA and Blackside, Inc. Distributed by PBS VIDEO).
42. C. E. Marsh, *From Black Muslims to Muslims* (Metuchen, NJ: Scarecrow Press, 1984), 112, 118.
43. Marsh, 118, 119.
44. J. Baxter and Jefri Aalmuhammed's film documentary, *BrotherMinister* (© BrotherMinister 1997). This film contains an extended clip from Louis Farrakhan's 1993 Savior's Day speech. The words from the epigraph are transcribed from that speech, which renewed the controversy surrounding the assassination of Malcolm X and the role that Louis Farrakhan may have played.
45. Shabazz, 9.
46. I have sought without success to corroborate this claim.
47. O. Davis, "Our Shining Black Prince." A eulogy delivered at the Funeral of Malcolm X, at Faith Temple Church of God, February 27, 1965. http://www.hartford-hwp.com/archives/45a/071.html (last accessed on December 27, 2007).
48. T. Insoll, *The Archaeology of Islam* (Oxford, UK: Blackwell Publishers, 1999), 176–7, 180, 183–6.
49. G. Orwell, *Shooting an Elephant, and Other Essays* (New York: Harcourt Brace, 1950), 171.
50. D. Chidester, *Patterns of Transcendence* (Belmont, CA: Wadsworth Publishing Co., 1990), 206–8.
51. J. Ashton and T. Whyte, *The Quest for Paradise: Visions of Heaven and Eternity in the World's Myths and Religions* (New York: HarperSanFrancisco, 2001), 95.
52. Chidester, 206–8.
53. K. Holloway, *Passed On: African American Mourning Stories* (Durham: Duke University Press, 2002), 207–9.

Part Two   The Spiritual Children of Malcolm X

1. See A. Rampersad, *Ralph Ellison: A Biography* (New York: Alfred Knopf, 2007).

Four   Julius Lester: Blackness and *Teshuvah*

1. J. Eisenberg and E. Scolnic, eds., *The JPS Dictionary of Jewish Words* (Philadelphia: Jewish Publication Society, 2001 * 5761), 164.
2. See J. Lester, *All is Well* (New York: William Morrow, 1976).
3. For a fascinating account of the way that boredom in contrast to Lester's claim can spur the religious imagination, see M. Raposa, *Boredom and the Religious Imagination* (Charlottesville and London; University of Virginia Press, 1999).
4. I have my doubts. On the other hand, Robert Cole suggests that young children may be more spiritually sophisticated than we imagine. See R. Cole, *Spiritual Life of Children* (Boston: Houghton Mifflin Company, 1991).
5. John Lewis, former head of the Student Nonviolent Coordinating Committee (SNCC), more or less confirms Lester's account of his role in the movement. See J. Lewis and M. D'orso, *Walking with the Wind: A Memoir of the Movement* (New York: Simon and Schuster, 1998), 394.
6. See J. A. Gordon, *Why They Can't Wait: A Critique of Black-Jewish Conflict over Community Control in Ocean Hill-Brownsville (1967–1971)* (New York: RoutledgeFalmer, 2001) for an insightful analysis.
7. See P. Chesler, *The New Anti-Semitism: The Current Crisis and What We Must Do about It* (San Francisco: Jossey-Bass, 2003), 78.
8. See F. Jameson, "The Vanishing Mediator: Narrative Structure in Max Weber," *Working Papers in Cultural Studies* 5 (1973): 111–49.
9. Kessler, 171.
10. Willis, 199.
11. Julius refers here to the Lakota Sioux's concept of "Wakan Tanka." According to Gary Kessler, "Wakan Tanka is better translated as 'Great Mysteriousness.' It is a collective name for a number of different '*wakan* (powerful and sacred) beings.'" See Kessler, 10. In a comment that seems apropos of Julius, Kessler adds: "To identify Wakan Tanka with the monotheistic god of nonnative religious traditions obscures important and instructive differences."
12. Compare Julius' statement with Emerson's famous claim: "I am God in nature; I am a weed by the wall." R. W. Emerson, "Circles" in *Emerson: Essays and Lectures* (New York: The Library of America, 1983), 406.
13. See T. Fitzgerald, *The Ideology of Religious Studies* (New York: Oxford University Press, 2003).
14. See M. S. Smith, *The Early History of God: Yahweh and Other Deities in Ancient Israel* (Grand Rapids, MI: Wm. B. Eerdmans, 2002).
15. *Totem and Taboo: Resemblances between the Psychic Lives of Savages and Neurotics*, trans. A. A. Brill (London: G. Routledge & Sons, limited, 1919). The subtitle of the book says all you need to know on this point.
16. See M. Torgovnick, *Primitive Passions: Men, Women, and the Quest for Ecstasy* (New York: Alfred Knopf, 1997).
17. For the sad case of an African man from the Congo who was displayed to white audiences in a cage along side "other" animals, see P. V. Bradford, *Ota Benga: The Pygmy in the Zoo* (New York : St. Martin's Press, 1992). Zoo officials placed him somewhere between monkey and man on the great chain of being. In fact, he was part of the Monkey House exhibit at the Bronx Zoo. Born in the Congo region of Central Africa in 1883, he committed suicide on March 20, 1916.
18. See Lester, 301, 307, 312.
19. Lester, 318.
20. Lester acknowledges this point elsewhere. See J. Lester, "Blacks and Jews: Where Are We? Where Are We going?" in *Strangers and Neighbors: Relations between Blacks and Jews in the*

United States, ed. M. Adams and J. Bracey (Amherst: University of Massachusetts Press, 1999), 814–16.

21. J. Lester, *Look Out Whitey, Black Power's Gon' Get Your Mama!* (New York: The Dial Press, 1968), 137–8.

22. See A. Camus, *Neither Victims Nor Executioners*, trans. Dwight McDonald (Philadelphia: New Society publishers, 1986).

23. For an unflattering portrait of King, see Lester, *All Is Well*, 218–26. Julius refers repeatedly to King's empty eyes (219–20). Eyes are commonly regarded as windows to the soul, revealing what is deep and essential about a person. In Julius' view, Kings' eyes were blank, void of spirit, and lifeless. He contrasts King invidiously with Fidel Castro: "[W]ith Fidel, I felt no distance between us. His eyes were not empty. There was very definitely a person in those big-pocketed Cuban military fatigues. I had no problem imagining him in bed with his girlfriend" (223). During his first encounter with King, he claims to have fallen asleep twice while King was speaking (218). He encounters him a second time in the mid-1960s and refers to him derisively as Christ (218). He refers contemptuously to the "old-line nigger," bourgeois-style and bearing of King and his entourage, to the royal way that King reacted to subjects such as Bayard Rustin, and to Rustin's inappropriate familiarity with King (219). Is this a homophobic jab at Rustin? Like many people, Julius was moved by King's eloquence; behind the words, however, was only death. Or as Julius puts it: "I couldn't feel a living person there" (222). King, he continues, had many defects: "I knew that he wasn't a great leader, and that history may determine that Martin King was the worst thing that had happened to black people since Booker T. Washington" (222). In death Malcolm X looked like the "shining black prince" that Ossie Davis said he was; In contrast, King looked like a lynching victim. A victim all the more because, "[u]nlike Malcolm, he did not immerse his being in the soul of his people. Failing to do this, he was forever lost" (225). Julius implies that King was slavish. With a Nietzschean jab, Julius writes: "On Martin Luther King's tombstone are inscribed the words: 'Free at last! Free at last! Thank God Almighty! I'm free at last!' Those are strange words for an epitaph. They're appropriate for King, though. He *is* free now. Myths can live more easily when there is no person who has to represent the myth. He is free now and I'm glad. He suffered long enough" (226). The point of these citations is not that King is above this sort of critique or that what Julius says is not true. My only point is to illustrate Julius's sensibility. He claims that his Soul did not believe in the movement. I have my doubts.

24. Compare the logic of this passage, where Julius conflates Palestinian identity and the merit of the Palestinians' claims with acts of terrorism with Adolph Reed's critique of the logic underlying the notion of "Blackantisemitism." See A. Reed, "What Color is Anti-Semitism" in *Strangers and Neighbors: Relations between Blacks and Jews in the United States*, ed. M. Adams and J. Bracey (Amherst: University of Massachusetts Press, 1999), 26.

25. Julius' assumption that his status as a black Jew was distinctive if not unique did not emerge out of thin air. Rather, it is part of a long-standing cultural common sense. Katya Gibel Azoulay underscores this point in *Black, Jewish, and Interracial: It's Not the Color of Your Skin, but the "Race" of Your Kin and Other Myths of Identity* (Durham, NC: Duke University Press, 1997), where she offers the following commentary: "The dispersion of Jews across the globe produced a diaspora of people whose skin color ranges from dark African and Asian to the pale northern European Jews. Why, then, are those who are identifiably black seen as 'different' or 'unique' when they present themselves as Jewish?" (11). While exploring the complexities of Black, Jewish, and Interracial identities, Azoulay identifies three conditions for the possibility of Black, Jewish, and Interracial identities. First, the Supreme Court in *Loving v. Virginia* struck down laws prohibiting marriages between blacks and whites. The male plaintive in the case, Richard Loving, was Jewish. Thus the Court gave constitutional legitimation to the idea that Jews were white, even if their whiteness was of a different shade and of an inferior kind (54–5). The second condition of possibility

214 *Notes*

is black people's status in America as "the primary racial other" against which the same, the normal, the racially neutral, "unmarked," and unremarkable is defined (55). Third, "*the idea* of 'Black and Jewish,' as a specific and unique identity, results from the political activities of Jewish radicals, particularly in the labor movement of the 1930s and '40s, the Communist Party (CP) of the 1950s and, most important, the civil rights movement of the 1960s" (60).

26. See Matthew Jacobson, *Whiteness of a Different Color: European Immigrants and the Alchemy of Race* (Cambridge, MA: Harvard University Press, 1998), where Jacobson presents this complex issue as follows:

> "Are Jews white?" asks Sander Gilman. The question gets at the fundamental instability of Jewishness as a racial difference, but so does its wording fundamentally misstate the contours of whiteness in American political culture. From 1790 [with the passage of the "Naturalization Act"] onward, Jews were indeed "white" by the most significant measures of that appellation: they could enter the country and become naturalized citizens. Given the shades of meaning attaching to various racial classifications, given the nuances involved as whiteness slips off toward Semitic or Hebrew and back again toward Caucasian, the question is not *are* they white, nor even how white are they, but how have they been both white and Other? What have been the historical terms of their probationary whiteness? (176).

27. Sammy Davis Jr. converted to Judaism in the 1950s.

28. Y. Chireau and N. Deutsch eds., *Black Zion: African American Religious Encounters with Judaism* (New York: Oxford University Press, 2000), 16.

29. "What do American Jews Believe? A Symposium." (part 2) P. Knobel; N. Lamm; R. Langer; D. Lapin; J. Lester; J. D. Levenson; N. Lewin; D. L. Lieber; M. Medved; M. A. Meyer; J. Neusner; D. Novak; J. A. Polak; D. Prager; R. L. Rubenstein; I. Schorsch; D. Singer; D. Steinmetz; S. L. Stone; D. A. Teutsch; H. J. Weschler; J. Wertheimer; E. H. Yoffie; S. Zimmerman; *Commentary* 102, no. 2 (1996): 57–96.

30. "What do American Jews Believe? A Symposium" (part 2).

31. See Jonathan Serna, *American Judaism: A History* (New Haven: Yale University Press, 2004). According to Serna, there was widespread "[i]gnorance of Jewish law and the absence of rabbinical authority" during the colonial period, which underwrote a diversity in "religious observances and attitudes" (22). The rhythms of American culture made keeping the Sabbath and observing Jewish holidays difficult (24). "[F]rom the very beginning of Jewish settlement, Jews and Christians... fell in love and married" (27). This violated the prohibition on intermarriage. Indeed, America's largely Protestant and "democratic" culture was unavoidable. Jewish law underwent a process of Americanization. "The freedom that produced this 'anyone can do what he wants' attitude reinforced the diversity in Jewish ritual practice that, we know, already existed in colonial times" (45). To be sure, this laissez faire situation provoked a traditional (Orthodox) movement and neotraditional (Conservative and Reconstructionist) movements in response. But these responses only confirmed the degree of actually exiting diversity within American Jewry. In addition to these circumstances, black Jews faced the full force of white supremacy.

32. On the occasion of Jimi Hendrix's death and several years before the earth-shaking death of his father, Julius describes the deaths of Malcolm X and John Coltrane as "the only deaths that I have ever felt in the fiber of my being." *All Is Well*, 254.

33. Elsewhere, Julius writes: "Malcolm was John the Baptist, preaching in the wilderness. We still wait for a savior and, this time, I don't think he's coming." See J. Lester, *The End of White World Supremacy* (review). *New York Times,* May 16, 1971.

34. See Lester, *All Is Well*, 105; *Falling Pieces of the Broken Sky* (New York: Arcade Publishing Inc., 1990), 134–5; "Beyond Ideology," *Whole Earth* (2000). http://findarticles.com/p/articles/mi_m0GER/is_2000_Summer/ai_63500750/print (last accessed on December 30, 2007.

35. See J. Lester, *The End of White World Supremacy* (review). *New York Times,* May 16, 1971.

36. According to Lester, "There was an occasional anti-Semitic remark in the speeches of Malcolm X but not until Louis Farrakhan did the anti-Semitism come to the forefront." See J. Lester, *Falling Pieces*, 161–2.

37. "Black Politburo" is Debra Dickerson's term. See D. Dickerson, *The End of Blackness* (New York: Pantheon Books, 2004), 250.

38. Lester speaks of a "politic of blackness." He claims that Jimi Hendrix helped him avoid the dehumanizing consequences of that politic: "I often referred to him jokingly to my friends as 'my leader.' But it wasn't a joke.... He helped me to keep struggling to be me because he chose to be himself." See Lester, *All Is Well*, 254.

39. Lester makes these points in a variety of places and ways. The following two will suffice: "The present generation of blacks is unworthy of its forbearers. That is a harsh judgment, but in finally letting ourselves be unashamedly angry after centuries of repressed anger, we have lost what was absolutely essential—a way of being in the world and living with adversity, without being controlled or dominated by it." To a group of black students at a small liberal arts college in Maine, upset by his marriage to a white woman, Julius remarks: "Love is its own justification.... To call myself black was to do no more than modify a definition imposed on me by centuries of Western history. If one knew himself as nothing but black, he'd simply inverted nigger, Negro, and colored, not transforming himself but continuing to live by someone else's description of his reality." "He who hates whites, however, may only be hating the whiteness in himself, thereby not loving black people, but loving hatred of whiteness.... One hates injustice, loves humanity and kills only because the killing is forced upon him" See Lester, *All Is Well*, 293, 285, 162.

40. The closest Julius comes to a radical revision of his views of Malcolm X occurs in fictional form when Malcolm X makes a cameo appearance in Julius' novel, *And All Our Wounds Forgiven* (1994). I hesitate to put Julius' views into the mouth of a character. However, this is not just any character but the protagonist and hero. In Julius' fictional judgment, Malcolm is held accountable for the deadly spirit of demonization, especially in-group, black-on-black demonization that he did more than anyone else to unleash, and that he polished with unmatched rhetorical skill.

41. http://findarticles.com/p/articles/mi_m0GER/is_2000_Summer/ai_63500750/print (last accessed on December 30, 2007.

Five   Jan Willis: *Duhkha* and Enlightenment

1. D. Keown, *A Dictionary of Buddhism* (New York: Oxford University Press, 2003), 81.

2. Cf. W. E. B. DuBois, *The Souls of Black Folks* (New York: Barnes & Noble Classics, 2003), 135–6 on the frenzy of the Black Church.

3. See R. Otto, *The Idea of the Holy* (New York: Oxford University Press, 1990) for an influential analysis of the concept.

4. A "taste of power" is the title that Elaine Brown chose for her memoir. She is the former girlfriend of Huey P. Newton, the cofounder of the Black Panther Party and the only woman to lead the organization. See E. Brown, *A Taste of Power: A Woman's Story* (New York: Pantheon, 1993).

5. M. Abu-Jamal, *We Want Freedom: A Life in the Black Panther Party* (Cambridge, MA: South End Press, 2004), 161–4, 174, 182.

6. Abu-Jamal, 162.

7. Abu-Jamal, 162.

8. Abu-Jamal, 184.

9. J. Guy, *Afeni Shakur: Evolution of a Revolutionary* (New York: Atria Books, 2004), 76–7.

10. Abu-Jamal, 182. This is not to say that men did not play "penis games." What it says, rather, is that gender relations are complex choices that both men and women make, even when these choices are structured by male dominance.

11. In his excellent study, *Waiting 'Til the Midnight Hour: A Narrative History of Black Power in America* (New York: Henry Holt, 2006), P. E. Joseph, apropos the gender politics of the Panthers, remarks: "Her [Kathleen Cleaver] glamorous public image did much to obscure the party's ambiguous treatment of black women. Internally, Panthers debated women's role in a revolution designed to provide black men with the positions of respect and authority that white society had historically denied them. Pivotal players in the development and maintenance of the organizations growing infrastructure, women in the rank and file waged an intense uphill struggle to be considered full partners in the revolution" (231).

12. The Sangha is the community of those who follow the Dharma—the teachings of the Buddha Shakyamuni.

13. See S. Kierkegaard, *Fear and Trembling/Repetition,* ed. and trans. Howard V. Hong and Edna H. Hong (Princeton, NJ: Princeton University Press, 1983), 11. This phrase suggests that we must make what we love unattractive (or, in the case of a baby, have it made unattractive; blackening the breast makes it appear odd and perhaps taste badly) to detach ourselves.

14. See G. Delueze and F. Guataari, *Anti-Oedipus: Capitalism and Schizophrenia* (Minneapolis: Minnesota University Press, 1983), 23.

15. M. L. King, Jr., *A Testament of Hope: The Essential Writings of Martin Luther King, Jr.,* ed. James Melvin Washington (San Francisco: Harper & Row, 1986), 295.

16. D. Brazier, *The New Buddhism* (New York: Palgrave, 2002), 146–7. For a scholarly treatment of karma see W. D. O'Flaherty, ed., *Karma and Rebirth in Classical Indian Traditions* (Berkeley: University of California Press, 1980).

17. Jan sometimes writes as if she were the only black Buddhist. In fact, there is a significant black Buddhist community, including a "cyber sangha" of which Jan is a member.

18. A "karma formation" is a set of habits, conditioned by past habits that influence future habits.

19. O. C. Cox, *Caste, Class, and Race* (New York: Doubleday and Company, 1948; repr. New York: Modern Reader Paperback Edition, 1970), 91.

20. As my colleague Charlie Orzech said to me in conversation, "no reputable scholar today accepts the Aryan thesis." For a critique of the Aryan thesis, see B. Lincoln, *Theorizing Myth: Narrative, Ideology, and Scholarship* (Chicago: University of Chicago Press, 1999).

21. Cox, 84, 89.

22. Cox, 93.

23. Cox, 93.

24. See Jones, *Is God a White Racist?*

25. Jones, 71, 80, 99, 122, 132, 156.

26. H. Dumoulin, *Christianity Meets Buddhism* (LaSalle, IL: Open Court Publishing Company, 1974), 35–42.

27. Dumoulin, 90–2, 96–7.

28. E. West, *Happiness Here & Now: The Eightfold Path of Jesus Revisited with Buddhist Insights* (New York: Continuum, 2000), 19.

29. T. Gyatso (Dalai Lama XIV), *The Good Heart: A Buddhist Perspective on the Teachings of Jesus* (Boston: Wisdom Publications, 1996), 105.

30. Malcolm X and A. Haley, *Autobiography of Malcolm X* (New York: Ballantine Books, 1992), 43.

31. Such experiences are often called "religious experiences." I understand such experiences as John Dewey rather William James understands them, certainly not as Richard Rorty and Robert Brandom do.

32. E. Dickinson, *The Complete Poems of Emily Dickinson* (Boston: Little Brown, 1960), 702.

Coda My Point of View as an Author

1. J. Dewey, *A Common Faith* (New Haven: Yale University Press, 1934), 10.
2. Dewey, 26.
3. L. Bennett Jr., *The Challenge of Blackness* (Chicago: Johnson Publishing, 1972), 305.
4. G. Santayana, *Interpretation of Poetry and Religion* (London: Adam and Charles Black, 1900), v.
5. J. Royce, *The Problem of Christianity* (Chicago: University of Chicago Press, 1968), 62.
6. See R. Corriginton, *Nature's Religion* (Lanham, MD: Rowman & Little field Publishers, 1997), 151.
7. I borrow this concept from R. Rubenstein, *After Auschwitz* (New York: Bobbs-Merrill, 1966), 152.
8. Dewey, 86, 87.
9. Friedrich Nietzsche, *Samtliche Werke: Kritische Studienausgabe* vol. 10, selection s[1] number 68, ed. Giorgio Colli and Mazzino Montinai (Berlin: de Gryter, 1980), 195. Unpublished fragments dating to November 1882 to February 1883.

SELECTED BIBLIOGRAPHY

Abu-Jamal, M. *We Want Freedom: A Life in the Black Panther Party.* Cambridge, MA: South End Press, 2004.

Adams, M. and J. Bracey, eds. *Strangers and Neighbors: Relations between Blacks and Jews in the United States.* Amherst: University of Massachusetts Press, 1999.

Armstrong, K. *Buddha.* New York: Penguin Putnam, 2001.

Ashston, J. and T. Whyte. *The Quest for Paradise: Visions of Heaven and Eternity in the World's Myths and Religions.* New York: HarperSanFrancisco, 2001.

Barbour, J. D. "Character and Characterization in Religious Autobiography." *Journal of the American Academy of Religion* 55, no. 2 (2001): 307–27.

Beal, T. K. *Religion and Its Monsters.* New York: Routledge, 2002.

Brazier, D. *The New Buddhism.* New York: Palgrave, 2002.

Brotz, H. *Black Jews of Harlem.* Knopf Publishing Group, 1998.

Camus, A. *Neither Victims Nor Executioners.* Trans. Dwight McDonald. Philadelphia: New Society Publishers, 1986.

Carew, J. *Ghosts in Our Blood: With Malcolm X in Africa, England, and the Caribbean.* Chicago: Lawrence Hill Books, 1994.

Chesler, P. *The New Anti-Semitism: The Current Crisis and What We Must Do about It.* San Francisco: Jossey-Bass, 2003.

Chidester, D. *Patterns of Transcendence.* Belmont, CA: Wadsworth Publishing, 1990.

Chireau, Y. and N. Deutsch, eds. *Black Zion: African American Religious Encounters with Judaism.* New York: Oxford University Press, 2000.

Cole, R. *Spiritual Life of Children.* Boston: Houghton Mifflin, 1991.

Collins, R. P. *Seventh Child: A Family Memoir of Malcolm X.* Secaucus, NJ: Carol Publishing, 1998.

Cone, J. *A Black Theology of Liberation.* Philadelphia: J. B. Lipincott, 1970.

Cotta, S. *Why Violence? A Philosophical Interpretation.* Gainesville: University Press of Florida, 1985.

Cox, O. C. *Caste, Class, and Race.* New York: Modern Reader Paperback Edition, 1970.

Cullen, C. *The Black Christ and Other Poems.* New York: Harper & Brothers, 1929.

Dray, P. *At the Hands of Persons Unknown: The Lynching of Black America.* New York: Modern Library, 2003.

DeCaro, L. A. *On the Side of My People: A Religious Life of Malcolm X.* New York: New York University Press, 1996.

Delong-Bas, N. J. *Wahhabi Islam: From Revival and Reform to Global Jihad.* New York: Oxford University Press, 2004.

Dewey, J. *A Common Faith.* New Haven: Yale University Press, 1934.

Du Bois, W. E. B. *The Negro Church: Report of a Social Study Made under the Direction of Atlanta University; together with the Proceedings of the Eighth Conference for the Study of the Negro Problems.* Atlanta: Atlanta University Press, 1903.

———. *The Souls of Black Folks.* New York: W. W. Norton, 1999.

Dumoulin, H. *Christianity Meets Buddhism.* LaSalle, IL: Open Court Publishing, 1974.

Esposito, J., ed. *The Oxford History of Islam.* New York: Oxford University Press, 1999.

———. *Islam: The Straight Path.* New York: Oxford University Press, 1991.

Fanon, F. *Black Skin, White Masks.* New York: Grove Press, 1967.

Fauset, A. H. *Black Gods of the Metropolis.* Philadelphia: University of Pennsylvania Press, 2001.

Fluehr-Lobban, C. *Islamic Society in Practice.* Gainesville: University Press of Florida, 1994.

Freud, S. *Future of an Illusion.* Trans. James Strachey. New York: W. W. Norton, 1961.

———.*Totem and Taboo.* Trans. A. A. Brill. New York: Vintage Books, 1918.

Gallen, G. and C. Carson *Malcolm X: The FBI File.* New York: Carroll & Graf Publishers, 1991.

Gates, H. L., ed. *Bearing Witness: Selections from African-American Autobiography in the Twentieth Century.* New York: Pantheon, 1991.

Gordon, J. A. *Why They Can't Wait: A Critique of Black-Jewish Conflict over Community Control in Ocean Hill-Brownsville (1967–1971).* New York: RoutledgeFalmer, 2001.

Guy, J. *Afeni Shakur: Evolution of a Revolutionary.* New York: Atria Books, 2004.

Gyatso, T. *The Good Heart: A Buddhist Perspective on the Teachings of Jesus.* Boston: Wisdom Publications, 1996.

Hall, R. E. "Skin Color as Post-Colonial Hierarchy: A Global Strategy for Conflict Resolution." *Journal of Psychology* 137, no. 1 (2003): 41–53.

Harris, T. *Exorcising Blackness: Historical and Literary Lynching and Burning Rituals.* Bloomington: Indiana University Press, 1984.

Harvey, V. *Feuerbach and the Interpretation of Religion.* Cambridge: Cambridge University Press, 1995.

Hegel, G. W. F. *Hegel's Phenomenology of Spirit.* New York: Oxford University Press, 1977.

Holloway, K. *Passed On: African American Mourning Stories.* Durham: Duke University Press, 2002.

Howard-Pitney, D. *Afro-American Jeremiad.* Philadelphia: Temple University Press, 1993.

Insoll, T. *The Archaeology of Islam.* Oxford, UK: Blackwell Publishers, 1999.

Johnson, C. H., ed. *God Struck Me Dead: Religious Conversion Experiences and Autobiographies of Ex-Slaves.* Philadelphia: Pilgrims' Press, 1969.

Jones, W. R. *Is God a White Racist?: A Preamble to Black Theology.* Boston: Beacon Press, 1998.

Joseph, P. E. *Waiting 'Til the Midnight Hour: A Narrative History of Black Power in America* New York: Henry Holt, 2006.

Khalidi, T. *The Muslim Jesus.* Cambridge, MA: Harvard University Press, 2001.

King, R. *Orientalism and Religion.* London: Routledge, 1999.

Lester, J. *Look Out Whitey, Black Power's Gon' Get Your Mama!* New York: Dial Press, 1968.

———. *All Is Well.* New York: William and Marrow, 1976.

———. *Falling Pieces of the Broken Sky.* New York: Arcade Publishing, 1990.

———. *And All Our Wounds Forgiven.* New York: Arcade Publishing, 1994.

Lewis, L. and M. D'orso. *Walking with the Wind: A Memoir of the Movement.* New York: Simon and Schuster, 1998.

Lincoln, B. *Theorizing Myth: Narrative, Ideology, and Scholarship.* Chicago: University of Chicago Press, 1999.

———. "Theses on Method." *Method & Theory in the Study of Religion* 8 (1996): 225–227.

Marsh, C. E. *From Black Muslims to Muslims.* Metuchen, NJ: Scarecrow Press, 1984.

Meier, A., E. Rudwick, and F. L. Broderick, eds. *Black Protest Thought in the Twentieth Century.* Indianapolis: Bobbs-Merrill, 1971.

Mitchell, R. A. *The Buddha: His Life Retold.* New York: Paragon House, 1989.

Nasa, S. H. *Islamic Spirituality: Foundations.* New York: Crossroad, 1987.

O'Flaherty, W. D., ed. *Karma and Rebirth in Classical Indian Traditions.* Berkeley: University of California Press, 1980.

Olney, J. *Metaphors of Self: The Meaning of Autobiography.* Princeton University Press, 1972.

Orwell, G. *Shooting an Elephant, and Other Essays.* New York: Harcourt Brace, 1950.

Pagels, E. *The Origins of Satan.* New York: Random House, 1995.

Patterson, O. *Rituals of Blood: Consequences of Slavery in Two American Centuries.* Washington, DC: Civitas/CounterPoint, 1998.

Perry, B. *Malcolm X: The Life of a Man Who Changed Black America.* Barrytown, NY: Station Hill Press, 1991.

Porter, R. and H. R. Wolf. *The Voice Within: Reading and Writing Autobiography.* New York: Alfred Knopf, 1973.

Raboteau, A. *Slave Religion: The Invisible Institution in the Antebellum South.* New York: Oxford University Press, 1978.

Rampersad, A. *Ralph Ellison: A Biography.* New York: Alfred Knopf, 2007.

Rickford, R. J. *Betty Shabazz.* Naperville, IL: Sourcebooks, 2003.

Ricoeur, P. "Narrative Identity." Trans. Mark S. Muldoon. *Philosophy Today* 35, no. 1 (1991): 73–81.

Royce, Josiah. *The Problem of Christianity.* Chicago: University of Chicago Press, 1968.

Rubin, D. C., ed. *Remembering Our Past: Studies in Autobiographical Memory.* New York: Cambridge University Press, 1995.

Rudwin, M. *The Devil in Legend and Literature.* La Salle, IL: Open Court Publishing, 1931.

Russell, J. B. *Satan: The Early Christian Tradition.* Ithaca: Cornell University Press, 1981.

Santayana, George. *Interpretation of Poetry and Religion.* London: Adam and Charles Black, 1900.

St. Clair, M. *Object Relations and Self-Psychology: An Introduction.* Belmont, CA: Wadsworth, 1986.

Segal, R. *Islam's Black Slaves.* New York: Farrar, Strauss and Giroux, 2006.

Shabazz, I. *Growing Up X: A Memoir by the Daughter of Malcolm X.* New York: One World/Ballantine, 2002.

Smith, M. S. *The Early History of God: Yahweh and Other Deities in Ancient Israel.* Grand Rapids, MI: Wm. B. Eerdmans, 2002.

Smith, T. *Conjuring Culture: Biblical Formations of Black America.* New York: Oxford University Press, 1994.

Strong, J. S. *The Buddha: A Short Biography.* Oxford, UK: Oneworld, 2001.

Taylor, M. C., ed. *Critical Terms for Religious Studies.* Chicago: University of Chicago Press, 1998.

Teresa of Avila. *The Life of Saint Teresa of Avila by Herself.* London: Penguin Books, 1957.

Washington, J. M., ed. *A Testament of Hope: The Essential Writings of Martin Luther King, Jr.* San Francisco: Harper & Row, 1986.

Watt, M. W. *Islamic Philosophy and Theology.* Edinburgh: Edinburgh University Press, 1985.

West, C. *Prophesy Deliverance! An Afro-American Revolutionary Christianity.* Philadelphia: Westminster Press, 1982.

———. *Prophetic Fragments.* Trenton, NJ: Africa World Press, 1990.

West, E. *Happiness Here and Now: The Eightfold Path of Jesus Revisited with Buddhist Insights.* New York: Continuum, 2000.

White, R. "Autobiography against Itself." *Philosophy Today* 35, no. 3/4 (1991): 291–303.

White, Jr., V. L. *Inside the Nation of Islam.* Gainesville: University Press of Florida, 2001.

Wilken, R. L. *The Christians as the Romans Saw Them.* New Haven: Yale University Press, 1984.

Wilson, David Sloan. *Darwin for Everyone*. New York: Bantam Dell, 2007.

Wolfenstein, E. V. *The Victims of Democracy: Malcolm X and the Black Revolution*. Berkeley: University of California Press, 1981.

Yousman, B. "Who Owns Identity? Malcolm X, Representation, and the Struggle over Meaning," *Eastern Communication Association* 49, no. 1 (2001): 1–18. http://libproxy.uncg.edu:4618/ ehost/pdf?vid=3&hid=14&sid=593e4aa4-5a81-4390-bc56-ead11ebc8011%40sessionmgr7 (last accessed on December 24, 2007).

INDEX